Inequality and Governance

Governance matters for social welfare. Better governed countries are richer, happier and have fewer social and environmental problems. Good governance implies that public sector agents act impartially. It manifests itself in the form of equality before the law, an independent and professional public administration and the control of corruption.

This book considers how economic inequality – both interpersonal and interethnic – can affect the quality of governance. To this end, it brings together insights from three different perspectives. First, a long-run historical one that exploits anthropological data on pre-industrial societies. Second, based on experimental work conducted by social psychologists and behavioural economists. Third, through cross-country empirical analysis drawn from a large sample of contemporary societies.

The long-run perspective relates the inequality-governance relationship to societal responses in the face of uncertainty – responses that persist today in the guise of cultural traits that vary across countries. The experimental evidence deepens our understanding of human behaviour in unequal settings and in different governance contexts. Together, the long-run perspective and the experimental evidence help inform the cross-country analysis of the impact of economic inequality on governance. This analysis suggests the importance of both economic inequality and culture for the quality of governance and yields several policy implications.

Andreas P. Kyriacou is Professor of Economics at the Universitat de Girona (Spain). Over the years, he has worked on a range of research topics mostly from the perspective of Institutional Economics. These include federalism and decentralisation, non-economic motives driving individual behaviour and, more recently, the causes and consequences of government quality.

T0382828

Routledge Frontiers of Political Economy

For more information about this series, please visit: www.routledge.com/books/series/SE0345

Inequality and Governance

Andreas P. Kyriacou

Routledge
Taylor & Francis Group

LONDON AND NEW YORK

First published 2020 by Routledge

2 Park Square, Milton Park, Abingdon, Oxon, OX14 4RN

605 Third Avenue, New York, NY 10017

Routledge is an imprint of the Taylor & Francis Group, an informa business

First issued in paperback 2020

British Library Cataloguing-in-Publication Data
A catalogue record for this book is available from the British Library

Library of Congress Cataloging-in-Publication Data
A catalog record has been requested for this book

ISBN: 978-1-138-69050-9 (hbk)
ISBN: 978-0-367-77767-8 (pbk)

Typeset in Galliard
by Wearset Ltd, Boldon, Tyne and Wear

For Arnau and Nico

Contents

Figures

Tables

Acknowledgements

I'd like to thank the staff at Routledge, specifically Andy Humphries, Anna Cuthbert and Laura Johnson, for proposing and shepherding through this book. Several people were kind enough to invite me for a short research stay, thus giving me quality time to think about the issues at hand: David Cameron and Dwayne Benjamin of the School of Public Policy and Governance at the University of Toronto, Niamh Hardiman of the Geary Institute of Public Policy at University College Dublin, and Alexandra Sandmark as well as Oisín Plumb of the Centre for Nordic Studies at the University of Highlands and Islands at Orkney. Thanks to Lluís Planas for reading through the whole manuscript and pointing out errors and potential improvements. Thanks also to Pedro Trivin for all his help with STATA. Finally, I would like to thank my family for their patience and support, especially during the summer of 2018.

1   Introduction

Economic inequality has been on the rise around the world over the last four decades. Facundo Alvaredo *et al.* (2018) show that income inequality has increased in almost all world regions since 1980, although at different speeds. The rising trend of income inequality has been attributed to a range of factors (for a summary, see Anthony Atkinson [2015] and François Bourguignon [2017]). In developed countries, these include technological change that is biased in favour of high-skilled workers, increased competition from countries with lower wages for unskilled workers, assortative mating, whereby individuals form relationships with people with similar incomes and, finally, the rise of single parent households. In developing countries, it is mostly seen as the result of changes in the sectoral composition of the economy due to economic development in line with Simon Kuznets's (1955) seminal argument regarding the shift from agriculture to industry. The level of economic development also partly explains why economic inequality varies so much across countries. Based on the average value of the Gini index of disposable income over the period 1996 to 2016 – a measure that I will fully explain in Chapter 2 – economic inequality in Swaziland and Namibia, is almost two and a half times greater than that in Iceland and Denmark.[1]

Large economic inequalities are bad news for a range of social, political and economic objectives. Kate Pickett and Richard Wilkinson (2009) relate income inequality across developed countries and within the United States to a range of health and social problems such as, life expectancy and infant mortality, mental illness and drug use, obesity, child well-being (including experience with conflict), academic performance, teenage births, homicides and imprisonment rates (see Wilkinson and Pickett [2017], for a recent survey of associated work). These authors identify increasing anxiety due to the greater salience of status in more unequal settings as a fundamental driver of many of these problems. Status, relative or positional concerns also help explain empirical evidence showing that inequality is associated with lower happiness levels in Western countries (for surveys, see Ada Ferrer-i-Carbonell and Xavier Ramos [2014] and Andrew Clark and Conchita D'Ambrosio [2015]).

Economic inequality can also affect democratisation and democratic political engagement. High levels of economic inequality may lead economic elites to oppose democracy because they are fearful of the redistributive pressures that are expected to emerge in the normal course of democratic politics (Carles Boix [2003], Daron Acemoglu and James Robinson [2006]). Within developed democracies, economic inequality may lead to unequal political participation. Drawing on a sample of industrialised democracies, Frederick Solt (2008) shows that higher levels of economic inequality reduce interest in politics, the frequency of political discussion and participation in elections of all but the wealthiest citizens. According to this author, this vindicates the relative power theory of political engagement, which holds that wealthier people can apply their superior resources to set the political agenda leaving poorer individuals to feel powerless and, as a result, to opt out of politics altogether (see, originally, Elmer Schattschneider [1960]). To the extent that poorer citizens are under-represented when political priorities are being set, this can potentially translate into policies that are biased in favour of wealthier citizens setting in place a negative feedback loop between economic and political inequality (see Solt [2010] and Aina Gallego [2015]). In the words of Joseph Stiglitz (2012) writing on democracy in the United States, "the median voter … is richer than the median American. We have a *biased* electorate, tilted toward the top" (Chapter 5, subheading, "The evisceration of our democracy", eBook, italics in the original).

Inequality is also inimical to economic growth. Andrew Berg *et al.* (2018) exploit a large number of country-year observations covering both developed and developing countries to show that higher net (after tax and transfer) inequality, as measured by the Gini index, is correlated with lower growth rates. Era Dabla-Norris *et al.* [2015] report similar findings based on the income shares of the top 20 and bottom 20 per cent. Berg *et al.* (2018) identify several channels, including imperfect credit markets and fertility. Poorer people have more limited access to capital and tend to have higher fertility rates. Because of this, they invest less in human capital to the detriment of economic growth. Another channel explored by these authors is income redistribution. A priori, inequality may lead to redistributive policies that may harm growth by dampening incentives to work and invest (see, originally, Arthur Okun [1975]). On the other hand, redistribution may promote growth insofar as it finances public spending in areas such as infrastructure, education and health. The authors do not find that redistribution is harmful to growth except when it is very extensive (top twenty-fifth percentile of all observations).

Most of the work analysing the consequences of inequality focuses on interpersonal inequality. But a growing body of work has turned its attention to the impact of economic inequality between ethnic groups. Such ethnic or horizontal inequalities as they are known, may lead relatively deprived groups to mobilise violently against the better off, thereby increasing the likelihood of civil war (Frances Stewart [2000]; Gudrun Østby [2008] and Lars-Eric Cederman *et al.* [2011, 2015]). Ethnic group inequalities have also been associated with transitions away from democracy. Christian Houle (2015) provides empirical evidence to support the argument that higher ethnic inequalities may lead to redistributive conflicts and, ultimately, the demise of democracy. This is especially likely if within-group inequalities are lower, since this increases cohesion within ethnic groups. Kate Baldwin and John Huber (2010) show that ethnic inequalities undermine public good provision and explain this by suggesting that income and ethnic differences are likely to make agreement over which public goods to provide more difficult. Alberto Alesina *et al.* (2016) focus instead on the link between ethnic group inequalities and economic development. Based on a cross-section of up to 173 countries, they show that income differences among ethnic groups are harmful for development.

In this book, I will turn my attention to the impact of economic inequality – both interpersonal and interethnic – on governance. As will be extensively discussed in Chapter 2, governance refers to the way public authority is exercised. Good governance implies that public sector agents act impartially or, in other words, without regards to personal relationships and preferences. It manifests itself in numerous ways including, an independent and professional public administration, equality before the law (including contract and property right enforcement) and, control of corruption or the misuse of public power for private or political gain. I focus on governance because a large and expanding body of work has linked good governance to a range of desirable social outcomes.

One notable outcome is economic development. An efficient public administration facilitates the cost-effective provision of public goods and, more generally, the formulation of sound policies and regulations to the benefit of sustained economic growth (Paolo Mauro [1995]; Peter Evans and James Rauch [1999]). Secure property rights and equality before the law encourage investments in physical and human capital and technology (Douglass North [1990]; Daron Acemoglu *et al.* [2005]; Stefan Voigt *et al.* [2015]). Control of corruption reduces the misallocation of resources that emerges either directly, because of the appropriation of public resources, or indirectly, due to sub-optimal public sector decisions (Andrei Shleifer and Robert Vishny [1993]; Pranab Bardhan [1997]). The quality of governance may also impact on income inequality. As I explain in Chapter 5, corrupt public officials may "shake down" poorer people for bribes and accept bribes from economic elites in exchange for policies that worsen the distribution of income. Moreover, voters are less likely to support redistributive programmes if they perceive the public sector to be biased, inefficient and corrupt.

Good governance has also been associated with greater reported happiness across countries perhaps because it implies fair treatment of individuals by the state (Jan Cornelis Ott [2010, 2011]). Good governance can, moreover, lead to better health, education and environmental outcomes (see Bo Rothstein [2011] for a review of related work and additional empirical evidence). Health and education policies are better designed and implemented, access to them is based on need rather than capacity to pay or personal connections, and more resources are available than would be in the presence of malfeasance. Better environmental outcomes emerge in part because of a more effective design of environmental policies and because good governance implies less corruption of public officials with the aim of circumventing environmental regulations.

To explore the relationship between inequality and governance, I will begin, in Chapter 2, by discussing how I define and measure each concept. To reiterate, governance refers to the exercise of public authority. As such, it is distinct from democracy, which is more concerned with access to public power. Democracy is a determinant of governance rather than governance per se. Governance is also related to, but distinct from, state capacity that is more concerned with government's ability to raise taxes and includes tax compliance by citizens. To measure governance, I will turn to the World Bank's World Governance Indicators. The advantages and disadvantages of these perceptions-based measures will be discussed. I then distinguish between structural and market inequality. The former emerges when some individuals or groups are endowed with more rights than others, while the latter emerges from market exchange. To measure economic inequality, I will focus on the distribution of income across individuals and ethnic groups. Moreover, I will also employ an indicator capturing perceived rather than actual inequality as well as a measure of (in)equality of opportunity. I will end Chapter 2 with a preliminary empirical analysis of the association between economic inequality and governance.

In Chapter 3, I consider the inequality-governance relationship in a long-run perspective going as far back as our hunter-gatherer ancestors. We will see that good governance as equality before the law, depends on the weakness of social stratification and ingroup favouritism or bias. Stratification and bias are societal responses to the existential uncertainty that emerges from the struggle for survival and reproductive success, as well as cognitive limits faced when trying to guess the intentions of others. I will identify four related factors affecting stratification and bias, namely, infectious disease, population growth, conflict and the nature of production. These factors, in turn, partly depend on the biogeographic conditions faced by social groups. When possible, I will make use of anthropological data on pre-industrial societies to flesh out some of the arguments. This analysis identifies the deep determinants of inequality and governance and, as such, reveals a set of exogenous variables that will be useful when considering the impact of inequality on governance in contemporary settings later on.

In Chapter 4, I review a range of insights that have emerged in the fields of social psychology and behavioural economics. The associated experimental evidence confirms the human tendency to favour ingroups – a tendency that can lead people to accept unethical behaviour from members of their group and endorse group leaders that discriminate outgroups. The evidence has also shown that the perceived legitimacy of social inequalities has a bearing on the salience of group boundaries between low and high status groups, as well as the degree to which low status groups abide by the law. Moreover, it has revealed that those endowed with power tend to view subordinates instrumentally, underestimate the individual merits of less advantaged people, and behave less ethically. Finally, the experimental evidence shows that individual expectations of corrupt behaviour by others may explain high and low corruption countries as alternative equilibria.

In Chapter 5, I examine the relationship between economic inequality and governance in contemporary settings based on cross-country data. This requires a discussion of the causal mechanisms through which inequality can affect governance which, in turn, emerges from an understanding of the behaviour of individuals arrayed across the income distribution. To isolate the impact of inequality on governance I review a set of potentially confounding variables and discuss the real possibility that the quality of governance can itself affect the degree of economic inequality. To account for such reverse causality, I rely on the long-run determinants of inequality identified in Chapter 3. The empirical analysis, based on a sample of up to 126 developed and developing countries, provides strong support for the expectation that economic inequality is bad for good governance. Moreover, I show that the impact of interpersonal inequality on governance is mediated by the level of democracy and, specifically, that the negative impact of interpersonal inequality on governance is stronger in more democratic settings.

The results reported in Chapter 5 ignore the confounding influence of a potentially crucial variable associated with both economic inequality and governance. This variable is culture. In Chapter 6, I will argue that the societal responses to existential uncertainty brought to light in Chapter 3, express themselves in contemporary settings as specific cultural traits that are inimical to good governance. These traits are related to both governance and economic inequality and, as such, their omission biases the empirical estimates reported in Chapter 5. I reconsider the impact of economic inequality on governance when accounting for culture and find that while both economic inequality and culture are relevant, the impact of culture may be stronger.

The analysis generates a series of policy implications that will be taken up in the concluding chapter of this book. I begin by defining the key variables and reviewing the available quantitative indicators that will be employed throughout the analysis.

Note

1 The first time an author is cited, I indicate his or her name and surname. In subsequent citations, only the surname is used.

2 Concepts, measures and correlations

Introduction

It is important at the outset to define the basic concepts that will be used throughout this book, namely, economic inequality and governance. What do I mean when I refer to good governance or the quality of governance? Good governance is defined as impartial governance or governance without regards to the personal preferences or relationships of those wielding authority. It manifests itself in the absence of corruption, a meritocratically selected and autonomous civil service and equality before the law. To measure governance, I will turn to the World Bank's World Governance Indicators. These indicators aim to capture different facets of governance based on perceptions held by experts, citizens and entrepreneurs. They have both strengths and weaknesses that will be discussed.

When referring to inequality, I differentiate between structural and market inequality. The former emerges outside the market and describes a situation where individuals or groups are afforded differential treatment by the law, slavery being the most infamous example. Alternatively, market inequality refers to inequality in income and wealth that emerges in the context of market exchange. It can be the result of individual effort as well as a range of uncontrollable factors. Market or gross inequality can be modified by public policy in which case it becomes net income or wealth inequality across individuals or groups. I will measure inequality by way of alternative indicators including the Gini coefficient, the shares of income of different quintiles of the income distribution and a measure of (in)equality of opportunity.

After presenting and discussing the indicators that will be employed to measure good governance and inequality, I take a first step towards analysing the relationship between these two variables based on simple correlations. This analysis suggests that good governance is negatively associated with inequality, whether this is measured across individuals or groups or in terms of disposable income, perceptions or inequality of opportunity. It is important to understand however, that this finding is extremely preliminary for at least three reasons. First, it tells us nothing about how inequality may impact on governance or, in other words, it does not explore the theoretical arguments that may reveal the causal channels going from inequality to governance. Second, it does not deal with the real possibility that good governance itself may affect income inequality. Third, it does not control for the confounding effect of variables that both theoretically and statistically may be associated with both governance and inequality and, as a result, whose omission may bias the estimated relationships. This said, I do begin to address this last problem by controlling for the level of economic development for reasons that are set out in the pages that follow.

Defining governance

Following Bo Rothstein and Jan Teorell (2008), good governance is impartial governance and more specifically, impartiality in the exercise of public authority. Defining governance in terms of the *exercise* of public authority differentiates governance from democracy, which is more concerned with *access* to public power. Impartiality exists if,

> [w]hen implementing laws and policies, government officials shall not take into consideration anything about the citizen/case that is not beforehand stipulated in the policy or the law ... [As Geoffrey Cupit (2000) writes] "To act impartially is to be unmoved by certain sorts of considerations – such as special relationships and personal preferences. It is to treat people alike irrespective of personal relationships and personal likes and dislikes".
> (Rothstein and Teorell [2008], page 170)

In other words, good governance emerges when the public sector treats all individuals "in the same empirical situation" equally (Max Weber [1922]).

Impartiality means that the selection of public administrators should be based on merits and qualifications previously stipulated in law, rather than on personal relationships, political affinity or group membership. Corruption or the misuse of public office for private or political gain implies a violation of impartiality since it means that public officials are acting in their own specific interest (see also, Nicholas Charron and Victor Lapuente, [2013]). Impartiality implies the rule of law insofar as the latter is a set of rules that are equally binding on all members of society, regardless of how powerful they are (see also, Francis Fukuyama [2011, 2014]). Impartial governance "requires that ... society be able to create and sustain impersonal categories – such as citizens – and then to treat everyone in the same category alike" (North *et al.* [2009], page 262).

Impartial governance is imbued with what Weber (1922) calls rational authority or legitimacy as opposed to traditional or charismatic authority. Rational authority imposes limits based on explicit (written) and impersonal rules, traditional authority imposes them by custom, and charismatic authority is not bounded by either rules or traditions. Rational authority implies impersonal bureaucratic relationships such that people obey superiors not as individuals but as members of an organisation. Traditional and, especially, charismatic authority is structured around relationships of personal loyalty. Finally, rational authority implies equality of treatment for "everyone in the same empirical situation" while, in the case of traditional and charismatic authority, treatment depends on custom, status, whim and personal ties to those yielding power.

While good governance from a Weberian perspective is associated with written law, it is important to consider that from a long-run historical perspective, written law has been neither a necessary nor a sufficient condition for equal treatment. By treating all (male) members equally, hunter-gatherer societies have been able to approach the rule of law even in the absence of writing (more on this in Chapter 3). Human history offers many examples of formal laws affording unequal treatment of individuals according to their social rank and, at most, equal treatment only within one's class (Samuel Finer [1997]). By way of illustration, the Hamurabi code of Babylonia dating back to the eighteenth century BCE applies different satisfactions and different penalties according to whether one is privileged, a commoner or a slave. According to Roman law, the lower classes in the Roman Empire (*humiliores*) were subject to corporal and capital punishment from which the upper classes (*honestiores*) were exempt. The T'ang Empire's law code emerging in seventh century CE China, was "inegalitarian, root and branch" with lighter and easily escapable punishments for the upper classes, heavier and inescapable ones for the common folk and "ferocious" punishments for the lower classes that included slaves. Finer also gives examples of societies with formal laws extending equality of treatment beyond social rank. The Mosaic code of the Jewish Kingdoms gave no special status to priests or aristocrats and protected even slaves. The written law of the Venetian Republic treated commoners the same as nobles and afforded free legal counsel to those too poor to pay for it. We could go on with other examples – mostly of unequal treatment across social groups – but the point is that there is nothing inherent in formal law that ensures equal treatment (see also, Bruce Trigger [2003]).

Rather than focusing on impartiality, Francis Fukuyama (2013) proposes that good governance is a reflection of "a government's ability to make and enforce rules, and to deliver services, regardless of whether that government is democratic or not" (page 350). In this context, the author focuses on two variables, namely, state capacity and bureaucratic autonomy. Capacity includes the ability to raise taxes and the education and professionalisation of the public administration. Autonomy refers to independence from politicians and is inversely related to the number and type of mandates issued by politicians. The relationship between autonomy and the quality of governance could be non-linear: quality will be low if autonomy is limited, as is the case when politicians staff public administrations with political appointees, or when autonomy is very high, since then bureaucracy is not subject to any political control. Greater capacity may increase the optimal level of autonomy insofar as better-educated and more professional civil servants internalise norms that reduce the possibility of malfeasance. Fukuyama argues that his approach to good governance differs from the "impartiality" approach. The emphasis on tax capacity is an obvious difference between the two. On the other hand, both his and the impartiality view separate democracy from governance. Moreover, the emphasis on a professional and independent civil service is a corollary of the application of impartiality – rather than personal, ideological or group criteria – when recruiting public servants.

The quality of governance has been defined much more broadly. Rafael La Porta *et al.* (1999) state that quality emerges when the public sector does not distort the proper functioning of the private sector (that is, it respects property rights and does not overregulate), is an efficient administrator (meaning that corruption and red-tape are low while tax compliance is high), provides public goods (such as education and health) and allows for and protects political freedoms. Similarly, Daniel Kaufmann *et al.* (2010) define governance as,

> the traditions and institutions by which authority in a country is exercised. This includes (a) the process by which governments are selected, monitored and replaced; (b) the capacity of the government to effectively formulate and implement sound policies; and (c) the respect of citizens and the state for the institutions that govern economic and social interactions among them.
>
> (Page 4)

Both these definitions include democracy as part of good governance and as such, diverge from those previously presented. On the other hand, the reference to property right protection, control of corruption and respect of citizens and the state for institutions overlaps with governance-as-impartiality while tax compliance and government capacity clearly coincides with Fukuyama's approach.

There is some confusion in scholarly work between the concepts of institutional quality on the one hand and the quality of governance on the other (see also, Andreas Kyriacou [2013a]). Most authors use the terms institutional quality and the quality of governance interchangeably. But North (1991) famously defines institutions as the "humanly devised constraints that structure political, economic and social interaction. They consist of both informal constraints (sanctions, taboos, customs, traditions, and codes of conduct), and formal rules (constitutions, laws, property rights)" (page 97). Defined in this way, institutions are more an input into the quality of governance. For example, formal protection of property rights and de jure institutional constraints more generally, may contribute towards better governance but they do not necessarily reflect the extent to which these formal rules are actually binding (Voigt [2013]). Informal rules and more generally cultural traits may influence the extent to which government acts impartially, including respect for the rule of law, control of corruption and meritocratic recruitment but, as will be explained in Chapter 6, they are clearly distinct from these governance outcomes.

Measuring governance

Because of their country coverage and over time comparability, most quantitative work has employed the World Governance Indicators published by the

World Bank (WBGI). The WBGI cover over 200 states since 1996 and are based on perceptions of experts, survey respondents, non-governmental and public-sector organisations. A key feature of the indicators is that all country scores are accompanied by standard errors that reflect the number of sources available for a country and the extent to which these sources agree with each other (Kaufmann *et al.* [2010]). The WBGI measure the quality of governance across six dimensions: (1) voice and accountability (VA) – the extent to which a country's citizens are able to participate in selecting their government, as well as freedom of expression, freedom of association, and a free media (as such it encapsulates the notion of democracy); (2) political stability and the absence of violence (PS) – the likelihood that the government will be destabilised or over-thrown by unconstitutional or violent means; (3) government effectiveness (GE) – the quality of public services, the quality of the civil service and the degree of its independence from political pressures, the quality of policy formulation and implementation, and the credibility of the government's commitment to such policies; (4) regulatory quality (RQ) – the ability of the government to formulate and implement sound policies and regulations that permit and promote private sector development; (5) the rule of law (RL) – the extent to which agents have confidence in and abide by the rules of society, and in particular the quality of contract enforcement, property rights, the police, and the courts, as well as the likelihood of crime and violence, and; (6) control of corruption (CC) – the extent to which public power is exercised for private gain, including both petty and grand forms of corruption, as well as "capture" of the state by elites and private interests.

It has been pointed out, based on partial correlations, that the first two indicators (VA and PS) are distinct from the last four (GE, RG, RL and CC), while the latter are strongly correlated with each other (Laura Langbein and Stephen Knack [2010]). According to these authors, one way of thinking about the six dimensions is to see VA and PS as inputs into the general notion of good governance that is captured by dimensions 3 to 6. Indeed, in my sample, the simple correlations among the last four dimensions range from 0.889 (p-value 0), between RQ and CC, to 0.945 (p-value 0), between CC and GE. One reason for these high correlations is that the different dimensions are capturing the same underlying variable which, given the previous discussion, could be impartiality in the exercise of public authority. Whatever the underlying variable connecting these dimensions, it makes sense to combine them to obtain an aggregate indicator of the quality of governance. I thus take the average values of the GE, RQ, RL and CC dimensions. The resultant variable can range from −2.5 to 2.5, with higher values reflecting higher quality.

In the empirical analysis, I employ the average value of the WBGI variables over 1996–2016 as well as the average values of the time variant variables (including the inequality measures discussed later) over the same period. I thus focus on the cross-section variation in the data and do not exploit the variation of the key variables over time. While this approach obviously sacrifices information gained from the time-dimension, it is important to note that the governance measures vary much more across countries than over time as attested by the between and within standard deviations (sd) of the aggregate governance indicator. Specifically, the overall sd is 0.968, the between sd is 0.958 and the within sd is 0.159 (see also, Kaufman *et al.* [2010]). Taking average inequality values for each country, moreover, reduces noise in the inequality measures described later, due to abrupt changes in the household surveys on which they are based (William Easterly [2007]). It also has the salutary effect of increasing the sample size since the inequality indicators are relatively scarce for some countries over time.

In Figure 2.1, I plot the aggregate governance measure against the VA dimension. The figure shows that there are important cross-country differences in the quality of governance. Quality is low in countries such as Somalia, South Sudan (SSD) and the Democratic Republic of Congo (ZAR), higher in ones like Armenia, Tunisia and Mexico, and highest in Denmark, New Zealand and Norway, amongst others. It also shows the merit of not including Voice and Accountability when generating the aggregate governance indicator. The quality of governance is positively associated with VA, but there are also some stark differences. The quality of governance is very high and VA relatively low in Singapore and Hong Kong while quality is low and VA high in countries such as the Marshall Islands (MHL), Palau (PLW) and Nauru (NRU).

Perceptions-based indicators have both strengths and weaknesses (for discussions see, for example, Daniel Treisman [2007]; Kaufmann *et al.* [2010]; Ray Fisman and Miriam Golden [2017]). One issue is the presence of systematic biases in perceptions. Biases could emerge because experts may read the same reports and even rely on each other's assessments. Moreover, a "halo effect"

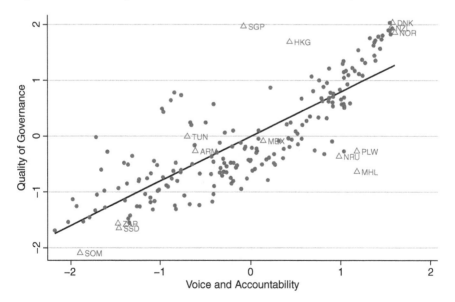

Figure 2.1 Measuring the quality of governance.

may exist such that a strong economy or democracy can elicit positive views on governance from those surveyed. In addition, ideological biases may also emerge insofar as those who express more (less) scepticism regarding a large economic role for government are more (less) likely to perceive problems in governance. Alternatively, perceptions-based indicators have a set of advantages. One is that perceptions are important since individuals base their decisions on them (see also, Kaufmann *et al.* [2010]). Another is that relying on more objective measures of governance such as, for example, corruption convictions, may be more indicative of the efficiency of police, courts and the media rather than the extent of corruption. Similarly, employing data on reported bribes paid can also lead to biases since individuals surveyed may underreport bribery incidents or, even worse, not report them at all (see Nathan Jensen and Aminur Rahman [2015] and Treisman [2015]). Finally, perceptions-based data have a much greater coverage than objective measures, which tend to be limited to specific-country cases, or reported bribery data, whose year and country coverage is much more limited (see, for example, the United Nations International Crime Victims Survey, Transparency International's Global Corruption Barometer and the World Bank's Enterprise Surveys).

Defining inequality

At the outset it is useful to distinguish between what Easterly (2007) calls structural and market inequality. Structural inequality emerges when non-market decisions grant individuals or groups more rights than others. Slavery is the clearest example since it deprives those subject to it of their right to life and freedom. Structural inequality was instituted by feudalism insofar as it assigned different rights and obligations to social groups leading to a steep social hierarchy. Hereditary kingdoms – both ancient and contemporary – are another case of structural inequality since kings and their heirs are afforded rights denied to others. Disenfranchisement of social groups based on gender or race is another example. South Africa's system of Apartheid or the Jim Crow laws in the United States, both of which institutionalised discrimination against people based on skin colour, are two notable cases. Arguably, a distinction should be made between de jure and de facto structural (in)equality. As previously stated, the absence of written laws enshrining equal treatment does not mean that it may not emerge in practice. Moreover, the adoption of equal treatment in formal law does not guarantee equal treatment in practice. While de jure inequality has been virtually eliminated since the twentieth century, de facto structural inequality persists wherever individuals or groups, who in principle are equal before the law, are afforded unequal treatment. In other words, de facto structural equality is synonymous with the rule of law and thus, good governance, while de jure equality before the law is not.

Market inequality on the other hand emerges when income and wealth diverge in the context of voluntary market exchange. It can be the result of effort but also a host of factors that are beyond one's control including initial resource endowments, innate cognitive capacities, noncognitive personality traits such as risk aversion or the capacity to defer gratification, cultural factors like the Protestant work ethic and social capital or, simply, chance (see, for example, Samuel Bowles and Herbert Gintis [2002] and Miles Corak [2013]). Thus, two individuals who are not legally discriminated because of their skin colour, may diverge economically because they do not have access to the same resources needed to develop their capabilities. Or two people with the same de jure rights and similar initial endowments may diverge in their incomes over time because of different innate capacities, personality traits, cultures, levels of effort or simply because of good or bad luck.

Equal opportunity policies such as public health and education can reduce market inequality insofar as they mitigate the impact of uncontrollable factors. But public policy can also reduce market inequality by changing the distribution of income and wealth through progressive redistributive policies on both the tax and spending sides. Obviously, the potential impact of equal opportunity and redistributive policies is especially large in societies where the experience of structural inequality was stronger and more recent. The economic inequality that emerges after public intervention is known as net inequality (market inequality is also known as gross inequality). Net inequality represents the economic inequality experienced by individuals or groups and as such will be more suitable to capture the causal arguments linking inequality with governance.[1]

Economic inequality can be interpersonal or intergroup. While the former generally refers to income or wealth differences among households, the latter deals with such differences across social groups. These groups can be defined in terms of some relatively mutable economic dimension such as social class, but they can also be defined by more immutable categories such as race, ethnicity or religion. Combining income or wealth differences with one or more of these relatively fixed categories or markers is likely to increase the saliency of social groups. In other words, group boundaries are likely to harden as we add group markers to intergroup income inequalities (Joel Selway [2011]). Conversely, interpersonal inequality within social groups will tend to undermine group boundaries.

Measuring inequality

The most widely used measure of economic inequality, the Gini index, is derived by plotting the cumulative share of the units of analysis (households or groups) ordered from lowest to highest incomes (x-axis) against the cumulative share of income earned by them (y-axis). Perfect equality is represented in this space by a 45° line starting at the origin, since this means that a given percentage of the population receives the same percentage of income. Inequality increases as the curve that emerges when plotting the two variables – known as the Lorenz curve – falls below the 45° line, although necessarily it, as well as the 45° line, must begin and end at the same point (since 0 per cent of the population will receive 0 per cent of income and 100 per cent receives all the income). The Gini index or coefficient is computed as the ratio of the area between the two curves (Lorenz curve and 45° line) to the area beneath the 45° line. It ranges between 0 and 1 (or 0 and 100) and a higher Gini coefficient represents a more unequal distribution. To measure interpersonal inequality, I turn to the Standardized World Income Inequality Database (SWIID) that combines household survey data from the Luxemburg Income Study (LIS) and the United Nations University–World Institute for Development Economics (UNU-WIDER) to provide the widest cross-country and time-series data on market and net income inequality (Solt [2016]).[2]

In Figure 2.2, I plot the Gini index of net income against that of market income from SWIID while at the same time halving the space in two by way of a 45° line. Redistributive policies reduce those inequalities that emerge in the market and, consistent with this, the figure clearly shows that for most of the countries in the sample, net income inequality is below market inequality. The figure also shows that reductions in market inequalities are more significant in wealthy countries and much less so in developing ones. This result may be driven by three complementary factors (see also, Houle [2017]). First, wealthier countries simply have more resources to redistribute. Second, they have more state capacity meaning that they are better able to raise taxes and to redistribute the available income. Third, poor countries may adopt less progressive policies because politics is less about the left-right ideological divide (less programmatic) and more about patronage (more clientelist). In Chapter 5, I will discuss the relationship between patron-client and redistributive politics. For now, the possibility that the former may be more important than the latter in poorer

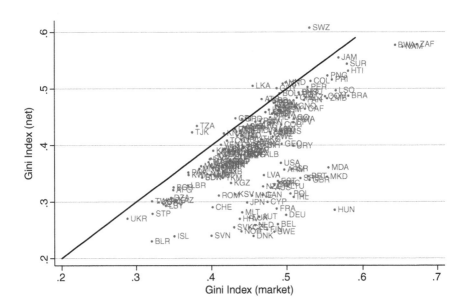

Figure 2.2 Market versus net income inequality.

countries, may be an important reason why net income inequality exceeds market inequality in countries like Tajikistan, Tanzania, Sri Lanka and Swaziland.[3]

The greatest advantage of the Gini index is that it is widely reported and is thus available for a large sample of countries (the SWIID provides data on 192 countries from 1960 to 2016). It does have disadvantages however; one of them being that changes in the index may represent different changes in the underlying distribution of income (see, for example, Klaus Deininger and Lyn Squire [1996] and Frank Cowell [2008]). For example, redistribution from the highest income earners to the middle class leads to the same change in the Gini coefficient as a redistribution of income from the middle class to the lowest income earners. To get a fuller picture of inequality, I will follow Deininger and Squire (1996) and additionally measure inequality based on income quintiles: one measure is the share of disposable income earned by the wealthiest 20 per cent on the share earned by the poorest 20 per cent (Q5/Q1) and another is the share of income earned by the middle 60 per cent (Q2, Q3 and Q4) – also labelled the middle class (for example, Easterly [2001] and Anthony Atkinson and Andrea Brandolini [2011]). For data on income shares, I turn to the World Bank's World Development Indicators (WDI) and specifically data from the World Bank's Development Research Group.

In Figure 2.3, I plot the net income Gini from SWIID against the Q5 to Q1 ratio from the WDI (again, always taking average values over the period extending from 1996 to 2016). The association is strong as attested by a simple correlation statistic of 0.663 (p-value of 0). This said, the figure shows a degree of

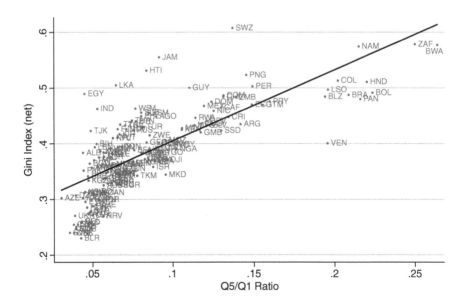

Figure 2.3 Gini versus Q5 to Q1 ratio.

dispersion confirming the idea that the two indicators represent different ways to measure income inequality. In Figure 2.4, I plot the net income Gini against the share of disposable income accruing to the middle class. The relationship is now negative indicating that a larger middle class is associated with less inequality. The association is even stronger now with a simple correlation of –0.856 (p-value of 0).

I also use a Gini indicator, available for a limited subset of countries, which reflects (mis)perceptions of income inequality (Vladimir Gimpelson and Treisman [2018]). This measure is based on the International Social Survey Project (ISSP [2009]) and specifically question 14a, which asked respondents to guess the distribution of resources in their country. Perceived rather than actual inequality is important since the former is more likely to affect behaviour. The data covers 40 countries and the year 2009. In Figure 2.5, I plot the SWIID Gini against this measure of perceived inequality in a space split into two halves by a 45° line. While the figure suggests that perceived inequality is broadly similar to actual inequality (in fact the simple correlation is 0.412 with a p-value of 0.008), it also points to important differences in some countries. For example, in countries such as Switzerland (CHE), France and Hungary where actual inequality is similar (Gini index of 0.290, 0.288 and 0.285 respectively), perceived inequality is 0.276 in Switzerland, 0.333 in France and 0.379 in Hungary. Alternatively, Slovakia and South Africa with similar levels of perceived inequality (0.363 and 0.366), vary significantly in actual inequality (0.255 and 0.578 respectively).

To measure (in)equality of opportunity I turn to an indicator proposed by Paolo Brunori *et al.* (2013). They differentiate inequality due to circumstances

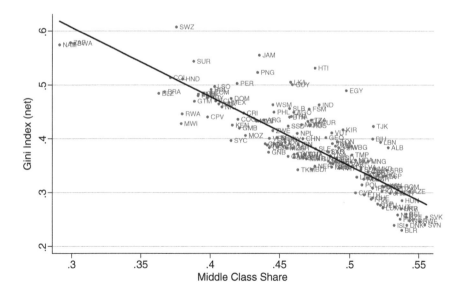

Figure 2.4 Gini versus middle class share.

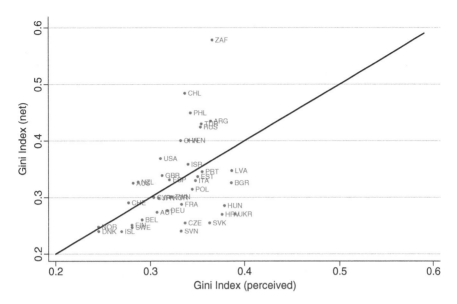

Figure 2.5 Actual versus perceived Gini.

beyond one's personal control (for example gender, age, ethnicity, place of birth, or parental background) from inequality due to effort. Equal opportunity policies aim to minimise the impact of uncontrollable circumstances on one's income prospects. By way of illustration, equality of opportunity would exist if, assuming the same level of effort, men and women earned similar wages. The index of inequality of opportunity, available for 41 countries, is obtained by regressing individual income on circumstances and an error term, assuming that the impact of effort on income is captured by the error, and using the estimated impact of circumstances to predict incomes. The resultant distribution of incomes reflects that which emerges due to different circumstances and thus is a measure of inequality of opportunity. Given the difficulty of accounting for all circumstances beyond one's control, the measure must be taken as a lower bound of the extent of inequality (for an extensive discussion of the concept of equality of opportunity, see John Roemer [2008]).

In Figure 2.6, I plot the net income Gini against the inequality of opportunity measure. The data reveal a positive association but the two indicators are clearly measuring different types of inequality as additionally attested by a simple correlation of 0.359 (p-value of 0). The figure shows that high income inequality countries like Egypt, Colombia, Panama and Brazil, differ markedly in the degree of equality of opportunities enjoyed by their citizens – relatively high in Egypt, much lower in Brazil. From another perspective, it also tells us that income inequality varies among countries that have similar levels of equality of opportunity. For example, the indicator of inequality of opportunity is

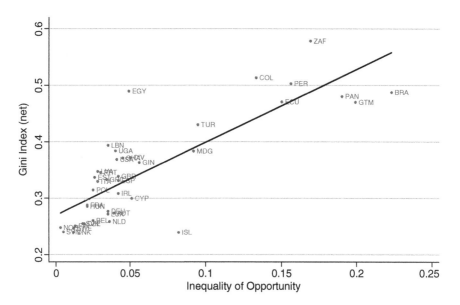

Figure 2.6 Gini versus inequality of opportunity.

around 0.035 for the Netherlands, Luxembourg, Germany (DEU), Greece and Lebanon, but the first three countries have significantly lower net income inequalities than the last two.

To measure ethnic group inequalities, I turn to two indicators proposed by Alesina *et al.* (2016). These authors combine ethnographic and linguistic maps on the location of ethnic groups, with satellite images of light intensity at night as a proxy for development, to generate Gini indicators capturing differences in mean income across ethnic groups. To identify the location of ethnic groups they employ the Geo-Referencing of Ethnic Groups (GREG), which is the digitised version of the Soviet Atlas Narodov Mira and provides information on ethnic groups in the early 1960s, as well as the Ethnologue that maps language groups in the mid to late 1990s (ETHG). The GREG strives to map major immigrant groups whereas Ethnologue generally does not, something that is relevant for New World countries. The ethnic inequality data covers up to 173 countries and three periods, namely, 1992, 2000 and 2012. I employ the average values over the three periods. The resultant indicators are similar as indicated by the simple correlation statistic of 0.770 (p-value of 0).

In Figure 2.7, I plot the Gini index measuring interpersonal income inequality against the ethnic inequality measure from GREG. The two variables are clearly measuring different types of inequality (simple correlation is 0.107 with a p-value of 0.170). Thus, ethnic inequality is 0 in the Bahamas and Jamaica while interpersonal inequality is 0.493 and 0.555 respectively. Conversely, interpersonal inequality is relatively low in Norway and Finland (0.248 and 0.251) whereas ethnic inequality is quite high (0.561 and 0.699 respectively).

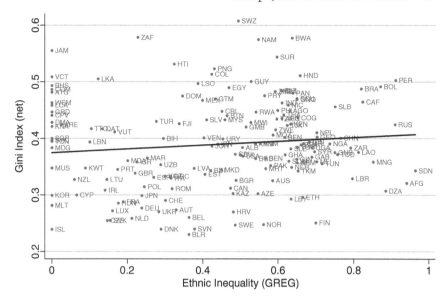

Figure 2.7 Interpersonal versus ethnic inequality.

Correlations

Having described the indicators measuring the quality of governance and eco-nomic inequality, I will now consider the extent to which (if at all) these indi-cators suggest an association between governance and inequality. In Figures 2.8 to 2.13, I plot the quality of governance indicator, against the various inequality measures. The figures clearly show a negative correlation between good govern-ance and inequality. Going from the weakest to the strongest correlation, the quality of governance is negatively correlated with the Q5/Q1 ratio (Figure 2.9, simple correlation = –0.184, p-value = 0.019, N = 160), negatively correlated with the Gini index of net income (Figure 2.8, simple correlation = –0.305, p-value = 0, N = 184), positively correlated with the middle class income share (Figure 2.10, simple correlation = 0.309, p-value = 0, N = 161), negatively correl-ated with ethnic inequality as measured via GREG (Figure 2.13, simple correl-ation = –0.516, p-value = 0, N = 172), negatively correlated with inequality of opportunity (Figure 2.12, simple correlation = –0.531, p-value = 0, N = 41) and, finally, negatively correlated with perceived inequality (Figure 2.11, simple correlation = –0.746, p-value = 0, N = 40).

The figures and simple correlations suggest that governance and inequality may be associated in some way. Two important points must be made here. First, association or correlation does not mean causation. Thus, knowing from Figure 2.8 that as interpersonal net income inequality increases the quality of govern-ance falls, does not mean that rising inequality worsens governance. It could also be the case that bad governance increases inequality. As will be explained in Chapter 5, it seems even more likely that the direction of causality goes in both

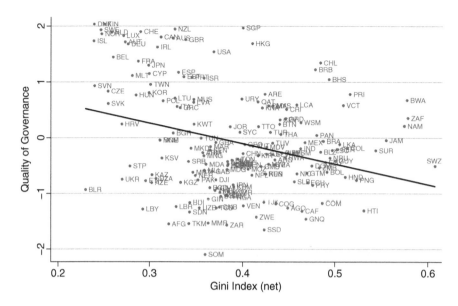

Figure 2.8 Quality of governance and inequality (Gini index).

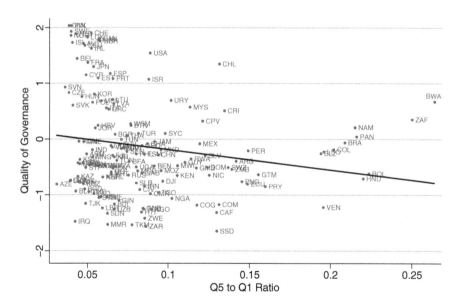

Figure 2.9 Quality of governance and inequality (Q5 to Q1 ratio).

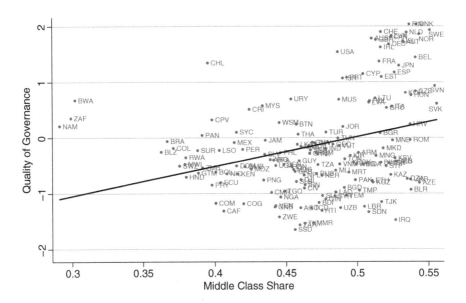

Figure 2.10 Quality of governance and the middle class.

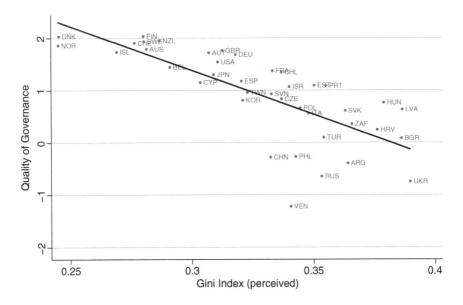

Figure 2.11 Quality of governance and perceived inequality.

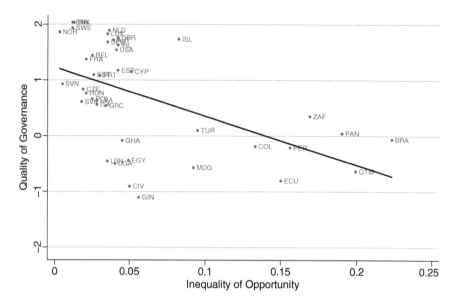

Figure 2.12 Quality of governance and inequality of opportunity.

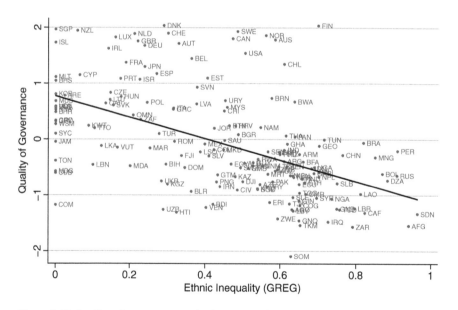

Figure 2.13 Quality of governance and ethnic inequality.

directions. Moreover, the simple associations ignore the influence of other factors that may be related to both good governance and inequality. One very important factor in this respect is economic development.

In Chapter 1, I have already reviewed work that has identified good governance as an important determinant of economic development. But economic development has, itself, been identified as an important determinant of good governance. Development may improve governance because it is associated with the spread of education and literacy thus increasing the odds that bad governance will be detected and contested (Treisman [2000]; Lorenzo Pellegrini and Reyer Gerlagh [2008]). Moreover, wealthier countries can pay public officials more, thus both selecting more competent ones, and weakening their incentive to abuse their power for private gain (Caroline Van Rijckeghem and Beatrice Weder [1997]; Gabriella Montinola and Robert Jackman [2002]; Fisman and Golden [2017]).

Economic development has also been linked to income inequality. I have already explained that wealthier countries may redistribute more because they have more resources and state capacity, and because politics in these countries tends to be more programmatic. But perhaps the most famous account of how development and inequality are linked is the Kuznets curve (see, originally, Kuznets [1955]). The shift from agriculture to industry that accompanies economic development leads to greater income inequalities because of a divergence between urban and rural incomes and because rural incomes are more equally distributed. As industrial employment increases, the income distribution improves since more and more workers earn their living in industry and because the fall of the labour force in agriculture drives up wages there. Thus, an inverted U-shape relationship is proposed with inequality increasing when economic development begins and eventually falling at higher levels of development. Finally, inequality may also impact on economic development in several ways previously mentioned. It can have a positive impact by sharpening incentives for innovation and entrepreneurship or facilitating saving and investment. But it can also affect development negatively, insofar as it begets class conflict that can lead to political instability, it reduces the health and education levels of the less well-off, it leads to redistributive policies that dull incentives to work and, the subject of this monograph, to the extent that it undermines the quality of governance (see Berg *et al.* [2018] for a review).

Whatever the causal relationship between economic development on the one hand, and the quality of governance and inequality on the other, the truth is that the most widely used measure of development, GDP per capita, and the governance and inequality measures are statistically associated. In Table 2.1, I display the simple correlations between the logarithm of real GDP per capita (taking average values over the period 1996–2014) and the governance and inequality measures described earlier. It shows that real GDP per capita is strongly correlated with governance and the perceived inequality indicator and it is also associated with the other inequality measures at statistically significant levels. Economic development is positively associated with governance and negatively with inequality.

Table 2.1 Correlation with real GDP per capita

	Log of real GDP per capita	P-value	Number of observations
Quality of governance	0.756	0.000	175
SWIID Gini index	−0.288	0.000	168
Q5/Q1 ratio	−0.155	0.060	148
Middle class share	0.369	0.000	149
Perceived Gini	−0.742	0.000	40
Inequality of opportunity	−0.373	0.016	41
Ethnic inequality (GREG)	−0.465	0.000	162

In view of these correlations, in Table 2.2, I regress the governance measure against the inequality indicators, first in the absence, and then in the presence of real GDP per capita, taking care to employ the same sample of countries in each case. At the outset, it is important to reiterate that the results reported in Table 2.2 are preliminary since they don't control for other confounding variables nor do they address the issue of two-way causality. Notwithstanding this, the results confirm the negative association between good governance and inequality suggested by Figures 2.8 to 2.13. The quality of governance is negatively associated with the Gini index measuring interpersonal (actual and perceived) and intergroup inequality, the Q5/Q1 ratio, and the inequality of opportunity measure, and positively associated with the middle class share of disposable income. However, the strength of the relationship and, at times, its statistical significance, is significantly reduced when controlling for real GDP per capita. The reduction of the point estimates corresponding to the inequality variables when including GDP per capita, together with the large increase in the adjusted R^2, suggests that it is an important confounding variable, the inclusion of which, provides an important step towards checking the robustness of the estimated effect of inequality on the quality of governance. It is for this reason that, in all the empirical estimates exploring cross-country differences in the quality of governance, I always control for the level of economic development of the countries included.

Conclusion

Good governance is impartial governance. It means that public officials are unswayed by personal preferences and relationships and, instead, take decisions based on laws and policies that treat people in the same empirical situation equally. It manifests itself in the absence of corruption, equality before the law and meritocratic recruitment of a civil service that is shielded from political meddling. Good governance is not the same as democratic governance as attested by empirical indicators measuring both concepts. While democracy is strongly and positively correlated with good governance, suggesting that it may be an important determining variable, the empirical measures also point to several

Table 2.2 Quality of governance and inequality

	Dependent variable: Quality of governance			
	Inequality measure	*Log of real GDP per capita*	*Adjusted R²*	*N° of observations*
SWIID Gini index	−4.150*** (0.943)		0.113	166
	−1.568** (0.639)	0.578*** (0.042)	0.594	166
Q5/Q1 ratio	−3.529** (1.514)		0.025	148
	−1.191 (1.013)	0.622*** (0.042)	0.602	148
Middle class share	5.428*** (1.544)		0.094	149
	0.602 (0.869)	0.618*** (0.044)	0.599	149
Perceived Gini	−16.855*** (1.921)		0.545	40
	−7.631*** (2.185)	0.823*** (0.138)	0.676	40
Inequality of opportunity	−8.779*** (1.555)		0.264	41
	−3.948*** (0.935)	0.727*** (0.073)	0.801	41
Ethnic inequality (GREG)	−1.971*** (0.232)		0.270	161
	−0.852*** (0.212)	0.595*** (0.051)	0.595	161

Notes
Regressions displayed horizontally. All regressions are OLS and include a constant (not shown). White heteroscedasticity consistent standard errors in parentheses. *, **, **** significance at the 10, 5 and 1 per cent levels respectively.

instances of democratic countries with low quality of governance and non-democracies with good governance.

Inequality can be structural or market-based. In the former case, this implies the existence of formal laws that discriminate in favour of individuals or social groups. Even when formal laws enshrine equal treatment, structural inequality exists when unequal treatment emerges in the application of the law. This, de facto structural inequality, is thus synonymous with the absence of impartial or good governance. Market inequality emerges in the context of voluntary exchange in the private sector. It can be the result of effort but also a range of factors beyond one's control. It can be reduced by redistributive policies, as well as policies like public health and education that aim to reduce the impact of uncontrollable factors on one's capacity to earn market income.

Inequalities in income and wealth emerge both across individuals and across social groups.

The available indicators measuring good governance on the one hand, and inequality on the other, suggest a negative association between the two. This association emerges when measuring inequality through several indicators. With the exception of the quintile-based measures, the negative association is robust to the addition of a very important confounding variable, namely, real GDP per capita as a proxy for the level of economic development. This does not mean however that we have a causal story linking inequality with governance. For that, we need to explore the channels through which inequality may undermine governance, at the same time as we consider the possibility that the quality of governance may influence economic inequality. Empirically this requires that we account for a range of additional covariates and, moreover, that we propose exogenous determinants of inequality in an effort to isolate inequality's impact on governance. The remainder of this book is devoted towards this theoretical and empirical exploration.

Notes

1 This is also one reason for not employing inequality data based on income tax statistics since they mostly employ gross (before tax) income (see Atkinson *et al.* [2011] for this and other shortcomings of tax-based data including, a limited availability of countries, information only on the top income shares, different definitions of income within and across countries and biases due to differential rates of tax evasion).
2 In the Appendix, I list the different country samples corresponding to each inequality indicator employed in the analysis.
3 Walter Scheidel (2017) states that, just like the case of many developing countries today, for most recorded history, the absence of extensive fiscal redistributive systems meant that there was little difference between market and disposable incomes. According to him "[r]egular income taxes rarely predate the twentieth century" (Introduction, subheading "How is it done?", eBook).

3 Insights from the past

Introduction

In this chapter, I will consider the relationship between inequality and governance from a long-run historical perspective. I will argue that the emergence of good governance in the guise of rule of law depends on the weakness of social stratification and ingroup bias. I will review four interrelated factors affecting stratification and bias, namely, infectious disease, population growth, intra and intergroup conflict and the nature of production. These factors, in turn, depend on the biogeographic conditions experienced by human societies making biogeography an ultimate cause of governance. In this respect, my approach here is similar to a growing body of work that has identified the impact of biogeography on contemporary social and economic outcomes (see Nathan Nunn [2009]; Enrico Spolaore and Romain Wacziarg [2013]; Nunn [2014]; and Quamrul Ashraf and Oded Galor [2018] for reviews).

This long-run perspective is justified for at least two reasons. First, pre-history and history provide a wealth of variation in the degree of inequality and governance regimes and can thus help illuminate our understanding of the relationship between these variables. Second, the identification of biogeographic factors can yield a range of exogenous determinants of inequality that may be useful when analysing the causal relationship between contemporary inequality and governance.

This chapter is structured as follows. In the next section, I will argue that at the most basic level, societal structures relevant to governance emerge in response to existential uncertainty. This uncertainty is driven by a Darwinian struggle for survival and reproductive success, as well as cognitive limits faced when trying to fathom the intentions of others. Social hierarchies and group bias emerge to reduce existential uncertainty. Having explained this, in the following section I will argue that the steepness of social hierarchy and the strength of group ties determine the extent to which societies have been able to move towards equality before the law. After that, we will see that these social responses to existential uncertainty have been shaped by four factors namely, disease, demography, conflict and production and that these factors, in turn, have been influenced by biogeographic conditions. I will end the chapter with a discussion of religion in this light before summarising the main findings.

Social responses to existential uncertainty

Human beings strive to reduce existential uncertainty. This uncertainty emerges from the natural environment and, as technology has granted humans greater mastery over nature and human societies have increased in size, especially from human interaction (North [2005]). At the most basic level, uncertainty due to human interaction derives from two sources: a Darwinian struggle for survival and reproductive success on the one hand, and cognitive limits on the other.[1]

Consider first the Darwinian struggle to survive and transmit one's genes to the next generation. In this struggle, the individual's relative position within the social group is important since individuals with more status are likely to be more successful in securing resources and mating partners. Status is what economists call a positional good such that its consumption by one person necessarily implies less for another (see, for example, Robert Frank [1985]). Higher status does not only bestow greater access to resources and mates. It can also improve one's health. Frank (1985) refers to research showing that when monkeys or humans attain high status this increases their level of serotonin, a neurotransmitter associated with happiness and well-being. Michael Marmot (2004) speaks of a "status syndrome" such that a person's health is directly affected by his status or social position. Higher status implies greater autonomy or control over one's life and more opportunities for social participation both of which are identified as important determinants of good health.[2]

The pursuit of status in the context of a Darwinian struggle for survival and reproductive success represents a basic driving force behind social hierarchies. Scholars have explained how our closest primate relatives – chimpanzees, bonobos and gorillas – are organised hierarchically with an alpha male (and female in the case of bonobos) at the top with greater or exclusive (in the case of gorillas) access to mating opportunities (see most recently, Gintis *et al.* [2015] for associated work). But being the alpha also entails obligations. Christopher Boehm (1999) explains that the alpha male has an important role in diffusing conflict among the group's members if necessary, through the use of force. He calls this "governance with authority" (page 27). Thus, the very same hierarchy that emerges in the context of a zero-sum game for status and ultimately reproductive success, can also potentially act as a mechanism to reduce that conflict and ensuing uncertainty that emerge from social interaction within groups.

Based on evidence from both primate and hunter-gatherer societies, anthropologists have shown that hierarchy will be contested (Robert Kelly [1995]; Boehm [1999]). Because of the benefits of higher status in primate communities, individuals will occasionally attempt to topple the alpha male and take his place. Moreover, in chimpanzee and bonobo groups, coalitions of lower ranked individuals will sometimes form to remove a dominant and abusive male. Similarly, hunter-gatherers strive to preserve their individual autonomy by enforcing reverse dominance hierarchies. Faced with despotic or aggrandising tendencies by individual members, hunter-gatherers apply levelling actions of various intensities: moderate (criticism, ridicule, disobedience), strong (ostracism, expulsion, deposition or desertion) or very strong (execution of up-starts). The egalitarian nature of hunter-gatherers is also reflected in their prac-tice of meat sharing and collective decision-making by consensus.[3]

In sum, social hierarchies are the result of the struggle for status and ultimately for survival and reproductive success. But they do not reflect a Hobbesian anarchy or the unregulated fight of all against all. On the con-trary, the hierarchical organisation of the group can reduce the conflict and resultant uncertainty that emerges from the Darwinian struggle for survival. Conflict can be reduced due to the peace-keeping intervention of dominant members of the group, and insofar as group members accept their relative position on the social ladder. Dominant members can diffuse intragroup conflict if necessary, by using force. Indeed, this is the basic justification for granting a monopoly of violence to rulers or the state. However, hierarchies will be challenged by other would-be alphas or, more interestingly, by group members who rebel against the abuse of power by high-ranking members. Insofar as they are successful in reversing the social hierarchy, individuals are moving towards the establishment of equality before the law.

Let us turn now to a second biological building block – cognitive limits. Evolutionary anthropologist Robin Dunbar (1992) has explained how the human brain allows us to keep track of social relationships in small groups of up to 150 individuals with whom we have face-to-face interactions. Within such groups, we can identify cooperators and defectors and act accordingly. In other words, in small social groups, the uncertainty that emerges from social inter-action is reduced by the personal knowledge of the different members of the group. Dunbar's insight is related to the concept of reciprocal altruism that describes the ability to sustain cooperation with non-kin in the context of repeated interactions and tit-for-tat strategies or norms: one cooperates as long as others do and ceases to do so when others do not (Robert Trivers [1971]; Robert Axelrod [1984]). Reciprocal altruism must be distinguished from kin selection according to which individuals will behave more altruistically towards kin the more closely related they are, since by doing so they are improv-ing the survival chances of their own genes (William Hamilton [1964a, 1964b]). By genetically aligning the self-interest of kin group members, kin selection makes social interaction more predictable.

Thus, in small group contexts the personal knowledge of the individual members of the group and repeated exchange increase predictability in social interaction, especially if the members of the group are genetically related. But as the size of the group increases, genetic proximity falls and personal knowledge of others is more difficult since, beyond the 150 person threshold, the computa-tional effort required to monitor direct relationships with others becomes over-whelming. Moreover, the likelihood of repeated interactions with other group members falls. This makes it increasingly difficult to sustain cooperative relation-ships. In an effort to reduce the ensuing uncertainty, people will tend to develop a dual strategy, namely, construct hierarchical personal relationships and adopt symbolic markers (Peter Turchin and Sergey Gavrilets [2009]).

Hierarchy allows people to maintain personal one-to-one relationships with others, even in large group contexts. Now, individuals can focus on their relationship with those immediately above or below them in the social hierarchy. This reduces the computational effort required to keep track of the intention of others. It also increases the likelihood of repeated interaction. As such, hierarchically ordered personal relationships will be a rational response to the increased uncertainty in social interaction that emerges in larger group settings.

The idea of symbolic markers on the other hand, refers to the classification of non-relatives by way of specific criteria such as language, ethnicity or religion. The symbolic marker acts as a screening device allowing individuals to predict the behaviour of others. In other words, people within one's ingroup are on average considered more predictable than those outside it. And this predictability facilitates social cooperation within groups, strengthening ties among group members, while its absence or relative scarcity when interacting with outgroup members undermines exchange or even promotes conflict between groups (see also, Kyriacou [2005], Robert Boyd and Peter Richerson [2005] and Charles Efferson *et al.* [2008]). The important point here is that people strive to reduce uncertainty in social interaction and in the absence of familial or personal relationships, will latch on to specific characteristics to demarcate strangers as "one of us" or "one of them". Symbolic markers and the resulting ingroup bias stem from the basic human need to make the environment more predictable.

In summary, individuals are driven to reduce the uncertainty that stems from the Darwinian struggle for survival and reproductive success, and the cognitive limitations that emerge when trying to fathom the intentions of others in increasingly larger groups. Social hierarchies and symbolic marking are a response to this uncertainty. Hierarchies allow dominant individuals to reduce intragroup conflict. Hierarchies allow individuals to monitor their dealings with others since they can maintain personal face-to-face relationships in increasingly larger groups. Markers can reduce uncertainty by screening non-relatives and assigning them to ingroups, and thus likely cooperators, or outgroups, and thus probable non-cooperators. Hierarchies will be contested to the extent that elites are tyrannical and unpredictable in their dealings with group members, and insofar as they fail to fulfil their obligation to reduce within-group conflict.

The foundations of the rule of law

As explained in the previous section, uncertainty in social interaction is reduced in small group contexts by kin selection, the personal knowledge of other group members and the disciplining effect of reciprocity. Indeed, Fukuyama (2011, 2014) identifies kin selection and reciprocal altruism as the default mode of human sociability – calling it "natural sociability". As the group expands, however, these mechanisms become less effective and raise the need for alternative sources of predictability.

One response to uncertainty is to bias interaction towards demarcated ingroups of non-relatives. Identifiable ingroups screen-out potential defectors in large group settings and sustain cooperation between ingroup members beyond familial and reciprocal relationships. Avner Greif (1994) differentiates between individualist societies characterised by weak ingroup ties and collectivist societies where ingroup ties are salient. He argues that, historically, salient ingroups have facilitated market exchange between their members by sharing information concerning the reliability of different commercial partners. This practice acted as an informal contract enforcement mechanism since reneging on the terms of a deal injured one's commercial reputation. The reputation mechanism depended on an extensive network of personal acquaintances such that even if one did not know the potential trading partner personally, he could get reputational information through this network. It also depended on a shared definition about what constitutes (in)appropriate behaviour. Where ingroups were weaker and thus informal enforcement was not possible, formal institutions eventually emerged to structure market exchange with strangers (Greif labels this impersonal exchange). These differential responses to uncertainty meant that market exchange was limited to ingroups in some societies, but could flourish across groups in others.[4]

A second response to uncertainty in larger group contexts also presented in the previous section are hierarchically ordered personal relationships of patrons and clients. The nature of these relationships has been illuminated by James Scott (1972) who identifies three particular features. First, patron-client relationships are reciprocal in that each party provides a valued service to the other. There may be a degree of coercion in the relationship but it also benefits the parties. As such the patron-client relationship is an instrumental one. Second, they are based in inequality: "[t]here is an imbalance in exchange between the two partners which expresses and reflects the disparity in their relative wealth, power and status" (Scott [1972], page 93). The individual with higher socio-economic status (the patron) provides protection or services to the person with lower status (client) in exchange for support and assistance. The services provided by the patron tend to be vital to the client and, as such, the latter faces an inelastic demand. Third, the relationship is a face-to-face personal one cultivated by continuing reciprocity over time, often creating trust between the partners. The degree of asymmetry in the relationship thus depends on the relative coercive power of each party and on how important the patron's services are to the client.

The emergence of patron-client relationships is facilitated by the ineffectiveness of kin selection and ingroup ties in reducing social uncertainty. Fukuyama (2011) states that the emergence of feudalism can be explained as a response to the weakness of kinship ties (see, originally, Marc Bloch [1961]). Feudalism is a personal and hierarchical relationship between lord and vassal entailing legal obligations on both sides – protection on the part of the lord and production services on the part of the vassal. Feudalism emerged at a time when kinship ties had been weakened and no centralised state could provide security. In places where tribalism was strong – in German lands on the shores of the North Sea, in Scandinavia and in Celtic areas in the British Isles – feudalism did not take root.

What can hierarchically ordered personal relationships and ingroup bias tell us about the emergence of the rule of law? Equal treatment of individuals in similar circumstances is more likely the less asymmetric the personal relationships between people or, stated differently, the more equal the distribution of power among society's members. And, as explained by Scott (1972), this distribution of power will be more equal if the relative coercive power of individuals is similar and individuals are less dependent on others for their existence (more on this later). Less obviously perhaps, equal treatment is also more likely to emerge when ingroups are weaker. On one level, this is simply because a weaker ingroup bias means that one discriminates less in favour of ingroup members. On another level, weak ingroups also increase the likelihood of formal rules emerging that facilitate impersonal relationships with strangers (Greif [1994]). The move towards impersonality is also one towards impartiality that, by definition, means treating people without regard to personal relationships and preferences. But it does not in itself imply equal treatment since, recall, that formal rules are neither a necessary nor a sufficient condition for the rule of law. For this, we also require that social relationships be relatively symmetric. The combination of weak social hierarchies and weak ingroup bias sets the stage for the emergence of formal rules that treat people equally.

In Figure 3.1, I schematically represent the two types of society characterised in the previous discussion. The points represent individuals. The vertical distance between the different points captures the steepness or asymmetry in hierarchically ordered personal relationships. The horizontal distance between them

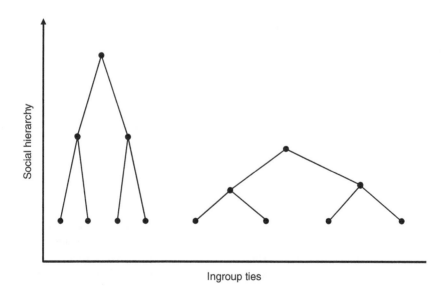

Figure 3.1 Two types of society.

reflects the strength of ingroup ties where a larger distance implies weaker ties. Thus, the society on the left is one with steep social hierarchy and strong ingroup ties while the one on the right enjoys more symmetric vertical relationships and weaker ingroup ties. It is my contention that the rule of law is more likely to emerge in the case of the latter society and, in societies with writing, it will be enshrined in formal laws.

This discussion begs the question: what determines the steepness of personal hierarchical relationships and the strength of ingroup ties? One productive and parsimonious way to examine this issue is by going back to the basic human need to reduce uncertainty in social interaction. From this perspective, I can identify four different but related long-run sources of existential uncertainty: the disease environment, population, intra and intergroup conflict and finally, the nature of production. These variables ultimately depend on the biogeographic environment within which each society is embedded. As illustrated in Figure 3.2, biogeographic realities determine the nature of different sources of existential uncertainty. These in turn determine the steepness of social hierarchies and the strength of ingroups and this determines the extent to which governance tends towards the equal treatment of individuals in similar circumstances.

The arrows in Figure 3.2 indicate a probabilistic rather than deterministic relationship. In other words, the identified variables affect the likelihood of different outcomes emerging allowing for the influence of alternative factors. With this qualification in mind, and as I explain later, the biogeographic environment has determined the infectious disease burden facing societies over time. Where this has been heavier, social groups have tended to limit interactions with strangers, increasing the salience of ingroups. Infectious diseases have also had an impact on the steepness of social hierarchy, by affecting the supply of labour and by extension its relative power. Disease has also influenced European colonisation strategies and the social structures that they gave rise to. The biogeographic environment has been, moreover, a fundamental determinant of the shift towards agriculture and, from there, population growth. By pushing against cognitive limits, population growth drives both hierarchy and ingroup bias. Because it puts pressure on the available resources, it can also set the basis for the emergence of property rights. Population increase – together with storable food surpluses – can also allow for specialisation in social roles, another source of social inequality. Hierarchical social relationships may also be directly related to the intensity of intra and intergroup conflict since this creates the need to empower individuals who can manage it. The impact of conflict on

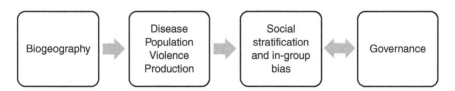

Figure 3.2 The basic story.

social stratification will also depend on the cost of violence technology, with cheaper technology equalising the ability to coerce and making it more difficult for any individual to accumulated power. How violence technology and conflict translate into social hierarchy depends in part on geography. Finally, biogeography determines the feasibility of autonomous production or, conversely, the extent to which individuals must coordinate to feed themselves (for example, coordination is more urgent with irrigated agriculture and less so with rainfed cultivation). Autonomy in production can contribute towards flattening social hierarchy as well as increasing the importance of individuals versus groups. In what follows, I will develop these ideas and, where possible, provide empirical evidence.[5]

Disease

The disease environment has been identified as a causal factor determining the relative strength of individuals versus groups. Specifically, Corey Fincher *et al.* (2008) have put forward a pathogen theory of group bias, arguing that in areas with historically higher infectious disease burdens, societies developed stronger ingroup biases as a defensive strategy (see Randy Thornhill and Corey Fincher [2014], for a review of work in this area). Because interactions with strangers are perceived to increase the risk of infection, people biased their dealings inwards in the context of identified ingroups. Over time, in areas characterised by a high/ low level of pathogen prevalence, a selection process favouring alleles probabilistically associated with strong/weak ingroups occurred. My chosen measure of infectious disease prevalence is from Damian Murray and Marc Schaller (2010) who employ epidemiological atlases to code the historical prevalence of nine infectious diseases across countries (the diseases are leishmaniasis, schistosomes, trypanosomes, leprosy, malaria, typhus, filariae, dengue and tuberculosis).

Geography is an important determinant of pathogen levels: countries closer to the equator have higher infectious disease burdens than countries further away. This can be appreciated in Figure 3.3, which plots country latitude (normalised so that 0 represents the equator) against historical pathogen prevalence, as well as the relatively large simple correlation coefficient between these two variables (−0.820 with a p-value of 0).

Historical pathogen prevalence could thus be a long-run determinant of governance through its effect on ingroup bias: a lighter disease burden, characteristic of areas further away from the equator, is likely to lead to weaker ingroups and these, in turn, will tend to contribute towards more impartial governance. In Table 3.1, I explore the link between pathogen prevalence, ingroup bias and governance through regression analysis. Specifically, I regress the governance indicator presented in Chapter 2, on a proxy of ingroup strength reported by Geert Hofstede (1980). Specifically, I rely on his distinction between individualist and collectivist societies. In collectivist societies, people are born into tightly knit ingroups that impose mutual obligations and expectations and share common fates and goals. Individualist societies have loose ties between

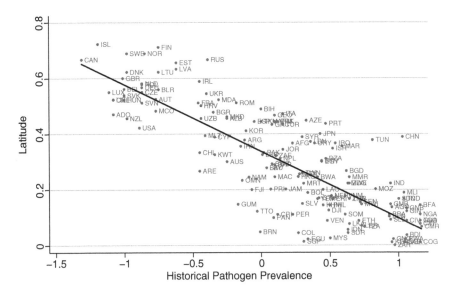

Figure 3.3 Geography and historical pathogen prevalence.

individuals, put rights above duties and emphasise personal control, autonomy and accomplishments (I will return to this variable in Chapter 6).

Again, I control for GDP per capita (in logs) with the aim of reducing the possibility of omitted variable bias. This may emerge because of the link between development and governance described in Chapter 2, but also because development has been linked to individualism. It has been argued, in the context of what is known as the modernisation hypothesis, that economic development increases existential security and thus reduces reliance on ingroups. Specifically, it generates a shift away from survival values towards self-expression values. Survival values emerge in a context of resource scarcity driving people into hierarchically organised ingroups such as the family or clan and, consequently, leading to a distrust of strangers with whom one competes for scarce resources. Self-expression values emerge when the resource constraint is relaxed thus reducing the competition for scarce resources and consequently leading to a lower reliance on ingroups in social interaction and a corresponding increasing trust of strangers (Harry Triandis [1995]; Ronald Inglehart and Christian Welzel [2005]; Hofstede *et al.* [2010]; Daniel Hruschka and Joseph Henrich [2013]).

In Table 3.1, I first regress the governance indicator presented in Chapter 2, on individualism and pathogen prevalence to see if the latter has an independent effect on governance. Pathogen prevalence has no relationship with governance in the presence of individualism which, taken together with its strong correlation with individualism (−0.672, p-value 0), suggests that to the extent that pathogen prevalence affects governance, it is through its effect on ingroup bias. I then employ historical pathogen prevalence as an instrument of individualism

Table 3.1 Pathogens, individualism and governance

	Dependent variable: Quality of governance	
	OLS	TSLS
Individualism	1.469***	2.506***
	(0.295)	(0.704)
Historical pathogen prevalence	−0.203	
	(0.120)	
N° of observations	98	98
R² adjusted	0.686	0.657
		First stage
Historical pathogen prevalence		−0.196***
		(0.035)
F-statistic first stage		40.695

Notes
Regressions displayed vertically. All regressions include a constant and control for GDP per capita
(not shown). White heteroscedasticity consistent standard errors in parentheses. *, **, **** significance at the 10, 5 and 1 per cent levels respectively. Historical pathogen prevalence is employed as an
instrument for individualism in the TSLS regression.

in the context of two-stage least squares (TSLS) regressions. I do so because of
the possibility that the quality of governance itself affects individualism (one
reason for the two-way arrow in Figure 3.2). Hruschka and Henrich (2013)
have explored this possibility. They argue and provide empirical evidence to
support the idea that the quality of governance, as measured by the Government Effectiveness variable from the WBGI, will tend to undermine ingroup ties
because it provides an alternative source of existential security.

The strength of the chosen instrument is supported by the first stage regression of individualism on pathogen prevalence and both the statistical significance of the latter and the resultant F-statistic (above the critical value of 10
advanced by Douglas Staiger and James Stock [1997]). Controlling for the level
of development moreover reinforces the exclusion restriction when using historical pathogen prevalence as an instrument for individualism. This requires that
the impact of pathogens on governance pass through the individualism-
collectivism dimension and not through some other, unaccounted for, channel.
One such channel could be economic development since scholars have linked
contemporary and historical disease burdens to under-development (see, respectively, John Gallup *et al.* [1999] and Acemoglu *et al.* [2001]).

The regression results provide support for the argument advanced here. A
lower pathogen prevalence means that a country will be more individualistic,
and a more individualistic country will tend to have better governance. The
results also indicate that reverse causality is not a problem. If it were, the
OLS point estimates would be higher than the TSLS ones since better governance should reinforce individualism. The fact that they are smaller suggest that

attenuation bias due to measurement error in the individualism-collectivism indicator is a bigger concern.

Disease prevalence may thus impact on governance by affecting the strength of ingroups. But disease may have had an impact on governance in other ways. In the following "Nature of production" section, we will see that disease, in combination with factor endowments, may have affected the colonisation strategies adopted by European powers across the world and, as a result, the governance structures that emerged in the colonies. Here, I want to focus on the impact of the plague on social hierarchies. With the breakdown of the Western Roman Empire, security in much of Western Europe was provided in the context of feudal ties. These were basically personal patron-client relationships in the context of which the king provided property rights to nobles in exchange for military muscle, and the nobles in turn provided protection to commoners in exchange for a share of their labour. The bubonic plague that affected feudal Europe in the fourteenth century, led to the death of around 25 to 45 per cent of the population. This created a situation of land abundance and scarce labour, increased the relative bargaining strength of peasants vis-à-vis lords, and, ultimately, contributed to the demise of master-serf relations (see North [1981]; Michael Mann [1986]). The plague hit even harder in the emergent cities of the time, decimating skilled craftsmen and merchants, leading to higher wages, increasing demands for a greater share of political power and attracting peasants thus weakening the bargaining power of the landed aristocracy even further (Ronald Rogowski and Duncan MacRae [2008]).

But the plague did not lead towards more equal social relationships everywhere. In Eastern Europe it had the opposite effect (Fukuyama [2011]; Acemoglu and Robinson [2012]; Scheidel [2017]). Faced with labour scarcity and upward pressure on wages, landowners in the East restricted the movement of workers and took over ever-larger pieces of land. One reason they could do so was that cities were smaller in Eastern Europe and so peasants' exit option was reduced compared to that enjoyed by commoners in Western Europe. And cities were larger in Western Europe because monarchs there found it useful to protect them to undercut the power of feudal lords. In the East, the state sided with the aristocracy to the detriment of peasants, and the (smaller) urban centres were administrative centres of the state.

In Egypt, something similar happened. While a declining population should have heralded higher wages for commoners, this was thwarted by the Mamluks, a militarily effective governing elite (Turchin and Sergey Nefedov [2009] who take this from Stuart Borsch [2005]). They applied their military strength to maintain resource extraction at pre-plague levels, despite the fall in population. They could do so because of the inability of peasants to flee coercion given Egypt's uninhabitable desert beyond the fertile land around the Nile. Thus, the bubonic plague led to more egalitarian social relationships in the West but it increased social hierarchies in the East and elsewhere. The effect of the plague depended in part on the capacity of peasants to flee coercion and we will return to the impact of the exit option on social structure shortly.[6]

Population

From a long-run, historical perspective, geography has been a key driver of population size. The reason is that biogeographic conditions have been identified as fundamental for the Neolithic or Agricultural revolution or the movement from a foraging, hunter-gatherer existence, towards settled agriculture. Jared Diamond (1997) has brilliantly explained that the speed at which different societies adopted agriculture depended on the availability of domesticable plant and animal species that, in turn, is geographically determined. Thus, agriculture was first taken up in the Fertile Crescent where domesticable species were relatively abundant. It then spread first along the East-West geographic axis, and then on a North-South direction since biogeographic conditions are similar along latitudes but differ along longitudes. The invention of settled agriculture led to population increases (see also, Gordon Childe [1936]; Elman Service [1975]). There are at least two reasons for this. First, it allows human beings to produce more food per acre. Second, for a hunter-gatherer who leads a nomadic existence, birth control and even infanticide is rational given that children reduce mobility.

The impact of population growth on aspects of societal organisation that determine the quality of governance has already been noted. Individuals seek to reduce uncertainty emerging from social interaction. Increasing group size reduces genetic proximity, pushes against cognitive abilities to monitor interpersonal relationships with others, and reduces the likelihood of repeated interaction. In response to this, ingroup bias and hierarchical personal relationships emerge as predictability-enhancing strategies. Taking Dunbar's community size threshold of 150 persons as a guide, this suggests that below this number, societies will tend to be more individualist and egalitarian. And, in fact, anthropological evidence has shown that in nomadic hunter-gatherer communities – whose average size is around 45 individuals (Patrick Nolan and Gerhard Leski [2009]) – males and females enforce an egalitarian ethos with the purpose of preserving individual autonomy (James Woodburn [1982]; Triandis [1995]; Boehm [1999]; Allen Johnson and Timothy Earle [2000]). This egalitarianism, insofar as it implies the equal application of rules to all members of the group, reflects a measure of rule of law in these societies.

This discussion indicates that, all else being equal, an important driver of social organisation and, ultimately, unequal treatment, is group size. Given Dunbar's low population threshold levels, above which hierarchy may emerge to facilitate social interaction in the face of uncertainty, it is useless to look for evidence on this issue in contemporary cross-country data. Population size in my cross-country sample ranges from 9,347 (Tuvalu) to 1.23 billion (China) with a mean value of around 29 million people. Fortunately, we can turn to anthropological data on pre-industrial societies some of which include communities with fewer than 100 members. Specifically, I exploit anthropological data from the Standard Cross-Cultural Sample (SCCS) that reports detailed ethnographic information on 186 pre-industrial societies sampled from the

Ethnographic Atlas initially compiled by George Murdock (Murdock [1967]; Murdock and Douglas White [1969]). The information corresponds to "the earliest date for which satisfactory ethnographic data are available or can be reconstructed [in order to] avoid the acculturative effects of contacts with Europeans" (Murdock and White [1969], page 340).

The SCCS reports a range of variables that reflect societal inequality between individuals. In particular, I rely on variables 158 and 270, labelled respectively social and class stratification that increase with the number of social classes or castes, variable 756, labelled political role differentiation and variable 759, called perceived power of leaders. In the case of variables 756 and 759, I have inverted the original scale and so higher values of these variables imply, respectively, greater differentiation and a situation where society perceives leaders to be very powerful. To measure societal size I turn to three variables: population density (v1130) starting at less than 1 person per square mile and ending at 500 persons or more per square mile, urbanisation (v152) starting at fewer than 100 persons and ending at 1000 people and, finally, mean size of community (v235), that starts with a community below 50 members and ends with one with one or more cities of more than 50,000. The regression results in Table 3.2 reveal a strong relationship between societal size and social inequality. Regardless of

Table 3.2 Population and social inequality

	Dependent variables:			
	Social stratification	*Class stratification*	*Political differentiation*	*Perceived power of leaders*
Panel A				
Population density	0.476***	0.451***	0.698***	0.223***
	(0.058)	(0.061)	(0.107)	(0.051)
N° of observations	186	186	90	90
R^2 adjusted	0.261	0.219	0.276	0.182
Panel B				
Urbanisation	0.511***	0.433***	0.693***	0.233***
	(0.068)	(0.073)	(0.123)	(0.054)
N° of observations	186	186	90	90
R^2 adjusted	0.234	0.156	0.193	0.141
Panel C				
Size of local community	0.463***	0.418***	0.505***	0.156***
	(0.027)	(0.032)	(0.084)	(0.034)
N° of observations	148	148	76	76
R^2 adjusted	0.527	0.419	0.272	0.178

Notes

Regressions displayed vertically. All regressions include a constant (not shown). The estimation method is OLS, with White heteroscedasticity consistent standard errors in parentheses. *, **, **** significance at the 10, 5 and 1 per cent levels respectively. Data comes from the Standard Cross-Cultural Sample: social stratification is v158, class stratification is v270, political role differentiation is v756, the perception of the power of leaders is v759, population density is v1130, urbanisation is v152 and mean size of local community is v235.

whether I measure group size in terms of population density, urbanisation or the mean size of the local community, this is always associated with greater stratification, political differentiation and perceived power of leaders.

The link between societal size and social inequality supports the idea that social hierarchy may be one response to the uncertainty that emerges in larger group contexts. However, population density can impact on social inequality through alternative channels. One channel are private property rights. Given the differential capacities of individuals to accumulate wealth and generate income, individual property rights will tend to widen wealth inequalities over time. This is especially so if primogeniture – or the practice of passing all of one's property to the eldest son – is the inheritance rule (Turchin [2006]).

It has been argued that population increases, led to the emergence of private property rights. According to North (1981), in hunter-gatherer societies with low population densities, there was no need for property rights. People simply took from nature. This practice continued as population increased, groups sub-divided and moved to new areas. But, at some stage, new areas where scarcer and hunter-gatherer groups came into increasing contact. In an effort to avoid the exhaustion of the resource base, groups initially adopted practices to limit population increase, including, infanticide and taboos. Eventually, groups adopted exclusive communal property arrangements thus both limiting the intensity of exploitation by insiders and the access to this base by outsiders. The move towards exclusive communal property is a first step towards individual property rights. Consistent with this account, Jean-Philippe Platteau and Yujiro Hayami (1998) suggest that compared to Asia, in Sub-Saharan Africa, low population densities led to the underdevelopment of property rights and con-sequently less social stratification and stronger redistributive norms.[7]

In Table 3.3, I explore the link between property rights and social stratifica-tion. The existence of private property rights is captured by variable 278 of the

Table 3.3 Population density, property rights and social inequality

| | Dependent variables: | | | |
	Social stratification		Class stratification	
Population density	0.477***	0.324***	0.448***	0.314***
	(0.062)	(0.075)	(0.066)	(0.083)
Property rights		0.479***		0.419***
		(0.125)		(0.141)
N° of observations	155	155	155	155
R² adjusted	0.265	0.320	0.217	0.255

Notes
Regressions displayed vertically. All regressions include a constant (not shown). The estimation method is OLS, with White heteroscedasticity consistent standard errors in parentheses. *, **, **** significance at the 10, 5 and 1 per cent levels respectively. Data comes from the Standard Cross-Cultural Sample: social stratification is v158, class stratification is v270, population density is v1130 and property rights is based on v278 (as explained in the text).

SCCS. Specifically, I recode this variable so that it takes the value of 1 (absence of property rights), 2 (heirs within the kin group but beyond sons or daughters, for example, sister's sons or younger brothers) and 3 (heirs are sons or daughters). The property rights variable is strongly correlated with population density (simple correlation is 0.566 with a p-value of 0). The results show that the inclusion of property rights reduces the estimated association of population density with social and class stratification (the results are maintained when measuring social inequality via v756 and v759). In each case, I am careful to employ the same number of observations to make sure that the result is not due to a change in the sample size. Taken together with the correlation between population density and property rights, these results are consistent with the argument that population density may contribute towards the emergence of property rights and these, in turn, may lead to social inequality.

In Table 3.4, I explore the relationship between population density, property rights, inequality and governance. In particular, I regress measures of governance on population density, property rights and my chosen indicators of social inequality. To measure governance I consider three variables from the SCCS: v764 measures how consensual or informal the decision-making process is, with higher values reflecting more consensus or informality; v761 refers to checks on the power of leaders and increases with more checks; and v1134, called despotic bias in conflict resolution, higher values of which indicate extreme bias in favour of elites when resolving disputes between individuals. Variable 764 reflects on what Rothstein and Teorell (2008) identify as the degree of equality in the access to public authority while variable 1134 captures the way that public authority is exercised. Variable 761 contains elements of the concept of rule of law since it measures the extent to which government or authority is restrained.

The results presented in the table indicate that social inequality is associated with less consensual or informal decision-making, fewer checks on elites and more unequal treatment when resolving disputes between individuals. They also suggest that societal size and property rights do not have an independent effect on governance. It is important to note however that the estimated effect of social inequality may be biased. One source of bias are alternative drivers of inequality. Specifically, I will argue that social inequality may also be the result of intra and intergroup conflict and the context within which individuals procure food. Later, I will revisit the relationship between social inequality and governance in the presence of these additional factors. Another source of bias could be reverse causality. It seems plausible that social inequality may increase when decision-making is biased in favour of an elite minority (a second reason for the two-way arrow in Figure 3.2). Ideally, to deal with this concern we require valid instrumental variables for social inequality. Unfortunately, a review of the SCCS does not yield variables that could be useful in this respect. As a result, the OLS point estimates of inequality reported in this chapter will tend to overestimate the impact of social inequality on governance. And it is because of this that I mostly talk of relationships or associations rather than causation.

Table 3.4 Social inequality and governance I

	Social stratification	Class stratification	Political differentiation	Perceived power of leaders	Population density	Property rights	Sample	R² adjusted
Consensual or informal decisions	-0.236 (0.146)				-0.167 (0.124)	-0.147 (0.219)	74	0.142
		-0.232* (0.119)			-0.179 (0.117)	-0.131 (0.220)	74	0.150
			-0.481*** (0.065)		-0.065 (0.103)	-0.152 (0.193)	74	0.453
				-0.940*** (0.180)	-0.086 (0.110)	-0.106 (0.205)	74	0.340
Checks on leader	-0.262*** (0.069)				-0.080 (0.070)	-0.055 (0.108)	73	0.309
		-0.260*** (0.056)			-0.093 (0.060)	-0.036 (0.103)	73	0.344
			-0.301*** (0.031)		0.028 (0.053)	-0.089 (0.091)	73	0.609
				-0.482*** (0.108)	-0.083 (0.059)	-0.089 (0.105)	73	0.371
Despotic bias in conflict resolution	0.048* (0.028)				-0.002 (0.030)	0.053 (0.033)	84	0.080
		0.078*** (0.028)			-0.014 (0.029)	0.038 (0.033)	84	0.123
			0.098*** (0.034)		-0.015 (0.052)	0.051 (0.062)	40	0.374
				0.215** (0.086)	0.001 (0.049)	0.054 (0.058)	40	0.326

Notes

Regressions displayed horizontally. All regressions include a constant (not shown). The estimation method is OLS, with White heteroscedasticity consistent standard errors in parentheses. *, **, *** significance at the 10, 5 and 1 per cent levels respectively. Data comes from the Standard Cross-Cultural Sample: social stratification is v158, class stratification is v270, political role differentiation is v756, the perception of the power of leaders is v759, consensual or informal decisions is v764, checks on leader is v761, despotic bias in conflict resolution is v1134, population density is v1130 and property rights is based on v278 (as explained in the text).

Conflict

Social hierarchy is, potentially, a response to the uncertainty generated by conflict. Recall that in our closest primate relatives, being higher up in the social hierarchy entails privileges but also obligations, one of which is the need to diffuse intragroup disputes (Boehm [1999]). With intragroup conflict, hierarchy can manifest itself in the guise of a leader with a monopoly of force. Moreover, intergroup conflict puts a premium on the hierarchical organisation of society since the latter may facilitate coordination (Stanislav Andreski [1968]). Hierarchy in the face of intergroup rivalry is all the more likely insofar as increasing the size of the ingroup becomes a rational response because of the benefit of size – larger groups will tend to dominate smaller ones, but their size also raises the need for greater hierarchy if they are to be effective (Turchin [2016]). Conflict between groups is also likely to increase the salience of group boundaries, thus strengthening within-group ties and weakening ties outside the group. Thus, we would expect both ingroup bias and social hierarchy to be rational responses to the uncertainty generated by intergroup violence.

One factor limiting intragroup conflict and thus reducing the need for hierarchy is the possibility that individuals may exit conflictual relationships by moving to another area. I have already mentioned how the possibility of fleeing to growing urban centres, available to peasants in Western Europe but less so to those in Eastern Europe, together with population reductions due to the bubonic plague, contributed towards the demise of feudalism in the former and facilitated its intensification in the latter. But from another perspective, the exit option can also reduce within-group conflict. In sparsely populated hunter-gatherer settings, intragroup conflict is reduced: through spatial avoidance, including changing bands; by preemptively suppressing deviant members and; by third party mediation without access to force (Nolan and Lensky [2009]; Boehm [2012]). Indeed, moving away in response to intragroup conflict may have been an important mechanism driving the gradual habitation of the world (Boix [2015]).

However, increasing population densities, especially after the Neolithic revolution, reduced the ability to respond to intragroup conflict by splitting from the group, at the same time as it increased the likelihood of conflict between groups for access to scarce resources. This brings me to an important theory of hierarchy and state creation, namely, the idea of environmental circumscription. Robert Carneiro (1970) explains that the first states that arose – in Egypt, Mesopotamia, India, China, Mexico and Peru – were delimited by mountains, seas or deserts. This reduced the area available for colonisation and cultivation and, with increasing population densities given the suitability of these areas for agriculture, raised the likelihood of conflict between groups over scarce resources. Environmental circumscription also undermined the capacity of individuals and groups to flee to avoid conflict. This was not the case in places like the Amazon basin or North America where resource abundance and vast expanses reduced competition over territory at the same time as it allowed individuals to flee conflictual situations (Eric Jones [1981] applies the same logic to Europe, while Fukuyama [2014] does so to Sub-Saharan Africa). In environmentally circumscribed areas, groups that were less successful in the fight over resources faced extinction or social sub-ordination in the context of larger units such as chiefdoms or kingdoms (see also, Diamond [1997]).

To consider the link between conflict and social hierarchy I again turn to the SCCS. As before, I measure social inequality by way of variables 158 and 270 (respectively increasing with social or class stratification) and variables 756 and 759 (respectively increasing with political differentiation and the perceived power of leaders). In addition, I turn to two variables that reflect on the capacity of individuals to avoid domination and conflict by moving away. The first variable (v785), labelled fission, increases with the frequency that dissatisfied persons move to other communities after disputes (this interpretation stems of the inversion of the original scale). The second (v786) is called mobility and is increasing with the degree of adult mobility. Moreover, I consider two variables capturing the presence and intensity of conflict between groups: v679 higher values of which reflect greater frequency of warfare or fighting and v901 that increases with the casualty rate of combatants (again, in the case of the latter variable, I invert the original scale).

The results in Table 3.5 provide support for the expectation that the capacity of individuals to exit their group reduces the need for social hierarchy to resolve intragroup conflict. More frequent fission and greater mobility are associated with less social inequality. Similarly, more warfare and more casualties are related to more social or class stratification. The results are robust to controlling for population density which, as previously argued, is likely to increase intragroup conflict, since it reduces the ability of individuals to move away to avoid it, and increase conflict between groups, because it puts a strain on the available resources. We have also seen that population density may lead to social hierarchy through its effect on societal uncertainty and the emergence of private property.[8]

There seems to be some evidence therefore that conflict and reduced spatial mobility are associated with social stratification. But do these variables have an independent effect on governance above and beyond their effect on stratification? I explore this in Table 3.6 by regressing the set of governance indicators previously employed – the extent to which decisions are consensual or informal, checks on leaders, and despotic bias when resolving conflicts between individuals – on the social stratification indicators, the frequency of warfare and population density. The results reaffirm the previous findings whereby population density impacts on governance through its effect on social hierarchy. They also indicate that – beyond its indirect effect on governance through social stratification – warfare may directly reduce checks on the power of leaders and increase the bias favouring elites when resolving disputes.

I will now turn to another factor shaping how conflict can impact on social inequality and governance, namely, the technology of violence. In the most

Table 3.5 Conflict and social inequality

	Dependent variables:							
	Social stratification	Class stratification	Political differentiation	Perceived power of leaders	Social stratification	Class stratification	Political differentiation	Perceived power of leaders
Panel A								
Fission	-0.294 (0.189)	-0.457** (0.216)	-0.625** (0.289)	-0.184 (0.117)				
Mobility					-0.400** (0.172)	-0.486** (0.196)	-0.552** (0.251)	-0.125 (0.104)
Population density	0.275*** (0.093)	0.234** (0.107)	0.526** (0.129)	0.191*** (0.061)	0.360*** (0.084)	0.333*** (0.099)	-0.623*** (0.123)	-0.198*** (0.058)
N° of observations	64	64	64	64	79	79	79	79
R² adjusted	0.167	0.147	0.252	0.184	0.281	0.239	0.309	0.178
Panel B								
Warfare or fighting	0.351* (0.194)	0.454** (0.208)	0.564 (0.358)	0.418** (0.165)				
Casualty rate					0.829*** (0.293)	0.938*** (0.326)	0.237 (0.556)	0.171 (0.223)
Population density	0.473*** (0.071)	0.477*** (0.073)	0.705*** (0.129)	0.232*** (0.054)	0.354*** (0.086)	0.317*** (0.095)	-0.546*** (0.136)	-0.150** (0.068)
N° of observations	133	133	78	78	79	79	47	47
R² adjusted	0.274	0.256	0.266	0.239	0.269	0.227	0.198	0.097

Notes

Regressions displayed vertically. All regressions include a constant (not show). The estimation method is OLS, with White heteroscedasticity consistent standard errors in parentheses. *, **, *** significance at the 10, 5 and 1 per cent levels respectively. Data comes from the Standard Cross-Cultural Sample: social stratification is v158, class stratification is v270 political role differentiation is v756, the perception of the power of leaders is v759, political fission is v785, mobility is v786, warfare or fighting is v679, casualty rate of combatants is v901 and population density is v1130.

Table 3.6 Social inequality and governance II

	Social stratification	Class stratification	Political differentiation	Perceived power of leaders	Population density	Warfare or fighting	Sample	R² adjusted
Consensual or informal decisions	-0.345** (0.144)				-0.147 (0.133)	-0.412 (0.379)	77	0.169
		-0.317** (0.125)			-0.151 (0.127)	-0.445 (0.370)	77	0.173
			-0.425*** (0.065)		-0.003 (0.083)	-0.327 (0.325)	77	0.381
				-0.929*** (0.208)	-0.091 (0.095)	-0.193 (0.344)	77	0.309
Checks on leader	-0.276*** (0.081)				-0.078 (0.072)	-0.295* (0.169)	75	0.302
		-0.273*** (0.067)			-0.072 (0.065)	-0.313* (0.164)	75	0.333
			-0.303*** (0.030)		0.013 (0.042)	-0.258* (0.130)	75	0.613
				-0.515*** (0.112)	-0.085 (0.055)	-0.214 (0.157)	75	0.366
Despotic bias in conflict resolution	0.057 (0.035)				0.038 (0.030)	0.156*** (0.053)	81	0.165
		0.072** (0.031)			0.031 (0.026)	0.140*** (0.049)	81	0.192
			0.109*** (0.031)		0.015 (0.037)	0.149** (0.071)	45	0.470
				0.207** (0.083)	0.042 (0.042)	0.134* (0.071)	45	0.354

Notes

Regressions displayed horizontally. All regressions include a constant (not shown). The estimation method is OLS, with White heteroscedasticity consistent standard errors in parentheses. *, **, *** significance at the 10, 5 and 1 per cent levels respectively. Data comes from the Standard Cross-Cultural Sample: v158 is social stratification, v270 is class stratification, v756 is political role differentiation, v759 is the perception of the power of leaders, consensual or informal decisions is v1130 and warfare or fighting is v679. population density is v1134, despotic bias in conflict resolution is v1134, population density is v1134, despotic bias in conflict resolution is v761, despotic bias in conflict resolution is v761, checks on leader is v764, checks on leader is v764, checks on leader is v764, checks is v764, checks on leader is v764.

general terms, where effective violence technology is only affordable to a small subset of society, this should sow the seeds of social hierarchy. Conversely, the more easily available and effective is this technology, the more egalitarian society should be. As an American saying goes: "God made men, but Sam Colt [who invented the revolver in 1830] made them equal" (Turchin, 2016, Chapter 5). As I explain next, an important factor mediating the impact of violence technology is geography.

At least 50,000 years ago, egalitarianism in hunter-gatherer settings was underpinned by the equal access of group members to simple but lethal projectile weapons (spears, bows and arrows) (Boehm [1999]; Gintis *et al.* [2015]). Projectile weapons made potentially dominant individuals vulnerable. In the not so distant past, around 350 BC, Aristotle relates the nature of military force – the cavalry, the heavy infantry, the light armed troops and the navy – to government types:

> When the country is adapted for cavalry, then a strong oligarchy is likely to be established. For the security of the inhabitants depends upon a force of this sort, and only rich men can afford to keep horses. The second form of oligarchy prevails when the country is adapted to heavy infantry; for this service is better suited to the rich than to the poor. But the light-armed and the naval element are wholly democratic...
>
> (*Politics*, Book 6, VII)

To understand the implications of Aristotle's statement I will turn to the work of Stanislav Andreski.[9] Andreski (1968) speaks of the military participation ratio (MPR) defined as the proportion of the total population enlisted in the military. Importantly, the more people that need to be mobilised for war, the more rights have to be granted to them in return, thus reducing social stratification. He gives numerous examples. In seventh century Byzantium, external threats led Emperor Heraclius to confiscate large domains, free serfs and distribute land to those willing to fight. In Prussia, the need to mobilise the masses in international conflicts led to the abolition of serfdom, the granting of ownership of lands to peasants, and the establishment of insurance schemes. Robert Bellah (2011) explains how during the Warring States period in ancient China, mass conscription was accompanied by the suppression of serfdom and the introduction of private property. Scheidel (2017) makes the same argument for the impact of mass mobilisation in countries participating in WWI and WWII: it contributed towards the expansion of the franchise, it increased workers' rights through unionisation and it led to more progressive taxation (see this author for a recent and extensive historical review of the link between military mobilisation and social levelling since classical Athens).

An important determinant of the MPR is the cost of armament such that, more expensive technologies, make weapons unaffordable and drive down the MPR. The introduction of initially costly bronze swords sometime around 3500 BC in Mesopotamia, reduced the MPR and strengthened the position of the elite. The same happened with the introduction by Eurosasian nomads of the horse and chariot in around 1800 BC as well as that of the short bow and the stirrup (first of leather and then of iron). The iron stirrup eventually led to the heavily armed mounted knight, highly effective against infantry, and under-pinned feudalism (see, originally, Lynn White [1962]).

Alternatively, the use of cheaper iron swords in fifth century BCE Greece and Rome, together with the Greek "phalanx" and Roman "testudo", raised the need for armed foot soldiers, increasing the MPR and contributing towards social levelling (see also, North [1981]; William McNeill [1982]). The effective-ness of the navy in ancient Greece, necessarily staffed by oarsmen, increased the MPR and contributed towards them gaining rights that previously were limited to the armed footsoldiers or "hoplites" that constituted the "phalanx" (see also, Bellah [2011] who, moreover, links the introduction of iron weapons to the demise of serfdom in China during the Warring States period). The effective use of the pike and the long-bow against armoured knights tilted the balance in favour of foot archers and contributed to the downfall of the medieval knight (see also, Mann [1986]). In England, the rise of (expensive) firearms and the end of the long-bow coincides with the enclosure movement during which communal land that was previously available to peasants, was fenced and assigned to a privileged minority. Everywhere, costly guns and canons increased the power of wealthy land-owning elites who could afford them, to the detri-ment of peasants and those cities too poor to defend themselves (Boix [2015]). Eventually however, the use of firearms increased the value of the footsoldier and heralded a period of economic and political enfranchisement (Andreski, 1968; Gintis *et al.*, 2015).[10]

While the cost of the technology of violence is an important factor explain-ing the MPR, we must not lose sight of the requirement that this technology be effective. In line with Figure 3.2, geography is crucial here. Andreski (1968) explains how rugged terrain and/or extensive forests undermined the strength of the cavalry in medieval Sweden, Norway, the Scottish Highlands and Switzerland, empowering instead a peasant militia of freemen. In Sweden, peasants were judged by tribunals composed mainly by their peers and took orders only from the king. Representatives of peasants sat in parliament. In Switzerland, war leaders were elected and vested with authority only during the duration of the military campaign. Geography there led to the "survival of tribal democracy amidst countries dominated by feudal lords" (page 62). Boix (2015) argues that it was not only the move from bronze to iron that reduced social hierarchies in ancient Greece. Another factor was Greek geography full of "fences, terraces, hills, small orchards, and vineyards" (Victor Hanson [1998] as cited in Boix [2015]) that made cavalry and chariots difficult to deploy. This was not the case in the plains of Thessaly, and the important role in this region of the cavalry meant that democracy did not take root there in the classical period (Andreski [1968]). Like the case of classical Greece, chari-ots were of little use in the forests of Germania and the peoples of this region organised themselves through assemblies of free warriors. In Africa, socially stratified cavalry states emerged in the savanna and could not expand into the thick tropical forests where moreover, the tsetse fly erected a disease barrier (Jack Goody [1971]).

Let us take stock of the discussion so far. Social hierarchy, with a monopoly of power enjoyed by leaders, may emerge as a response to the uncertainty generated by intragroup conflict. Hierarchy may also emerge from intergroup conflict since war puts a premium on group size and effective coordination. Alternatively, social equality will tend to be promoted when a large proportion of the population must be mobilised for war since this may lead to the enfranchisement of the population in exchange for their participation. I will now argue that war has the potential to contribute towards social levelling because it puts a premium on meritocracy in the military and the public administration more generally. It does so in the military since an incompetent leader makes the group vulnerable to extinction. It can do so in the public administration since a successful defence or attack depends on the volume of financial resources mobilised for war. To see this, we must turn to work that has considered the historical emergence of state capacity.

State capacity has generally been defined as the ability of the state to project its authority, for example, by raising taxes (Fukuyama [2011]). Crucially, Weber (1922) states that the rise of a more rational bureaucracy "has been promoted by needs arising from the creation of standing armies, determined by power politics, and from the related development of public finances" (page 972). As notably put by Charles Tilly (1975): "war made the state, and the state made war" (page 42). There are several examples of war leading to meritocracy in both the military and the public administration. It did so in nineteenth century Sweden after military defeat by Russia and the resultant loss of Finland, in Britain after the Crimean War and in Denmark after a series of defeats in the seventeenth and nineteenth centuries (Rothstein and Teorell [2015a, 2015b]). Defeat was blamed on the incompetence of the officer corps and this was associated with nepotism in recruitment and promotion. The argument whereby war leads to the adoption of merit based autonomous bureaucracy can also be extended to ancient China, and Prussia and Japan in the nineteenth century (Fukuyama [2014]).

It is important to note that insofar as meritocracy is by definition recruitment and promotion on the basis of merit rather than personal connections, it represents a move towards impartial governance. But it does not imply the general application of the rule of law in the sense of all individuals being treated equally in the public sphere (Fukuyama [2011, 2014]). The relevant example is ancient China. It was the first society to introduce meritocratic recruitment in the public administration but that in no way meant equal treatment of individuals. In the words of Finer (1997),

[t]hroughout all the changes in the form of the state … certain characteristics continued to prevail … [c]ollective and mutual responsibility, not individualism; authoritarianism, paternalism, and absolutism, not selfdetermination;

inequality and hierarchy, not equality before the law; subjects not citizens, duties not rights.

(Page 455)

Indeed, the link between the quality of governance and state capacity, as measured by the State Antiquity variable proposed by Valerie Bockstette *et al.* (2002) that reflects the existence of a centralised state since 1 CE (applying the standard 5 per cent discount factor), is 0.187 (p-value 0.022) and disappears when controlling for GDP per capita.

So, state capacity does not imply the rule of law. Instead, the latter is driven by deeper factors that affect societal responses to existential uncertainty. To complete my account of why some societies were able to make the shift towards the rule of law, I will now turn to a fourth factor impacting on social organisation, and from there governance, namely, the nature of production.

The nature of production

At the risk of repetition, humans identify with symbolic ingroups and adopt social hierarchies in an effort to reduce uncertainty in social interaction. So far, I have explained how the steepness of these hierarchies and the salience of ingroups depends on three underlying factors, namely, the disease environment, group size and intra and intergroup conflict. In this section, I will consider how the process through which food resources are extracted from nature, affects these uncertainty-moderating strategies and, ultimately, governance outcomes.

It is revealing to start by considering the nature of production in the small group settings characteristic of simple hunter-gatherers (Woodburn, [1982]; Boehm [1999]; Kent Flannery and Joyce Marcus [2012]). While simple hunter-gatherers may keep those plant-based resources gathered by them, they share animal-based ones. This is because animal-based resources are both variable and, lacking appropriate technology, impossible to store thus making risk pooling a rational strategy. And this risk pooling, together with the inability to accumulate wealth and transmit it intergenerationally, reinforces egalitarianism (see also, Eric Smith *et al.* [2010] and Boix [2015]).

A direct implication emerging from this is that as food resources become more predictable and storable, risk pooling should be less rational and social hierarchy more likely. This is exactly what happens in complex hunter-gatherer societies that are characterised by a more predictable resource base, storage and, as expected, a degree of social stratification (Woodburn [1982]; Bruce Knauft [1991]; Brian Hayden [1995]). A case in point are the Native Americans of the Northwest Pacific Coast before European contact (Kenneth Ames [1994]; Boix [2015]). These peoples lived in an environment rich in salmon. Its exploitation – fishing and storage – required controlling the specific location where this resource was abundant. Flannery and Marcus (2012) suggest that an important factor determining control is who got to the prime locations first. Individuals with access to these resources were able to accumulate wealth and this explains social stratification in these societies.

The shift to settled agriculture leads to increases in food production and consequently population densities. Higher population densities can lead to social hierarchy for a range of reasons, some of which have already been mentioned. Large societal size weakens kinship ties, pushes against cognitive constraints when trying to fathom the intention of others, and reduces the likelihood of repeated interactions thus increasing uncertainty in social exchange and opening the way towards hierarchically ordered personal relationships. Higher population densities have been linked to private property and, from there, economic inequality. Moreover, higher population densities increase the likelihood of both intra and intergroup conflict and thus put a premium on hierarchy as a way to reduce it. To these rationales, we can now add another: larger societies have a greater scope for specialisation in economic and social roles (see, for example, Childe [1936]). To the extent that different activities offer different returns, this can lead to inequality. This may happen simply because some types of economic activities may be more profitable than others. But it is especially likely if different activities afford different opportunities for economic and political control.

One factor conducive to control is the storability of food surplus. In simple hunter-gatherer settings storage of food is not possible. Food is consumed immediately or soon after being collected. Because of this, simple hunter-gatherers have been labelled "immediate return societies" as opposed to those practicing agriculture that are described as "delayed return" in nature (Woodburn [1982]). Food storage would be unfeasible for hunter-gatherers who are permanently on the move (Diamond [1997]). The absence of food storage undermines the capacity of ambitious individuals to accumulate resources and power (see also, Boehm [1999]). As previously stated, storability of food resources facilitated the emergence of hierarchy in complex hunter-gatherer societies. It did so even more forcefully in societies practicing settled agriculture. Centralised food storage may have been socially desirable since its redistribution allowed for consumption smoothing. However, it also opened the door to control of a vital resource and thus the appropriation of ever larger portions of societal surplus and, ultimately, the concentration of power (Diamond [1997]; Johnson and Earle [2000]).

Another factor that facilitates control is the need to mobilise the group to obtain food resources. At the outset, it is important to state that group mobilisation in itself does not imply elite control. In simple hunter-gatherers, hunting for big game is a cooperative endeavour but no hierarchy exists, probably because of the small societal size, the unpredictable nature of food resources and the absence of storage. However, in societies where food is more predictable and storable, the need to mobilise the group to obtain it opens up the possibility of elite control (Paul Hooper *et al.* [2010]). One example were the Eskimo communities of Alaska as observed by Europeans around the mid-nineteenth century. Mobilisation was necessary to hunt whales successfully since hunting was undertaken by organised boat crews of 7 to 10 men led by an umialik or whaling captain. The umialik financed the construction of the boat, and managed both the hunt and the distribution of the catch – assigning to himself a disproportionate share. Eskimo society was stratified, with the umialik and his family at the top (Boix [2015]).

A further, notable example of social hierarchy emerging from the need for collective action to obtain food is Karl Wittfogel's (1957) "hydraulic hypothesis". In areas with little rainfall but large rivers, social coordination to build large-scale irrigation projects was necessary to increase agricultural productivity. This empowered enterprising individuals able to organise and later control access to water resources, thereby laying the basis for social stratification (the examples are Mesopotamia, Egypt, China and Mexico). Empirical evidence has been provided by Jeanet Bentzen *et al.* (2016) who show that countries with a higher irrigation potential – land where irrigation can more than double yields as a share of land suitable for agriculture – are less democratic today. These scholars identify historical land inequality – from 1880 up to the mid-twentieth century and thus, before major land reforms in the 1960s and 1970s – as an important transmission channel.[11]

While irrigated agriculture has been associated with more social stratification, rainfed agriculture has been linked to more equality (see Jones [1981]). In areas with sufficient rainfall, autonomous production is feasible thus reducing the capacity of ambitious individuals to accumulate resources and power compared to societies relying on irrigation-fed agriculture. Thus, societies relying on rainfed agriculture should, all other thing being equal, be less hierarchical. But they should also be more individualist than regions practicing irrigated agriculture since sufficient rain reduces the need to coordinate within ingroups to access water resources. Individualism is, moreover, likely to be promoted insofar as it is not necessary for farming households to cooperate with each other during planting and harvesting.

Evidence on the link between rainfed agriculture and individualism has emerged from China and specifically a comparison of rice-growing regions south of the Yangtze river that rely on irrigation, and regions in the north of the river that grow rainfed cereals (Thomas Talhelm *et al.* [2014]). Rice is much more labour intensive than wheat and requires farmers to cooperate especially during planting and harvesting thus potentially strengthening societal ties. Consistent with this, these authors show that people in regions where irrigated rice farming is prevalent are more collectivist while those in rainfed wheat-growing regions are more individualist.

Cross-country empirical work supports the link between rainfed agriculture and political equality. Stephen Haber (2012) reports a non-linear relationship between rainfall levels and democracy. He argues that in arid areas practicing irrigation agriculture or tropical areas where plantation agriculture is suitable, the resultant social inequality led to autocratic regimes. Alternatively, in areas with moderate rainfall, agriculture was undertaken in the context of family farms, and this underpinned greater social equality and, ultimately, democracy. Welzel (2013) puts forward the cool water (CW) condition that is fulfilled in areas with moderately cold temperatures, continuous seasonal rainfall and permanently navigable waterways. In areas where the CW condition is satisfied, production can be both greater (these areas are more productive) and more autonomous (family farms are the norm and access to navigable rivers democratises market access). The greater availability of resources together with a degree of autonomy in obtaining and trading them, contributes towards the development of contractual society where social exchange is voluntary. Alternatively, social relationships in irrigation-based societies will tend to be coercive (see also, John Powelson [1997]). Contractual relationships will, in turn, contribute towards the emergence of "emancipatory values" that include individualism. Because of the underlying existential autonomy of individuals in these areas, if a state emerges (with a monopoly of force) it will take a more representative form. Welzel (2013) provides cross-country empirical evidence showing that the CW condition is positively associated with empancipatory values.

Scholars have also offered numerous historical examples linking rainfed agriculture to equality. Writing on Athenian democracy, Finer (1997) explains that until the fifth century BCE, the economy was largely based on rainfed cereal farming. This set the basis for autonomous production and family farms illustrated by the estimate that in the fifth century BCE, three quarters of citizens owned land. Larry Patriquin (2015) states that farm sizes ranged between 20 and 60 plethora (one plethora was around 900 square metres) and that in the late fourth century BCE, the wealthiest 10 per cent of citizens owned 30 to 35 per cent of land and 70 per cent was owned by 70 per cent of citizens. While estimates of land distribution may vary depending on the source, there is strong evidence of economic equality in Athenian society. And according to Patriquin (2015), economic equality was the basis of political equality, most notably in the Assembly and the courts that were open to all male citizens (the Council was not open to the lowest classes). Any citizen could bring a case to court, including one against the state. In fact, "impersonal principles of law and citizenship were taking precedence over the personal rule of kings and lords" (page 16). Moreover, taxation was progressive since taxes fell almost entirely on the rich. Haber (2012) frames the wars between the ancient Greeks and Persians as clashes between egalitarian and democratic societies dependent on rainfed agriculture and autocratic ones based on irrigated agriculture. Writing on ancient Israel, Finer (1997) explains that it was a relatively egalitarian society of pastoralists and farmers dependent on rainfed agriculture.

Russia had neither irrigation agriculture nor the conditions for autonomous production. John Etty (2007) explains that, historically, the most abundant rain fell on regions worst suited for agriculture. In those regions best suited for agriculture, it rained less and, when it did, it was torrential thus ruining one in three harvests. The growing season was short (six months compared to nine in Europe) meaning that agricultural activity was concentrated, received less rain and this was highly concentrated in the warmer months. This required labour pooling and made extended families rational. Resource scarcity combined with the difficulty of autonomous production is likely to have contributed towards the emergence of a hierarchical and inward looking society, despite the absence of irrigation agriculture.

Another notable example is Italy. Anthropologist Edward Banfield (1958) coined the term "amoral familism" to describe social interaction in a southern Italian village in the mid-1950s. Amoral familism is an ethos of strong suspicion of non-(nuclear) family members and the legitimacy of behaviour as long as it promotes family interests. Inspired by Banfield's insight, Robert Putnam *et al.* (1993) report empirical evidence of the presence of social capital, mainly gener-alised trust or trust in strangers, as well as horizontal social relationships in the north of the peninsula, while in the south particularised trust is the norm and hierarchy much more prevalent (more on this in Chapter 6).

Putnam *et al.* (1993) trace these differences to the eleventh century. In the north, relatively civic and self-governing communities emerged in the context of republican city-states, most notably in Florence, Venice, Bologna, Genoa and Milan (see also, Alina Mungiu-Pippidi [2015]). In the south, the Norman con-quest established a centralised and hierarchical state dominated first by a king and, over time, a landed aristocracy. Turchin (2006) argues that the origins of these differences are older and date to the collapse of the Roman empire in the sixth century CE during which the north was settled by relatively egalitarian and high trust Germanic tribes most notably the Lombards. While these historical explanations are illuminating, they may not be the ultimate causes for the observed differences. A deeper and complementary cause for the differences between the north and south could be geography. Thomas Sowell (1981) explains that the north concentrates most of the arable land and enjoys higher and more frequent rainfall while in the south arable land is scarce and rainfall low and highly variable. Luigi Guiso *et al.* (2006) explain that the South has historically been characterised by latifunds, while in the north, cultivation has been undertaken in the context of smaller plots. Thus, the differences between the north and south could also be due to the possibility that biogeography allowed for relatively more autonomous production to take root in the former.[12]

In view of these arguments, I revisit the empirical evidence from the SCCS presented earlier, by adding variables capturing the nature of production. As before v158 and v270 measure stratification, v756 is political role differenti-ation, v759 is the perception of the power of leaders, v1130 is population density and v676 the frequency of warfare or fighting. In addition, I include two variables that capture the transition to agriculture – v3 that increases with the importance of agriculture and v246 that increases as the economy moves from hunting and gathering to agriculture. Moreover, with variables v20 and v681, I consider the impact of the growing importance of food storage and the presence of irrigation respectively. Finally, I also regress the social inequality indicators on variables that capture whether the major crop type is cereals or root/tubers. I do so since cereals are storable while roots or tubers are not (Haber [2012]) and, recall, storability allows potential dominants to appropriate social surplus and consolidate their power (see Joram Mayshar *et al.* [2016] for empirical evidence).

The results in Panel A of Table 3.7 strongly confirm the importance of population for social stratification. Population density is always associated with more stratification at statistically significant levels. Moreover, the fact that the estimated effect of agriculture is not statistically significant, together with the fact that this effect is always significant in the absence of population density (not shown), is consistent with the idea that one way agriculture has impacted on social stratification is by increasing population densities. The regression results in panel B show weak evidence that cereals are positively associated with social hierarchy while roots or tubers are negatively so. That this is picking up the impact of storage on stratification is suggested by panel C where I moreover control for storage and find it be positively associated with hierarchy and, moreover, the estimated effect of cereals and roots or tubers largely disappears. Finally, in panel D, I also consider the impact of irrigation on social stratification and find it to have a positive and statistically significant effect (I do not show the results for v756 and v759 since the sample size in these cases is drastically reduced making statistical inference unviable). Panel D also shows that population density and storage are robust to the introduction of irrigation in the regressions.

In light of these results, in Table 3.8, I consider the impact of social stratification on governance in the presence of population density, war and, now, storage. The results are consistent with those previously reported. The impact of population and storage on governance seem to pass through their effect on social inequality. The results also suggest that above and beyond its indirect effect through social inequality, conflict will tend to directly reduce checks on leaders and increase despotic bias when resolving conflict between individuals.

The nature of production has also had an impact on social inequality and governance through its effect on the colonisation strategies adopted by Europeans since the sixteenth century CE. Stanley Engerman and Kenneth Sokoloff (1997, 2000, 2002) have argued that in areas in the Americas where the geographic conditions were suitable for mining or cash crops subject to economies of scale (such as sugar, coffee and cotton), and where indigenous labour was abundant (or slave labour was imported from Africa), large plantations or mines were established. Such was the case of the Spanish colonies in Mexico and Peru, Portuguese colonies in Brazil, but also English, French, Dutch and Danish colonies in the Caribbean and, to a lesser extent since they were not suitable for growing sugar, the English and French colonies in the US south (see also, Fukuyama [2014]). This production structure led to elites that were able to establish formal institutions (including political disenfranchisement) and policies (including biased land and education policies) that excluded the masses from economic opportunities thus contributing to the persistence of inequality over time. Conversely, further north, a temperate climate suitable for crops subject to constant returns to scale (cereal grains such as wheat and barley), together with an abundance of land and the scarcity of indigenous labour led to the establishment by English, French and Dutch colonists of family farms. The colonists demanded property right protection, the rule of law and, over time, democratic rights and resisted the efforts of elites to institutionalise their power

Table 3.7 Social inequality and the nature of production

	Dependent variables:							
	Social stratification	Class stratification	Political differentiation	Perceived power of leaders	Social stratification	Class stratification	Political differentiation	Perceived power of leaders
Panel A								
Importance of agriculture	0.034 (0.062)	0.026 (0.065)	0.134 (0.125)	0.029 (0.050)				
Hunter gathering to agriculture					0.067 (0.050)	0.062 (0.052)	0.008 (0.096)	0.040 (0.039)
Population density	0.446*** (0.090)	0.457*** (0.093)	0.598*** (0.157)	0.208*** (0.067)	0.422*** (0.078)	0.430*** (0.082)	0.699*** (0.149)	0.200*** (0.064)
Warfare or fighting	0.334* (0.198)	0.441** (0.212)	0.475 (0.383)	0.399** (0.166)	0.311 (0.197)	0.417** (0.210)	0.561 (0.383)	0.402** (0.165)
N° of observations	133	133	78	78	133	133	78	78
R² adjusted	0.269	0.251	0.266	0.232	0.275	0.256	0.256	0.237
Panel B								
Cereals	0.607** (0.235)	0.450 (0.275)	-0.373 (0.470)	-0.174 (0.196)				
Roots or tubers					-0.609** (0.234)	-0.575* (0.296)	0.416 (0.530)	0.128 (0.219)
Importance of agriculture	-0.037 (0.059)	-0.026 (0.067)	0.178 (0.141)	0.050 (0.057)	0.082 (0.069)	0.071 (0.071)	0.102 (0.131)	0.019 (0.052)
Population density	0.432*** (0.085)	0.445*** (0.090)	0.602*** (0.154)	0.210*** (0.064)	0.416*** (0.091)	0.428*** (0.094)	0.615*** (0.153)	0.214*** (0.066)

	(1)	(2)	(3)	(4)	(5)	(6)	(7)	(8)
Warfare or fighting	0.283	0.403	0.514	0.417**	0.303	0.412*	0.483	0.401**
	(0.196)	(0.213)	(0.384)	(0.163)	(0.197)	(0.212)	(0.377)	(0.165)
N° of observations	133	133	78	78	133	133	78	78
R² adjusted	0.298	0.262	0.262	0.230	0.290	0.266	0.261	0.225
Panel C								
Food storage	0.540***	0.628***	0.611**	0.221**	0.562***	0.629***	0.544**	-0.187*
	(0.109)	(0.108)	(0.233)	(0.101)	(0.109)	(0.107)	(0.239)	(0.105)
Cereals	0.432*	0.253	-0.624	-0.270				
	(0.234)	(0.267)	(0.494)	(0.199)				
Roots or tubers					-0.460*	-0.399	0.501	0.155
					(0.237)	(0.290)	(0.535)	(0.218)
Importance of agriculture	-0.033	-0.021	-0.166	0.045	0.052	0.039	0.058	0.004
	(0.056)	(0.064)	(0.144)	(0.059)	(0.067)	(0.069)	(0.136)	(0.053)
Population density	0.361***	0.363***	0.542***	0.188***	0.345***	0.349***	0.563***	0.195***
	(0.088)	(0.092)	(0.159)	(0.066)	(0.092)	(0.094)	(0.158)	(0.067)
Warfare or fighting	0.360*	0.479**	0.572	0.443***	0.377*	0.482**	0.512	0.416**
	(0.188)	(0.199)	(0.386)	(0.163)	(0.187)	(0.198)	(0.378)	(0.166)
N° of observations	131	131	77	77	131	131	77	77
R² adjusted	0.379	0.360	0.281	0.249	0.378	0.365	0.273	0.235
Panel D								
Irrigation	1.317***	1.358**			1.317***	1.331**		
	(0.484)	(0.519)			(0.480)	(0.506)		
Food storage	0.402**	0.381**			0.401**	0.378**		
	(0.173)	(0.173)			(0.171)	(0.171)		
Cereals	0.147	0.080						
	(0.409)	(0.448)						

continued

Table 3.7 Continued

	Dependent variables:							
	Social stratification	Class stratification	Political differentiation	Perceived power of leaders	Social stratification	Class stratification	Political differentiation	Perceived power of leaders
Roots or tubers					-0.320 (0.288)	-0.304 (0.355)		
Population density	0.198* (0.112)	0.227* (0.124)			0.216* (0.112)	0.240* (0.120)		
Warfare or fighting	0.244 (0.297)	0.455 (0.308)			0.246 (0.277)	0.442 (0.290)		
N° of observations	61	61			61	61		
R² adjusted	0.436	0.424			0.441	0.428		

Notes

Regressions displayed vertically. All regressions include a constant (not shown). The estimation method is OLS, with White heteroscedasticity consistent standard errors in parentheses. *, **, **** significance at the 10, 5 and 1 per cent levels respectively. Data comes from the Standard Cross-Cultural Sample: social stratification is v158, class stratification is v270, political role differentiation is v756, the perception of the power of leaders is v759, importance of agriculture is v3, hunter-gathering to agriculture is v246, population density is v1130, warfare or fighting is v679, food storage v20, cereals and roots or tubers are dummy variables based on v233 and irrigation is v681.

Table 3.8 Social inequality and governance III

	Social stratification	Class stratification	Political differentiation	Perceived power of leaders	Population density	Warfare or fighting	Food storage	Sample	R² adjusted
Consensual or informal decisions	-0.333** (0.158)				-0.150 (0.134)	-0.403 (0.383)	-0.036 (0.242)	76	0.156
		-0.305** (0.138)			-0.153 (0.130)	-0.440 (0.374)	-0.040 (0.241)	76	0.158
			-0.437*** (0.066)		-0.001 (0.085)	-0.286 (0.328)	-0.008 (0.181)	76	0.388
				-0.957*** (0.214)	-0.083 (0.099)	-0.143 (0.347)	-0.066 (0.189)	76	0.315
Checks on leader	-0.269*** (0.096)				-0.070 (0.071)	-0.302* (0.170)	-0.058 (0.144)	74	0.296
		-0.277*** (0.080)			-0.061 (0.066)	-0.321* (0.166)	-0.041 (0.137)	74	0.331
			-0.304*** (0.033)		0.017 (0.046)	-0.247* (0.131)	-0.042 (0.101)	74	0.611
				-0.504*** (0.118)	-0.069 (0.057)	-0.201 (0.157)	-0.138 (0.113)	74	0.367
Despotic bias in conflict resolution	0.059* (0.035)				0.039 (0.031)	0.155*** (0.053)	-0.007 (0.062)	81	0.154
		0.076** (0.032)			0.033 (0.028)	0.138*** (0.049)	-0.019 (0.063)	81	0.183
			0.108*** (0.032)		0.013 (0.037)	0.148** (0.072)	0.017 (0.092)	45	0.457
				0.203** (0.080)	0.034 (0.042)	0.127 (0.072)	0.071 (0.085)	45	0.350

Notes

Regressions displayed horizontally. All regressions include a constant (not shown). The estimation method is OLS, with White heteroscedasticity consistent standard errors in parentheses. *, **, *** significance at the 10, 5 and 1 per cent levels respectively. Data comes from the Standard Cross-Cultural Sample: social stratification is v158, class stratification is v270, political role differentiation is v756, the perception of the power of leaders is v759, consensual or informal decisions is v764, checks on leader is v761, despotic bias in conflict resolution is v1134, population density is v1130, warfare or fighting is v679 and food storage is v20.

(for fascinating examples of such efforts, see Acemoglu and Robinson [2012] who moreover extend this approach to Australia and New Zealand).

In addition to factor endowments, Acemoglu *et al.* (2001) suggest that the differential colonisation strategies adopted across European colonies were driven by the local disease environment. Where it was favourable, it made mass settlement possible (the neo-Europes: USA, Canada, Australia and New Zealand) and led to the establishment of inclusive economic and political institutions. Where it was hostile to mass European settlement (much of Latin America and Sub-Saharan Africa), a small European elite established extractive economic and political institutions à la Engerman and Sokoloff. This suggests an additional channel through which the disease environment may have had an incidence on governance.

Easterly (2007) argues that the "factor endowments" hypothesis is likely to explain the degree of economic inequality across the world and not just in European colonies. To this end, he reports that the ratio of land suitable for growing wheat versus sugar cane is significantly and positively correlated with the share of family farms in the nineteenth and twentieth centuries (data from Tatu Vanhanen [1997]) with the relationship peaking around 1958 when the sample grows to include many developing countries. He then shows that historical inequality as captured by the share of family farms, is significantly and negatively associated with contemporary inequality measures (the relationship is strongest around 1928). Moreover, using the wheat versus sugar ratio as an instrumental variable for contemporary inequality measures, he shows that contemporary economic inequality undermines both economic development and contemporary quality of governance and education levels.

I take a cue from Easterly (2007) and also explore the relationship between biogeography, historical land inequality and contemporary economic inequality. In Table 3.9, I regress two measures of historical land inequality on a set of biogeographic indicators. First, a land Gini from Ewout Frankema (2010) that reflects inequality and access to land rather than ownership and, as such, represents a lower bound on the degree of inequality (see also, Bentzen *et al.* [2016]). The earliest observation is from 1880 but most of the data is before the 1960s and 1970s and thus, again, before major land reforms. Second, I follow Easterly (1997) and employ the share of family farms reported by Vanhanen (1997). The earliest observations are from 1850 and most of the data comes from the late nineteenth century and the first half of the twentieth century. I regress these land inequality measures on, cool water (Welzel [2013]), irrigation potential (Bentzen *et al.* [2016]) and the (log) ratio of wheat versus sugar (Easterly [2007]). The results reported indicate that irrigation potential is positively related to the land Gini, while cool water and wheat versus sugar are positively associated with family farms.

In Table 3.10, I consider the relationship between historical land inequality and measures of interpersonal inequality described in Chapter 2, namely, the net income Gini from SWIID and the Q5/Q1 ratio and middle class share from the WDI. The results show that historical land inequality is significantly associated with contemporary inequality: a higher level of historical inequality in the

Table 3.9 Biogeography and historical inequality

	Dependent variables:	
	Gini land	*Family farms*
Cool water	0.033	21.784***
	(0.057)	(5.789)
N° of observations	105	111
R² adjusted	0.000	0.097
Irrigation potential	0.116***	0.190
	(0.039)	(4.226)
N° of observations	109	118
R² adjusted	0.024	0.000
Wheat/sugar ratio	−0.089	18.489**
	(0.073)	(7.962)
N° of observations	88	96
R² adjusted	0.003	0.036

Notes

Regressions displayed vertically. All regressions include a constant (not shown). The estimation method is OLS, with White heteroscedasticity consistent standard errors in parentheses. *, **, **** significance at the 10, 5 and 1 per cent levels respectively.

distribution of land predicts a higher level of current interpersonal inequality and a smaller middle class. Taken together, the results in Tables 3.9 and 3.10 are in line with those reported by Easterly (2007) and suggest that biogeography may potentially impact on contemporary governance through its effect on historical land distribution and, from there, through current interpersonal inequality. This points to the potential usefulness of the biogeographic variables as instruments when trying to isolate the causal impact of contemporary economic inequality on governance and indeed, I will employ this strategy in Chapters 5 and 6.

Table 3.10 Historical and contemporary inequality

	Dependent variables:		
	Gini index	*Q5/Q1 ratio*	*Middle class share*
Gini land	0.171***	0.128***	−0.115***
	(0.044)	(0.029)	(0.026)
N° of observations	105	99	99
R² adjusted	0.478	0.282	0.438
Family farms	−0.141***	−0.127***	0.109***
	(0.033)	(0.030)	(0.028)
N° of observations	110	107	107
R² adjusted	0.439	0.247	0.337

Notes

Regressions displayed vertically. All regressions include a constant and control for GDP per capita and GDP per capita squared to account for the Kuznets curve (not shown). The estimation method is OLS, with White heteroscedasticity consistent standard errors in parentheses. *, **, **** significance at the 10, 5 and 1 per cent levels respectively.

From a slightly different perspective, Eric Uslaner and Rothstein (2012, 2016) identify the prevalence of family farms as a factor contributing towards higher historical levels of education (in 1870) and, moreover, report that higher education levels in the latter part of the nineteenth century help predict lower contemporary levels of corruption. Galor *et al.* (2009) have explained the link between land inequality and weaker investments in public education, in the context of the transition from an agrarian to an industrial economy. Specifically, large land owners – who were against education since it increased the mobility and ultimately the cost of the rural labour force – were able to neutralise calls for education by emerging capitalist elites who wanted to promote education since it increased the productivity of labour in industrial production.

Uslaner and Rothstein put forward several reasons for the impact of education on corruption. Mass education increased the employment options available to individuals and consequently reduced reliance on personal patron-client networks that are antithetical to impartial governance. Moreover, establishing broad-based and free education may have signalled to people that the state was moving towards universalism and impartiality thus creating the expectation of, and a demand for, equal treatment by government. Finally, higher literary levels allowed people to read newspapers that try to keep government accountable.

I examine Uslaner and Rothstein's suggestion that one channel through which historical education may have impacted on contemporary governance is by weakening patron-client networks. In Table 3.11, I regress the quality of governance on historical education and two proxies for the importance of patron-client relationships. One is simply the Gini index of disposable income from SWIID, on the assumption that patron-client relationships are more likely in economically unequal settings. The other is another cultural variable proposed by Hofstede (1980) called power distance and defined as the extent to

Table 3.11 Governance and historical education

	Dependent variable: Quality of governance			
Education 1870	0.223***	0.159***	0.129**	0.095**
	(0.059)	(0.058)	(0.054)	(0.048)
Education today	0.551**	0.499*	0.508**	0.478**
	(0.263)	(0.252)	(0.227)	(0.224)
Gini index		−2.159**		−1.673*
		(1.070)		(0.894)
Power distance			−1.597***	−1.340***
			(0.463)	(0.445)
Nº of observations	62	61	62	61
R² adjusted	0.748	0.772	0.798	0.806

Notes
Regressions displayed vertically. All regressions are OLS, include a constant and control for GDP per capita (not shown). White heteroscedasticity consistent standard errors in parentheses. *, **, **** significance at the 10, 5 and 1 per cent levels respectively.

which the less powerful members of institutions and organisations within a country expect and accept that power is distributed unequally (again, more on this in Chapter 6). The estimated impact of historical education is always positive and statistically significant at the highest level, but it is markedly reduced in the presence of the Gini index or power distance and, especially, when both these proxies are included in the regression. This, together with the fact that historical education levels are correlated with the Gini index and power distance (the correlation after controlling for GDP per capita is, respectively, −0.457 and −0.450 with a p-value of 0), provides some support for the argument that historical education impacts on contemporary governance, partly through its deleterious effect on patron-client relationships.

The place of religion

In the previous pages, I have argued that the nature of governance depends on social responses – hierarchically ordered personal relationships and ingroup bias – that emerge to reduce uncertainty stemming from social interaction. In this same vein, religious beliefs can emerge to reduce existential uncertainty by linking observable events to non-observable forces (Fukuyama [2011]). They are difficult to falsify thus reinforcing social conservatism. But they facilitate social interaction by structuring rewards and punishments so that they reinforce the gains from cooperation. In this section, I will consider religious beliefs in light of the basic framework developed in this chapter. I will argue that the nature of these beliefs reflects social inequalities and the strength of identifiable ingroups – variables that, in turn, emanate from the long-term factors I have identified earlier.

Bellah (2011) argues that religions emerged to legitimise the existing distribution of wealth and status differences among individuals (see also, Diamond [1997]; Nolan and Lensky [2009]; Mark Aldenderfer [2010]; Flannery and Marcus [2012]). These differences where, moreover, reflected in the nature of each religion. Thus, in egalitarian hunter-gatherers the whole society participates in religious rituals. In more stratified societies, religion was also more hierarchical. For example, the Hawaiian paramount chief (and his priests), as documented in the nineteenth century, had exclusive access to deities and had power over life and death over both chiefs and commoners. Indeed, the paramount chief was considered a god. Consistent with my earlier account, Bellah puts forward three reasons for the absolutism of the paramount chief: it was made possible by "the increasing size of the social unit with its attendant loss of face-to-face community, by the increased surplus due to agricultural intensification, and by the rise of militarism now that there was so much to fight over" (page 208).

In a similar vein, Bellah (2011) documents divine kingship in the "hydraulic empires" of Mesopotamia, Old Kingdom Egypt, the Americas and Zhou China where the king was the "Son of Heaven" and he alone could perform the sacred rituals. Confucianism in ancient China was, in the words of Finer (1997), unabashedly a doctrine of inequality. The "five relationships", which it preaches as the basis for all social interaction, are all relationships of subordination: wife to husband, son to father, younger to older brother, and friend, and all to the emperor. The highly stratified and unequal society was legitimated by the Confucianist canon, and both together legitimated the absolutism of the emperor.

(Pages 30–31)

Things were very different in classical Greece. We previously saw that fifth century BCE Athens was characterised by relative economic and political equality among male citizens, which itself partly depended on the importance of "hoplites" and oarsmen as well as the viability of rainfed agriculture. Religion here established a hierarchy between immortals and mortals and was reflected in society by the distinction between nobles, small farmers and the propertyless (Bellah [2011]). However upward social mobility between these groups was possible. Moreover, individuals could mediate directly with the Gods – there was no specialised priestly cast or royal monopoly. Anyone could communicate with God as long as they respected the nomos, or "customs law".[13]

What of the three major monotheistic religions, Judaism, Christianity and Islam? Consider Judaism first. Finer (1997) describes ancient Israel as an egalitarian society consisting of a free peasantry and a popular militia side by side a royal mercenary army. Religion reflected this relative equality. The Jewish monarch was not divine. Nor was he an intermediary between the community and God. All individuals participated in religious rites even if they were performed by the king or the priests. The king was subject to the same God-given laws as all the members of the community. This made the ancient Jewish king "history's first limited monarch" (page 239). When the king was seen to breach the Law, he was denounced by the prophets.

Insofar as Islam and Christianity are concerned, they differ in at least one important dimension that is relevant to my discussion here, namely, the importance afforded to the individual versus the kin-group. Uniquely in the case of Christianity, Goody (1983) explains how in the sixth century CE, the Christian Church came out against marriages between close kin, marriages to the widows of dead relatives (levirate), the adoption of children and divorce. All these practices were "strategies of heirship" whereby kinship groups are able to keep property under the group's control. The Church had an economic interest to oppose these practices since it expected to be bequeathed the properties of those Christians who died without heirs. Alternatively, in Muslim societies, endogamy or marriage within kin-groups was encouraged or even enforced, and this allowed the kin-group to maintain control of a member's patrimony. The differential approach to marriage drove individualism in Christian Europe and promoted collectivism in Muslim societies.

The practice of exogamy in Christian Europe and endogamy in Muslim society explains the relatively high proportion of consanguineous marriages (between second cousins or closer) in contemporary Muslim countries: between

20 and 50 per cent of marriages as opposed to less than 1 per cent of marriages in Western and Eastern Christian countries. Spain, where between 1 and 10 per cent of marriages are consanguineous, is an exception (see Alan Bittles [1994]). Ashley Hoben *et al.* (2010) put forward a "parasite hypothesis of inbreeding" such that consanguineous marriages may arise because they confer immunological resistance to local pathogens (see also, Thornhill and Fincher [2014]). In support of this argument, they provide empirical evidence from a sample 72 countries, linking historical pathogen prevalence to the prevalence of consanguineous marriage. This opens up the possibility that biogeography could be one factor behind the different approaches to marriage in Christian versus Muslim societies.

There are also differences within Christianity regarding the individualism-collectivism dimension. Steve Bruce (2004) argues that the Protestant Reformation gave a boost to individualism since it emphasised individual responsibility by putting an end to the possibility that the good could pass on religious merit to the less good by performing religious acts on their behalf. According to Benito Arruñada (2010), Catholicism prioritises the family, thus reinforcing the natural tendency to favour kin and close friends over strangers, whereas Protestantism places obligations to strangers at the same level as those with family members (see also, Rachel McCleary [2007]). Hofstede *et al.* (2010) argue that, like Catholic societies, Orthodox ones also emphasise ingroup ties and point, as an example, to the institution in both of godfathers and godmothers as a way of strengthening group ties beyond biological kin.

The relationship between secular and religious authority represents another notable difference between the major monotheistic religions. In Muslim and Christian Orthodox societies (as well as China for most of its history), religious authority has historically been subordinate to the secular ruler – an arrangement known as ceasaropapism (Finer [1997]; Fukuyama [2011]). The intertwining of secular and political authority was strongest in the Muslim world whose rulers initially united both political and religious power. Over time political and religious offices were separated but the political authority appointed the religious leader. While political rulers were limited by Islamic law (sharia) in family, religious and civil matters, they could invoke the doctrine of necessity (siyasa) giving them unlimited power in areas like taxation, law and order, and conscription. And the Sunni doctrine of passive obedience meant that

> any Muslim ruler, whoever he was and however he came to power – who was able to protect the territories of Islam and impose civil peace was entitled to obedience. Obedience to such a ruler, whether bad or mad, was a religious duty.
> (Elie Kedourie [1989] as quoted in Finer [1997], page 1302)

Caesaropapism, although actively resisted, existed in the Byzantine empire and, especially, in Tsardom Russia as of the sixteenth century (see also, Encyclopaedia Britannica, online version). In the Western Christian Church, the investiture crisis in the latter part of the eleventh century, eventually gave the pope sole right to fill religious positions. The growing institutional independence of the Catholic Church together with its elaboration of canon law (based on the redis-covery of the Justinian Code), laid the foundations of the emergence of legal constraints on rulers. This did not happen in Byzantium, despite the continuous application of the Justinian code there. According to Fukuyama (2011), the reason why caesaropapism took hold in Byzantium but not in the West was that the latter was politically fragmented, thus allowing the Church to play off one polity against another for its benefit. In the East, the relative unity of the Byzan-tine Empire offered no such opportunities.

The previous discussion suggests that individualism will tend to be strongest in Protestant societies and weakest in Muslim ones, while Orthodox and Catholic societies should have moderate levels of individualism or collectivism. Moreover, all other things being equal, checks on leaders should be strongest with Protes-tantism and Catholicism and weaker under Orthodoxy and, especially, Islam. In Table 3.12, I regress contemporary indicators of the cultural dimension of indi-vidualism from Hofstede (1980) as well as executive constraints from Polity IV on religious affiliations in 1900 from Charles North *et al.* (2013). The executive con-straints measure is increasing with institutionalised constraints on the decision-making powers of chief executives. The results are as expected. The estimated impact of religion on individualism is positive in the case of Protestantism and negative in the case of Islam while it is not statistically significant for Catholicism or Orthodoxy. Moreover, Protestantism and Catholicism are strongly and posi-tively related to checks on the executive. Orthodoxy is also positively related but the estimated impact is significantly smaller. Islam, on the other hand, is strongly but negatively associated with institutional checks on executive power.

While this analysis is suggestive of the impact of religion on the strength of ingroups and – insofar as checks on the executive is a reflection of rule of law – governance, it does not explain why the different religions emerged in some societies and not others. Bruce (2004) states that the Protestant Reformation took root in areas already characterised by individualism but does not elaborate further. And recall that Goody (1983) identifies the origins of individualism in the sixth century and relates it to the material interests of the Christian Church. Greif and Guido Tabellini (2017, page 16) push the origins of individualism even further back when they state that "the Church built on earlier Greek, Roman, and Jewish traditions of individual-level universal moral responsibility and moral obligation toward the community as a whole". While not denying the role of the Greeks, Romans, Jews and the Church in boosting individualism, I have suggested earlier that individualism may ultimately depend on factors related to biogeography: a lower pathogen prevalence or higher capacity for autonomous production is likely to reinforce individualism or, conversely, undermine collectivism. As such the roots of Protestantism may ultimately be found in a biogeographic environment favourable to individualism (see also, Welzel [2013]), while an environment that made collectivism a rational strategy may have facilitated the rise of Islam.[14]

Table 3.12 Monotheistic religions, individualism and checks on the executive

	Dependent variables:				
	Individualism		Checks on the executive		
Protestant	0.346*** (0.069)		2.245*** (0.522)		
Catholic		-0.025 (0.047)		2.075*** (0.323)	
Orthodox		-0.070 (0.048)			0.858* (0.517)
Muslim			-0.140** (0.054)		-2.907*** (0.368)
N° of observations	100	100	100	152	152	152
Adjusted R²	0.462	0.290	0.292	0.327	0.155	0.233	0.087	0.390

Notes
Regressions displayed vertically. All regressions include a constant and control for GDP per capita (not shown). The estimation method is OLS, with White hetero-scedasticity consistent standard errors in parentheses. *, **, *** significance at the 10, 5 and 1 per cent levels respectively. The religious variables capture the share of the population affiliated with each religion in 1900.

Conclusion

In the previous pages, I have argued that cross-society differences in governance are the result of different societal responses that have emerged over time to make social interaction more predictable. Specifically, I have suggested that the move towards equality under the law has occurred in societies with flatter social hierarchies and weaker ingroup ties. Conversely, the rule of law is less likely to take root in societies with more significant social stratification and more salient ingroups. The steepness of hierarchies and the strength of ingroups evolved over time in the context of four fundamental and interrelated factors, namely, disease, population growth, conflict and production.

Thus, in societies facing a higher infectious disease burden, exchange with strangers was avoided, and this reinforced within-group interactions to the detriment of outgroup exchange. Disease has also had an impact on social inequality through its effect on labour supply. The bubonic plague increased labour scarcity thereby increasing the bargaining power of serfs and contributing to the demise of (hierarchical) feudal relationships in Western Europe. Disease, together with resource endowments determined the nature of European colonisation and the governance structures that emerged in the New World.

Population growth has been an important driver of social hierarchy. As societies moved away from hunter-gathering towards settled agriculture, increasing populations, reduced the strength of kinship ties, pushed against cognitive limits facing individuals when monitoring interactions with others, and reduced the likelihood of repeated interactions. Hierarchically ordered personal relationships and ingroup bias emerged to increase predictability in social exchange. Population growth also led to an increase of socio-economic inequalities by contributing towards the emergence of private property rights. In addition, greater numbers made specialisation in economic and social roles possible. Since different activities offer different returns, specialisation contributed towards the emergence of economic and social inequalities in the very distant past.

Higher population densities also increased the likelihood of intergroup conflict for scarce resources that, in turn, puts a premium on the hierarchical organisation of the group under competent military leadership. Intergroup conflict also increases the salience of group boundaries. Intragroup conflict creates a demand for leaders who can reduce it, possibly by endowing them with a monopoly of force. Elites are less likely to consolidate their power in the context of intra and intergroup conflict insofar as violence technology is relatively cheap, since cheaper technology makes weapons available to a larger share of society, at the same time as it increases the efficient size of armies and thus the need to compensate the masses to get them to fight. Insofar as success in battle also requires the efficient mobilisation of society's fiscal resources, it can also contribute towards meritocracy in the public administration (a dimension of state capacity). Intergroup conflict can thus undermine impartial governance insofar as it contributes towards the emergence of societal responses (hierarchy and ingroup bias) that are inimical to it (and this is more likely the less affordable the technology of violence), at the same time as it can contribute towards the emergence of a specific expression of impartiality in the form of meritocratic recruitment in the military and public administration.

A final long-term factor affecting social responses relevant to the rule of law is what I have called the nature of production. In complex hunter-gatherer societies and even more so in agricultural ones, the availability of food surplus and storage facilitated the emergence of an elite, initially entrusted with redistributing food in hard times but, eventually appropriating an ever-larger share to cement its position at the top of the social hierarchy. The possibility of controlling social surplus is facilitated by the need for social coordination to obtain the surplus in the first place. This was the case in areas where agricultural production depended on irrigation projects. It was also the case when biogeographic conditions were favourable to cash crops subject to economies of scale. Conversely, the possibility of control and thus social hierarchy is reduced if autonomous production was possible, something that depended on regular rainfall and the suitability of cereal crops that can be produced in the context of family farms. Autonomous production also undermined ingroup ties insofar as it obviated the need to cooperate with others to secure food.

Notes

1 It is useful to distinguish between risk and uncertainty. Unlike uncertainty, risk can be insured against on the basis of a probability distribution of outcomes (see North [2005] who takes this from Frank Knight [1921]).
2 This discussion is consistent with Weber's (1922) view that power can be valued for its own sake, and not necessarily only as a means to wealth.
3 Egalitarianism in nomadic foraging bands refers to relationships between male household heads, not within households where relationships are more hierarchical (Boehm [1999]). Moreover, egalitarianism does not imply equality in resources or prestige. Rather, it refers to equal access to resources, technology to acquire them, and the paths leading to prestige (Kelly [1995]).
4 Another response to uncertainty in the context of market exchange are informal fairness norms regarding the distribution of the gains from trade. Joseph Henrich *et al.* (2004, 2010) provide evidence to support the idea that fairness norms may have emerged in large group contexts because they facilitate market exchange with strangers by providing focal points that coordinate expectations. Arguably, this idea complements that in Greif (1994). Fairness norms in market exchange will tend to emerge as all societies become larger. But in some societies, this exchange will be informally regulated by ingroups and, consequently, will tend to be limited to them, while in others it will be regulated by formal rules and because of this, will be able to break beyond the boundaries of ingroups.
5 Ola Olsson and Christopher Paik (2016) have similarly linked the emergence and persistence of hierarchically ordered social relationships and ingroup bias to the very distant past. Thus, the first agricultural societies to emerge in the Fertile Crescent had a relatively heavy infectious disease burden, relied on irrigated agriculture and were at risk of attack from hostile neighbours. Hierarchy and ingroup bias were social responses to this environment. Independent-minded individuals were more likely to leave such societies – moving further and further away in successive waves. Those that entered Western and Northern Europe found an environment with fewer pathogens and rainfed agriculture allowing for less hierarchy and weaker ingroup ties.

6 The link between social hierachy and the exit option has also been made by Boehm (1999) who explains how despotism in chimpanzee communities is buttressed by the inability of subordinate males to exit since they would in all likelihood be killed by other chimpanzee groups. A more general argument has been made by Albert Hirschman (1970) who famously argued that the exit option – together with the voice option – has the potential to reverse a deterioration in the performance of firms, organisations and states.

7 North (1981) also suggests that agriculture emerged in the context of exclusive communal property since planting made no sense in the absence of some type of enclosure (see also, Bowles and Jung-Kyoo Choi [2013]). In a similar vein, Woodburn (1982) explains how redistributive pressures in the !Kung and Hadza hunter-gatherer communities, are inimical to farming activity since other members of the group demand a share of the surplus thus undermining incentives to farm.

8 Although not shown, the findings are even more robust when employing urbanisation and the size of the local community as measures of population.

9 See also, Finer (1997), Rogowski and MacRae (2008) and Boix (2015) for reviews of the literature and additional evidence.

10 From a slightly different perspective, it has been suggested that enfranchising the masses makes society more cohesive and thus more effective militarily. This argument has been explicitly formulated by Mann (1986) who explains that the effectiveness of the Greek "phalanx" and the medieval pikemen depended on each soldier in the formation, trusting the one to his left and right. Crucially, he sees this trust as the result of the relative equality enjoyed by the members of each society. Similarly, Turchin (2006) makes the case that the Roman Republic's military power was founded on a relatively low degree of income inequality something that increased the cohesiveness of Roman society.

11 Bentzen *et al.* (2016) relate their analysis to previous ones that have associated oil, minerals, and plantation crops with poor governance. What these resources have in common with water from irrigation is that they are "point-source" or extracted from a specific point, and thus easy to monopolise. See Finer (1997), for descriptions of the social structure of "hydraulic empires" in antiquity.

12 It is worth pointing out that, consistent with Inglehart and Welzel (2005), Banfield (1958) identified resource scarcity as an important driver of amoral familism. This raises the question as to whether north-south differences in the levels of social capital are due to different levels of development. But economic differences between the north and south only emerged after 1920 while Putnam *et al.* (1993) documents differences in social capital at least since 1860. This suggests that differences in social capital are a cause rather than a consequence of different growth trajectories (Turchin [2006]).

13 In a fascinating discussion, Bellah (2011) explains the etymological origins of the word *nomos* which derives from the verb *nemein*, "to distribute". Thus, *nomos* implied the principle of distribution and, indeed, he points to Richard Seaford (2004) who argues that the word originated in the widespread practice of distributing meat.

14 Stelios Michalopoulos *et al.* (2016) have similarly argued that the rise of Islam can be partly traced to geographic conditions in the Arabian Peninsula. Specifically, this region is endowed with agricultural areas that are relatively productive (oasis) and arid areas that are much less so (deserts). At the time of the Prophet, there were increasing trade opportunities but for these to be realised, safe passage had to be secured when moving from the productive to the less productive areas. This was difficult since individuals living in the latter (nomads) had an incentive to steal the transported goods. To secure safe passage in the face of such incentives, these individuals had to be bought off through redistributive transfers. But those receiving them had an incentive to renege on such arrangements. Islam emerged to make these agreements time consistent or credible, since it institutionalised redistribution from the wealthy to the poor through explicit redistributive mechanisms (most notably, the obligatory *zakat* and the voluntary *sadaqa*).

4 Insights from social psychology and behavioural economics

Introduction

In this chapter, I will consider the relationship between inequality and governance based on evidence from the fields of social psychology and behavioural economics. Both these research programmes explore human behaviour in experimental settings. Experimental or laboratory settings allow researchers to control for a range of confounding variables and thus zero in on the causal effects of interest, but there are also concerns about the extent to which the observed behaviour can be extrapolated beyond the lab into the real world (Stephen Levitt and John List [2007]). At the outset, it must be said that there is a scarcity of experimental work directly dealing with the impact of economic inequality on governance outcomes. Some studies have considered how low or high social status may influence the observance of the law. This work identifies the perceived legitimacy of the distribution of resources as an important variable affecting individual behaviour. It also indicates the corrupting influence of power.

The chapter is structured as follows. In the first section, I will review work that has explained the phenomenon of ingroup favouritism. In the previous chapter, I explained that ingroup favouritism is a response to societal uncertainty. I also made the obvious point that ingroup favouritism is antithetical to impartial governance. Here, I will review experimental work that has confirmed the generalised human tendency to identify with ingroups and, moreover, has shown that ingroup favouritism can lead people to accept unethical behaviour by ingroup members and endorse leaders that discriminate outgroups. Having done this I will turn to evidence that has revealed a crucial factor driving peoples' actions, namely, perceptions of legitimacy. Illegitimate laws are less likely to be followed. Illegitimate social inequalities may harden low and high status group boundaries and reduce respect for the law by low status groups. This said, people also have a tendency to "believe in a just world" and to this aim, tend to underestimate the extent of social inequality, overestimate social mobility and justify perceived social inequalities by attributing them to capacity differences between individuals. I will then consider the impact of power on corruption. Power leads people to view subordinates instrumentally, leads them to underestimate the merits of less advantaged individuals, and increases unethical behaviour among powerholders. In the last section, I will explain the existence of high and low corruption countries as a multiple equilibrium phenomenon that depends on individual expectations concerning the likelihood of corrupt behaviour by others. I will conclude the chapter by bringing the different insights together with the aim of informing the inequality-governance relationship.

Ingroup bias and unethical behaviour

Social psychologists have put forward several theories to explain ingroup favouritism including the realistic group conflict theory and the social identity theory. In realistic group conflict theory, ingroup favouritism and cohesion emerge from zero-sum competition for material resources or positional goods. Experimental evidence has been provided in the form of the Robbers Cave experiment, conducted in the summer of 1954 by Muzafer Sherif and associates (1961). The subjects were twenty-two 11 and 12-year-old boys with similar backgrounds and characteristics who did not previously know each other. The researchers, posing as counsellors in the summer camp, divided the boys into two different groups and assigned them to cabins far apart from each other so that the groups did not know of the other's existence. During the first week of the camp, the children interacted only within their assigned groups (ingroup formation phase). After this, a series of intergroup competitions were set up with prizes for the winners. Prejudice emerged first in the form of taunting and name-calling, but this eventually degenerated into more significant acts like burning down the other group's flag, ransacking their cabin and steeling private property. The mechanisms behind this type of behaviour are described by Jim Sidanius and Felicia Pratto (1999) as follows:

> [T]he perception that one group's gain is another's loss translates into perceptions of group threat, that in turn cause prejudice against the outgroup, negative stereotyping of the outgroup, ingroup solidarity, awareness of ingroup identity, and internal cohesion, including intolerance of ingroup deviants, ethnocentrism, use of group boundary markers, and discriminatory behaviour.
>
> (Page 17)

While competition over valued resources is a sufficient condition for ingroup favouritism, it is not, unfortunately, a necessary one. The presence of ingroup favouritism even in the absence of intergroup competition was confirmed in an experimental setting by Henri Tajfel and colleagues (1970, 1971). They took boys aged 14 and 15 years old and randomly assigned them into two groups. The boys were aware of which group they were in, but did not know who else was in their group. They were asked to allocate a non-trivial (to them) amount of money to the other boys who were only identified by a number and their group membership. This anonymity thus excluded the possibility that money be allocated based on interpersonal favouritism. Moreover, the boys could not assign money to themselves thus excluding self-interested allocations. A large majority of the participants gave more money to members of their own group than to members of the other group and did so even when favouring the ingroup meant relatively less money for both groups. According to these authors, the results reveal that ingroup favouritism does not require that the groups be competing or that there be a previous history of intergroup hostility. Simply randomly assigning individuals into distinct groups triggers ingroup favouritism.[1]

These findings led Tajfel and associates to propose the "social identity theory of group behaviour" (see, for example, Tajfel and John Turner [1986]). They argue that people strive to maintain or enhance their self-esteem, self-image or social identity. A positive social identity "is based to a large extent on favourable comparisons that can be made between the ingroup and some relevant out-groups: the ingroup must be perceived as positively differentiated or distinct from the relevant out-groups" (page 284). Thus, in the pursuit of self-esteem, people tend to identify themselves as members of specific ingroups, presume that these groups are superior to others, and reinforce ingroup and outgroup categories by favouring their ingroup. Interestingly, it follows that if a group's status is perceived to be low then the group will tend to undermine one's self-image, something that provides an incentive to individuals to abandon it and try to join a high status one. However, if intergroup mobility is limited, and social inequalities are perceived to be illegitimate, this will instead reinforce ingroup bias in low status groups (see also, Jolanda Jetten *et al.* [2017]). This said, all other things being equal, social identity theory would predict that ingroup favouritism is more likely to emerge in high status groups and less so in low status ones because of the perceived "inferiority" of the latter (see Itesh Sachdev and Richard Bourhis [1987] for experimental evidence).

Based on social identity theory, several scholars have considered the impact of either unfair or unethical behaviour (cheating) in the context of ingroups and outgroups. Michael Platow *et al.* (1997) examine responses to unfair treatment by leaders. On an interpersonal level, individuals tend to endorse leaders who treat individuals fairly or impartially. But in the context of social identity theory, these scholars show that leaders who distribute resources to favour their ingroup and thus, necessarily, to the detriment of outgroups, enjoy greater support from ingroup members. Francesca Gino *et al.* (2009) hypothesise that the behaviour of others will have a larger influence on one's perception of appropriate behaviour if they are members of one's ingroup. Specifically, when the person engaging in unethical behaviour is an ingroup member, individuals are more likely to consider this as acceptable and engage in unethical behaviour themselves. Alternatively, if the person who cheats is a member of an outgroup, "individuals may want to distance themselves from this 'bad apple' in order to maintain a distinctive and positive social identity" (page 394). In another study, Bram Cadsby *et al.* (2016) ran experiments with students from two comparable Chinese Universities to consider whether people cheat to favour a member of an ingroup to the detriment of outgroup members. They found that people lie to increase the payoff of ingroup members. Their experimental design rules out the possibility that this result may be due to an expectation of reciprocity: I'll cheat to favour you today because you may cheat to favour me tomorrow.[2]

While not framed in terms of ingroups and outgroups, Adam Waytz *et al.* (2013) consider the impact of loyalty on the likelihood that people will report unethical behaviour based on the premise that whistleblowing can promote ethical behaviour, but it can also be disloyal. In one of their studies, participants were differentially primed in favour of fairness or loyalty by being randomly assigned to write short essays on the importance of fairness/justice or the importance of loyalty. They were then asked how likely they were to blow the whistle in a range of scenarios. They found that people primed towards fairness are more willing to report unethical behaviour. Based on these results, they suggest that whistleblowing is more likely in individualist rather than collectivist societies given the premium placed on group loyalty in the latter.

Finally, scholars have also explored the extent to which a group-based versus an individualist mindset can affect corruption. Nina Mazar and Pankaj Aggarwal (2011) randomly assigned 140 business students into two priming conditions: either an individualist mindset involving identifying individualist pronouns like *I* and *mine* in a paragraph, or a collectivist mindset were subjects looked for words like *we* and *ours*. They were then put in a scenario where they assumed the role of a sales agent competing to win a contract to earn a commission. They were given the possibility to offer a bribe to the potential buyer and, moreover, they had to indicate the perceived responsibility for their decisions. The authors found that people primed with a collectivist mindset were more likely to offer a bribe and, importantly, identify a reduced perceived responsibility for their actions as the mediating channel (see also, Valentina Rotondi and Luca Stanca [2015] but based on individual-level data from 25 European countries).

Inequality, legitimacy and behaviour

In his essay on why people obey the law, Tom Tyler (1990) distinguishes between instrumental and normative motives. The instrumental motivation is, essentially, an extrinsic incentives-based argument that individuals obey the law because they calculate the private costs and benefits of deviating from law-abiding behaviour (see, seminally, Gary Becker's [1968] economic theory of crime). From this vantage point, increasing the cost of committing a crime is an effective way to deter criminal behaviour. The normative motivation on the other hand, sees people as intrinsically motivated to obey the law. From this vantage point, people may obey the law even when it is personally profitable for them not to do so and even in the absence of sanctions. The normative motivation reflects both a commitment to obey the law because of a perception that the law is just, and a commitment to obey it because the authority enforcing the law has the right to do so or, in other words, is legitimate. Legitimacy can be enhanced insofar as authorities follow clear norms of procedural justice (Tyler

[1990]). Compared to a legal system that assumes that individuals only respond to external sanctions and whose enforcement by agents of the law needs to be financed by the public purse, a legal system that is sensitive to the idea that individuals may be intrinsically motivated to obey the law can reduce the cost of compliance.[3]

The distribution of resources is perceived to be legitimate insofar as it adheres to procedural justice or, specifically, insofar as it emerges in a context that provides people with equal opportunities to compete for wealth and status (Tyler [2011]). Conversely, the distribution of income is likely to be seen as illegitimate if it is "the result of unfair wealth acquisition such as corruption, fraud, exploitation, nepotism, or mere chance or luck" (Jetten *et al.* [2017]). In a range of experiments, Aldo Rustichini and Alexander Vostroknutov (2014) report that individuals are more likely to reduce the winnings of others at a cost, if these winnings are the result of chance rather than merit. They argue that this is because individuals considered favourable outcomes due to chance (merit) to be undeserved (deserved), and thus felt more (less) justified in punishing winners. In the context of social identity theory, Simon-Pierre Harvey and Bourhis (2013) conduct several experiments and reveal that when wealth differences are perceived to be the result of individual merit rather than chance, individuals from wealthy groups tend to discriminate more against members of lower wealth groups while members of poorer groups are more accepting of wealth differences.

The importance of the perceived fairness of the rules of the game for the acceptance of societal outcomes has also been revealed in the context of dictator and ultimatum games. In the standard dictator game, the first player (the dictator) determines how to split an endowment between himself and another player. In the ultimatum game, the second player chooses to either accept or reject this proposal. If the second player accepts, the money is split according to the proposal. If the second player rejects, neither player receives any money. The game is typically played only once so that reciprocation is not an issue. Dictators give on average around 28 per cent of the sum of money to the second player (Christoph Engel [2011]) while the vast majority of offers to the second player in the ultimatum game are between 40 per cent and 50 per cent with no offers below 20 per cent (Ernst Fehr and Klaus Schmidt [1999]). Both these results go against expected profit-maximising behaviour and suggest an aversion to inequality. However, these games have been criticised in that they tend to neglect how the money is allocated in the first place (Clark and D'Ambrosio [2015], page 1166): "money appears here out of nowhere as 'manna from heaven' … so that having more than others is not seen as being deserved". When instead the experiment is set up so that income reflects effort rather than luck, the results change. Dictators allocating earned wealth were much less generous and when the income distributed by the proposer in the ultimatum game is earned rather than randomly assigned, less is offered and unequal offers are more likely to be accepted (Elizabeth Hoffman *et al.* [1994]; Todd Cherry *et al.* [2002]).

The relationship between rule observance and notions of justice and legitimacy in the context of social inequalities can be informed by two related strands of work, namely, social dominance and system justification theories. Social dominance theory dwells on the importance of ideology when explaining intergroup relations in socially unequal settings (Sidanius and Pratto [1999]). It starts by arguing that societies are structured in terms of group-based social hierarchies with higher placed groups having access to more material resources, power and status. Social dominance theory suggests that ideology is framed by ruling elites to justify social inequalities. Ideology, or legitimising myths, can serve to justify inequality in the minds of both high and low status groups. In the case of the latter, it implies that they accept their relative social position as fair and legitimate, an attitude labelled "false consciousness". The acceptance of social inequality is, moreover, buttressed by a psychological trait they call, "social dominance orientation" that reflects the "desire and support [of] group-based hierarchy and the domination of "inferior" groups by "superior" groups" (page 48). Indeed, individuals with such an orientation are more likely to endorse inequality-legitimising ideologies that, according to these scholars include, sexism, racism, individual responsibility and the Protestant work ethic. Moreover, recent work has shown that people with a social dominance orientation are likely to perceive smaller inequalities between social groups and, relatedly, will tend to reject egalitarian social policies aiming to reduce inequalities (Nour Kteily *et al.* [2017]).

In a similar vein, system justification theory builds on the insight that people prefer to believe that existing social systems are fair and legitimate (John Jost and Mahzarin Banaji [1994]). Specifically, people have a basic motivation to "believe in a just world" to reduce the psychological cost of an uncertain, uncontrollable and unjust environment (Melvin Lerner [1980]; Jost [2001]; Aaron Kay and Justin Friesen [2011]). Applied to the legal system, system justification implies that people may resist evidence that suggests that laws and their application may be neither fair nor legitimate (Tyler [2007]). One way that individuals justify a status quo characterised by social inequality is by stereotyping members of disadvantaged groups as less hard-working or intelligent. This stereotyping is undertaken by people in both high and low status groups. Thus, low status groups may justify existing social inequalities by internalising negative stereotypes of themselves and positive stereotypes of high status groups. High status groups may even ascribe social inequality to genetic differences between individuals (Michael Kraus and Dacher Keltner [2013]). Consistent with system justification and based on evidence from the United States, low status groups tend to endorse meritocracy and believe that large differences in pay are necessary to foster motivation and effort (Jost *et al.* [2003]), while people in general perceive lower inequalities than those that actually exist (Michael Norton and Dan Ariely [2011]), and tend to overestimate the degree of social mobility (Shai Davidai and Thomas Gilovich [2015]). This said, Benjamin Newman *et al.* (2015) have shown that low income earners are more likely to reject meritocracy if they reside in areas with high inequality since this increases the saliency of social inequality, leading them to reject the status quo as unfair.

Central to Newman *et al.*'s (2015) findings is the notion that low income individuals experience a sense of relative deprivation. One early approach to relative deprivation is Robert Merton's (1938) strain theory, which argues that low status individuals, especially when faced with the relative success of others, feel frustrated, alienated and resentful and, as a result, may be driven to commit crimes. The choice of criminal behaviour emerges because of social pressures to succeed that cannot be fulfilled through legal acts given the limited opportunities available to disadvantaged individuals. Frustration is less likely to emerge in structurally unequal societies where individuals may not face social pressure or expectations to move upwards into higher social classes. Rather,

> it is only when a system of cultural values, extols, virtually above all else, certain common symbols of success for the population at large while its social structure rigorously restricts or completely eliminates access to approved modes for acquiring these symbols for a considerable part of the population, that antisocial behavior ensues on a considerable scale.
>
> (Page 680)

In their review of the concept of relative deprivation, Heather Smith *et al.* (2012) distinguish between individual and group relative deprivation. In the case of the former, the individual believes that he or she is relatively deprived, while in the latter case he or she considers that his or her ingroup is (see, originally, Walter Runciman [1966]). For relative deprivation to emerge, three steps have to be taken. First, the individual must compare. Second, the individual must perceive he/she or his/her group is at a disadvantage. Third, this disadvantage must be seen to be unfair something that will lead to resentment. The perceived unfairness of the situation is likely if people view the process that generated the deprivation as illegitimate. According to these authors, resentment due to a feeling of individual relative deprivation may lead individuals to respond by, among other things, commit crimes. Group relative deprivation may lead them to participate in collective action aimed at improving the situation of one's ingroup. One form that this collective response may take is by calling for income redistribution (see, for example, Gerald Eisenkopf *et al.* [2011], who relate inequality of education opportunities to redistributive preferences in experimental settings). Conversely, relatively advantaged group members may mobilise to maintain ingroup privileges as long as they perceive these to be legitimate or, when these are seen to be illegitimate, because they fear that disadvantaged group members will act to erode their privileges (Tajfel and Turner [1986]; Silvia Moscatelli *et al.* [2014]; Jetten *et al.* [2017]).

Power and corruption

Lord Acton famously stated that "power tends to corrupt and absolute power corrupts absolutely". In an early article, David Kipnis (1972) asked "Does power corrupt?" His analysis is conducted in an interpersonal rather than inter-group framework. Specifically, he recruited 28 university students to act as managers of workers in a simulated company. The subjects did not know that, in reality, the workers did not exist, and that their output was simulated by the experimenters. They were split into two groups: the no-power group that could manage workers by persuasion and the power-group that could do this but also employ a set of instruments including promising and awarding a pay rise, giving additional instructions, deducting pay or threatening to do so, or firing a worker or threatening to do so. The results show that the subjects with power tried to influence the workers more than those without power, and did so by using the instruments available to them beyond persuasion. Moreover, those with power tended to devalue the value of the workers, even though all worker output exceeded minimum company standards. In addition, managers without power were more willing to meet socially with workers than those with power – the latter wanted to maintain social distance. Those with power felt that an important skill needed to be a successful manager was the ability to manipulate others. And subjects with power viewed the workers being extrinsically motivated by the instruments applied, rather than intrinsically so. Kipnis suggests that power triggers the following train of events:

> (a) With the control of power goes increased temptations to influence others' behaviour, (b) As actual influence attempts increase, there arises the belief that the behaviour of others is not self-controlled, but is caused by the power holder, (c) hence, a devaluation of their performance. In addition, with increased influence attempts, forces are generated within the more powerful to (d) increase psychological distance from the less powerful and view them as objects of manipulation.
>
> (Page 40)[4]

Susan Fiske (1993) expands our understanding of how power affects behaviour by emphasising the role of stereotyping and attention. Stereotyping refers to the tendency to evaluate people according to their membership of a group rather than their individual characteristics. Attention refers to the effort people exert to understand others. According to Fiske, "attention is directed up the hierarchy" (page 624). By this, she means that people with less power have an incentive to pay attention to those with more power since the latter have, by definition, a measure of control over them. Conversely, the powerful do not need to pay attention to the less powerful since they cannot be affected by them. This, together with the fact that the powerful have more people competing for their attention, leads them to rely on stereotyping when interacting with less powerful people. Stereotyping can maintain power relationships by limiting the stereotyped individual's options: an individual from a low status group may be negatively evaluated based on group status, rather than on his or her merits.

In his book, *The Power Paradox*, Dacher Keltner (2016) reports evidence from a range of experiments that indicate that power tends to increase unethical behaviour (the original studies are reported in Paul Piff *et al.* [2012]). In one experiment, research assistants were positioned at a four-way stop where, according to law, those who arrived earlier should be the ones to continue first. The research assistants classified the status of the drivers based on the make, prestige and age of the car. They found that drivers with more expensive cars were nearly four times more likely than those with cheaper cars to break the law, that is, arrive later but cut in front of another driver. In a related study, an assistant was positioned at a pedestrian crossing where the law requires that drivers yield to the pedestrian. Again, drivers of more expensive cars were more likely to violate the law and ignore the pedestrian. None of the drivers of the cheapest cars ignored the pedestrian but 46.2 per cent of the drivers of the most expensive cars did so. In another experimental setting, subjects were asked to identify where they fall along the income distribution by marking an X on a 12-rung ladder. A few days later, they played a game on a computer that gave them the opportunity to misreport their scores and thereby increase their chances of winning a cash prize. The wealthier participants were more likely to lie. In yet another related study, after identifying their social class through the same ladder, participants completed a variety of tasks and, as they departed the lab, were confronted with a bowl full of candy with a label indicating that these were for children participating in experiments. The wealthier participants took almost twice as much candy as the less wealthy.

In another set of studies, Joris Lammers *et al.* (2010) provide evidence that power leads people to impose strict moral standards on others but to apply less moral behaviour to themselves (a phenomenon they call moral hypocrisy). Specifically, in one experimental setting, they were primed to have more or less power and then asked to consider a range of moral dilemmas: speeding with little traffic to make an appointment; not reporting additional wages earned during spare time on a tax return or; whether it is appropriate for a poor person to keep an abandoned bike. Moral hypocrisy emerged among high power participants: they criticised this behaviour in others but not in themselves. These scholars suggest that feelings of power lead people to feel that they are entitled to judge others at the same time as they feel less bound by social disapproval in response to socially unacceptable behaviour. Moreover, they report evidence that shows that when entitlement is reduced by framing power as illegitimate, moral hypocrisy disappears: powerful people who perceive their position to be illegitimate are less likely to judge others for not following social norms at the same time as they are more likely to follow the norms themselves.[5]

Fang Wang and Xunwei Sun (2015) argue that the relationship between power and corruption is mediated by whether individuals hold a personalised power concept (the belief that power should be used to satisfy personal goals), or a socialised one (where power is to be used to achieve collective goals framed in terms of improving the welfare of others). To pursue this intuition, they conduct three studies: one relating self-reported measures of power (either personalised or socialised) to attitudes towards corruption, and two where experimental subjects are primed in these different power concepts and then their attitudes towards corrupt behaviour are calibrated. They find strong support for the expectation that power corrupts depending on the power concept held. Individuals who envision power through the self-interest prism are more likely to engage in corruption and more willing to accept corruption by others. The opposite happens when power is seen as something that should be used for societal benefit. In this case, individuals are even willing to forego income to punish corruption by others. By implication, adopting education and information policies that emphasise the notion of socialised power could help curb corruption.

Good or bad governance as alternative social equilibria

Fisman and Golden (2017) explain corruption as a multiple equilibrium phenomenon (see also, Jens Christopher Andvig [1991]; Bardhan [1997]; Rasma Karklins [2005]; William Miller [2006]; Rothstein [2011]; Anna Persson *et al.* [2013]). They start by clarifying that most people in most countries disapprove of corruption. If people condemn corruption, why do they engage in it? Part of the answer lies in the realisation that there are always at least two parties to corruption: one from the private sector seeking favourable treatment, and another in the public sector who can offer the benefits. In a setting where corruption is endemic, potentially corrupt individuals from the private and public sector have an abundance of partners in crime. In an environment where corruption is scarce, so too are potential parties on either side of a corrupt transaction. Moreover, the prevalence of corruption in one setting and its scarcity in the other means that the probability of being caught is higher in the latter. In addition, uniquely in a corrupt setting, those who abstain from corruption can be "priced out" from accessing scarce public resources. Finally, insofar as corruption violates internalised ethical norms, the prevalence of corruption reduces the psychological cost of participating in corrupt acts (see also, Bin Dong *et al.* 2012).

The move from a corrupt setting to a clean one is hampered by the fact that any individual who unilaterally decides to abstain from corruption may be at a disadvantage insofar as access to scarce public resources is concerned. Given the potential private or individual costs of foregoing corruption in corrupt settings, it will only make sense to eschew corrupt behaviour when you expect most individuals to behave in the same way (see also, Rothstein [2011] and Persson *et al.* [2013]). This same argument has been used to explain tax evasion or compliance. People are less likely to pay their taxes if they believe others are not fulfilling their tax obligations (John Scholz and Mark Lubell [1988]; George Klosko [1992]; Rothstein [2000]; Fehr and Urs Fischbacher [2005]).

Nan Zhang (2015) and Nils Köbis *et al.* (2015) consider the extent to which the expectation of others' behaviour affect corruption in experimental settings.

Zhang (2015) sets up a corruption game in a simulated hospital environment where participants are allocated into three roles, namely nurses, early patients or late patients. Late patients have the possibility to bribe nurses to skip the line and reduce their waiting times to the detriment of early patients. Nurses accepting the bribe faced the risk of being reported by the early patients (at a cost to them), and thus being sanctioned. He finds that participants cheated in direct proportion to their expectation that others would also cheat, and this result also stands for individuals who clearly believed that accepting gifts was inappropriate. Köbis *et al.* (2015) put subjects in a setting where they were the CEO of a construction company with the option to bribe the Minister of Public Affairs who allocates a bridge building contract. The bribe involves an invitation to a company banquet (labelled "ambiguous corruption" since this could also be a legal lobbying activity) or paying for the Minister's private vacation from the company budget ("severe corruption"). They find that people engage in both more ambiguous and severe corruption if they perceived corruption to be more prevalent.

Conclusion

The experimental evidence reviewed in this chapter reveals that individuals tend to identify with groups. Even in the absence of competition for resources, individuals randomly assigned to artificial groups practice a degree of ingroup favouritism. A driving force behind this behaviour is the need for positive social identity. With this aim, individuals identify themselves as members of specific groups, consider these groups to be better than others, and reinforce group categories by favouring their group. Ingroup favouritism is intensified in contexts characterised by intergroup competition for resources and, more generally, insofar as groups feel threatened by others.

Favouring an identified ingroup is opposite to impartial treatment of individuals or, stated differently, treating people in the same empirical situation similarly. Ingroup favouritism leads individuals to support leaders who unfairly distribute more resources to them compared to members of outgroups. It leads people to underplay and even follow unethical behaviour by ingroup members and, relatedly, makes it more likely that they turn a blind eye when observing such behaviour. Moreover, it leads individuals to lie to increase the pay-off of their ingroup and it reduces the perceived responsibility of unethical actions such as bribing.

Members of low status groups are, a-priori, less likely to favour their group because of the negative self-image attached to it. Their search for a positive social image may lead them to strive to join higher status groups. But this depends on the perceived legitimacy of the status quo and the possibility of upward mobility. When social inequality is perceived to be illegitimate and upward mobility is limited, ingroup bias by low status groups will tend to be reinforced. The perceived legitimacy of inequality depends on context: if people in either low or high status groups believe there are equal opportunities and that one can improve his or her social position through hard work, they will tend to see inequality as more legitimate. On the other hand, individuals are likely to consider inequalities that emerge from corruption, nepotism and chance as illegitimate. High status groups have an interest to expound ideologies that help legitimise social inequalities. Low status groups will be receptive to these legitimising attempts since people are motivated to believe the world is a fair place – that inequalities are lower than they are, that mobility is higher than it is, and that effort pays – to reduce the psychological cost of uncertainty.

The likelihood that individuals in low status groups will justify social inequality through legitimising myths is inversely related to their direct experience with inequality. Moreover, in societies where upward mobility is expected of individuals but unequal opportunities mean that it is difficult to fulfil these expectations, people will tend to be frustrated and may turn to crime or, more generally, may reduce their adherence to the law. Similarly, frustration in low status groups may lead to collective action to change the status quo (for example, redistributive demands), something that may mobilise relatively advantaged groups to take action to maintain their privileges.

The behaviour of high status individuals has been illuminated by studies considering the impact of power on behaviour. Powerful people tend to view subordinates as a means to an end and to judge them based on their membership of lower status groups rather than based on their individual merits. Powerholders are more likely to adopt unethical behaviour and, especially when they consider their power to be legitimate, to justify such behaviour in themselves while severely criticising it in less powerful individuals. Powerful individuals primed to think in terms of social welfare rather than self-interest are less likely to engage in unethical behaviour.

Finally, the experimental evidence reviewed points to the importance of expectations about others' behaviour on one's decision to engage in unethical acts. People are more likely to bribe others when they expect others to do the same. The reason could be because this signals the availability of "partners in crime", because it reduces the expectation of getting caught and punished, because it increases the possibility of honest people being out-competed and, finally, because it reduces a sense of guilt from bending internalised moral constraints. Whatever the reason, the important insight from this line of research is that countries can be trapped in a bad governance equilibrium. Specifically, while it may be in everyone's interest that governance be improved, no one has an incentive to unilaterally behave impartially unless most other people also do the same.

Can this analysis help inform empirical predictions about the impact of inequality and governance based on the cross-country indicators presented in Chapter 2? At the outset, it must be said that the experimental evidence points to the importance of qualitative factors that are difficult to account for in cross-sectional empirical work. Most notably, it reveals the role of the perceived legitimacy of the process generating inequality. This focuses attention to perceptions concerning equality of opportunities and the capacity to improve one's prospects through hard work. If inequality is perceived to emerge in an environment in which people can get ahead based on their own effort, then it is less likely to affect individual and group behaviour. Moreover, individuals may underestimate the real extent of inequality and overestimate social mobility. This points to the usefulness of the measures of perceived interpersonal inequality presented in Chapter 2.

This does not mean that standard quantitative inequality indicators are not useful. Arguably, the success of ideologies legitimising inequality is likely to be reduced as inequality increases. Similarly, the illusion of "a just world", where effort pays, is more difficult to sustain in a context of high inequalities. The same can be said of perceptions about the extent of inequality and social mobility. As such, as interpersonal inequality increases, governance may deteriorate since low status individuals may see unethical behaviour as justified thereby reducing their adherence to the law. On the other side of the income distribution, high income individuals may reduce their adherence to the law because of the corrupting effect of power. From a group perspective, increasing intergroup inequality may lead to calls for income redistribution that may be resisted by high status groups through both legal and – given evidence that power loosens ethical constraints – illegal means. In more collectivist societies, where a premium is placed on loyalty to the group, individuals may turn a blind eye to unethical acts by group members, especially if this behaviour is perceived to benefit the ingroup.

Notes

1 Because of these minimal group differentiation criteria, scholars refer to these set-ups as "minimal group experiments".
2 Gino *et al.* (2011) conducted the experiment at Carnegie Mellon University and to elicit group identity in their experiment, the "cheater" either wore a T-shirt from this University (ingroup scenario) or one from the University of Pittsburgh (outgroup). In Casby *et al.* (2016) ingroup and outgroups were generated by selecting students from two different universities.
3 Rui Costa-Lopes *et al.* (2013) suggest that one reason justice norms emerge is that "the fulfillment of justice standards brings with it a sense of control, predictability, satisfaction, and trust in the complexity of social interaction, and this, in turn, enhances mental and physical well-being" (page 229). For a more general discussion of how intrinsic motivation can reduce the cost of collective action, see Kyriacou (2010).
4 For experimental evidence on the tendency of those in power to see subordinates as a means to an end see also, Deborah Gruenfeld *et al.* (2008). Power also leads people to attribute acts of generosity by others to instrumental motivations (M. Ena Inesi *et al.* [2012]).
5 These scholars also find, albeit less robustly, that low power subjects tend to be more critical of their own transgressions than those of other people, a finding they label hypercrisy from the Greek *hyper* or "too much", and *kritein* or "being critical".

5 Economic inequality and governance in contemporary societies

Introduction

Good governance, as I define it here, is impartial governance. It emerges when politicians and bureaucrats apply rules and regulations so that people in the same situation are treated equally. It is violated when public officials appropriate public resources for private or political gain, when courts apply laws differently to individuals or groups and when public administrators are not recruited on the basis of merit. In Chapter 2, we saw that a widely used perceptions-based governance measure is negatively associated with a range of indicators of interpersonal and intergroup inequalities. This association was robust when controlling for a country's level of economic development, an important consideration since development has been identified as a basic driver of both good governance and, in the context of the Kuznets curve, economic inequality.

In this chapter, I will consider the possible impact of economic inequality on governance in contemporary settings in a much fuller way. With an eye on parsimony, I will examine the theoretical or causal mechanisms through which inequality can undermine good governance. This requires an understanding of the behaviour of individuals arrayed across the income distribution. It also requires that we appreciate the real possibility that governance itself can influence the evolution of economic inequalities. To deal with such reverse causality, I will propose and apply TSLS regressions that rely on exogenous determinants of economic inequality. For these, I will turn to the biogeographic variables that have already been identified in Chapter 3. To further isolate the impact of economic inequality on governance I will explain the need to control for a range of variables that, like economic development, may be associated with both governance and inequality and, consequently, whose omission is likely to bias the estimated impact of the latter.

My findings, based on a sample of up to 126 countries (depending on the inequality indicator used), unequivocally support the expectation that economic inequality is bad for the quality of governance. The causal mechanisms linking the two variables raise the possibility that the impact of interpersonal inequality on governance may be mediated by the level of democracy and, specifically, that democracy may amplify the negative effect of inequality on governance.

Consistent with this, my empirical results show that the negative impact of interpersonal inequalities on governance is stronger in more democratic countries.

Economic inequality will undermine good governance

A good starting point for understanding how economic inequality may affect governance in contemporary settings is Acemoglu *et al.*'s. (2005) discussion of the interplay between economic inequality, political institutions and political power. These authors argue that the quality of governance, basically the degree of protection of private property and the provision of equal opportunities, depends on the relative political power of different social groups. This relative power emanates from, on the one hand, the political institutions in place, and on the other hand, the distribution of economic resources. Political institutions, most notably, democracy versus dictatorship, determine the *de jure* distribution of power in society. In turn, the de jure distribution of power feeds back on the nature of political institutions since those endowed with legal authority will deploy this to shape political institutions that sustain their power. Economic inequalities on the other hand determine the de facto distribution of power. Economic elites can employ their superior resources to bias political decisions in their favour. The distribution of resources can also affect the nature of political institutions meaning that economic inequalities can impact on both the de facto and the de jure distribution of power. From this vantage point, economic elites can undermine the rule of law by either influencing the institutions in place or by putting into place institutions that represent their interests. This can lead to a popular backlash in the form of revolution – communist or populist (Edward Glaeser *et al.* [2003]). The subsequent expropriation of elite assets to redistribute resources to the poor will undermine property rights. And in many cases, these revolutions simply replace existing economic elites with new ones thus implying the continued capture of governance.

The experimental evidence reviewed in Chapter 4 allows us to expand our understanding of economic elite behaviour. Social identity theory yields three insights that may be relevant here. One idea is that members of high status groups are more likely than low status group members to identify and ultimately favour their ingroup, because the high status of the group enhances one's self-image. Second, ingroup favouritism may lead members of high status groups to support leaders that advocate discriminatory or unfair treatment of outgroups. Moreover, in the face of rising inequalities, high income group members may be increasingly fearful of envy and antagonism from members of low income groups and as a result mobilise to maintain the status quo distribution of resources. Finally, high status groups may promote stories or ideologies that justify the existence of inequalities. Another relevant strand of work is that examining the corrupting influence of power. This work indicates that power or status tends to loosen ethical standards. Thus, more powerful people are more likely to break the law, lie, appropriate a larger share of common resources and view low status people both instrumentally and – through the application of social stereotypes – in a negative light. Taken together, these insights tend to reinforce the idea that economic elites may undermine good governance to maintain or further their privileges to the detriment of lower income groups.

Inequality can be bad for governance from another perspective – that afforded by considering the incentives facing the relatively poor. Societies with large economic inequalities tend to be ones where public goods or services like education and health are under-provided. Indeed, because these policies help determine the extent of equal opportunities, their under-provision is likely to be an important factor driving economic inequalities. You Jong-sung and Sanjeev Khagram (2005) suggest that in unequal societies with deficient public services, the relatively poor may turn to petty corruption to obtain these (see also, Uslaner [2008]). Moreover, the under-supply of public services creates bottle-necks and thus opportunities for corrupt behaviour from public officials who can use their public authority to increase their income.[1]

Allen Hicken (2011) explains that interactions between poor individuals and public officials may occur over time in the context of patron-client relationships wherein public officials-as-patrons, offer benefits to the poor-as-clients, in exchange for, bribes, their loyalty and support. These benefits include material goods ranging "from cash to cookware to corrugated metal", and nonmaterial benefits such as public sector jobs, access to public services or interventions with the bureaucracy on one's behalf. The provision of particularised public benefits based on personal relationships is, of course, antithetical to impartial govern-ance. Clientelism is not exclusive to democracies. Hicken (2011) explains that patron-client interactions occur in "both autocracies and democracies (and in everything in between)" (page 290). However, there are also important differ-ences. In democracies, clientelism is an instrument to shore up political support in the context of elections while in autocracies it is a way of creating socio-economic dependence on, and political subservience to, the regime (more on clientelism in democracies later).

The view of petty corruption emerging from the efforts of relatively poor individuals to meet their basic needs can be expanded upon by considering differences in time preferences with respect to income. More limited resources mean that poorer individuals tend to have higher discount rates or, in other words, are more concerned by immediate consumption and less by the future benefits that can be obtained if consumption is deferred in favour of investment in, for example, human capital. Individuals may have higher discount rates because of low absolute incomes, but also because of lower relative incomes, since a feeling of relative deprivation may also drive up immediate consumption as a compensating mechanism, to the determinant of investment (for experi-mental evidence linking relative deprivation to higher discount rates, see Mitchell Callan *et al.* [2011]). Evidence of higher discount rates among the poor has been provided by Emily Lawrance (1991) who – based on a panel of US families, reports that discount rates of poorer households are three to five percentage points higher than those of the richest families (see also, Tomomi Tanaka *et al.* [2010], who exploit data on Vietnamese villages).

The time preference approach to understanding the link between income and governance is useful because it generates the expectation that as individual incomes rise, people may increasingly value "medium to long-term investments in administrative capacity (develop a meritocratic recruitment system, start the legal steps for enacting and implementing rule of law, fight favouritism and corruption)" (Charron and Lapuente, [2010], page 451). These authors associate discount rates with a country's level of development since poorer countries should, on average, have higher discount rates. However, for any given mean level of income, discount rates could also vary across the income distribution, being highest for the relatively poor and falling as we move to the right of the distribution. Thus, as more people move up into the middle class, discount rates should fall and the quality of governance should improve (Marcus Tannenberg [2014]). Consistent with this, Fukuyama (2014) explains that the shift from patronage based organisations towards meritocratic ones in the UK and the US took place, respectively, in the late nineteenth and early twentieth centuries, in the context of economic development due to industrialisation and the associated emergence of an urban middle class (see also, Arthur Goldsmith [2007]).

Both Jong-sung and Khagram (2005) and Uslaner (2008) suggest that petty corruption is more likely if people perceive the status quo distribution of resources to be illegitimate. This could be because they perceive that economic elites employ their superior resources to bias laws, the bureaucracy and the courts in their favour, just as predicted by the description of elite behaviour earlier. Again, my discussion in Chapter 4 may be useful here. The distribution of resources will be perceived as illegitimate if people believe that they do not enjoy equal opportunities or if it is seen to be the result of corruption, fraud, exploitation, nepotism or luck rather than merit. Relative deprivation theory suggests that a combination of inequality of opportunities and social pressures to climb the social ladder, may lead poorer individuals to engage in illegal acts or underprivileged groups to mobilise against the status quo. On the other hand, social dominance theory indicates that economic elites will expound legitimising myths to justify social inequalities including merit-based explanations. System justification theories suggest that people may prefer to believe merit-based explanations of the distribution of resources and resist accounts that institutions are stacked against them. This said, the impact of legitimising myths and "beliefs in a just world" is likely to be inversely related to direct experience with relative income differences.

In Chapter 4, I also reviewed evidence suggesting that people are more likely to engage in corruption if they think that other people are doing the same. Behind this evidence was the notion of corruption as a bad social equilibrium. Individuals may consider corruption to be inappropriate but engage in it so as not to be priced out of scarce public resources. While everyone would benefit from shifting towards a setting where corruption is limited, it only makes sense to reduce corruption if most other people do the same. From this vantage point, relatively poor people may be forced to engage in corruption or seek particular-ised benefits from public officials because they fear that if they don't do so, they will not access vital public resources while others will (see also, Uslaner [2008]). Relatively wealthy people are also more likely to employ their superior resources to influence public officials if they think that most economic elites are doing so.

The discussion so far has been generally framed in terms of individual rather than group inequalities. A similar dynamic might emerge in the latter case. Rel-atively wealthy ethnic groups may employ their superior resources to bias public sector decisions for their benefit. The members of poor ethnic groups will be forced to resort to petty corruption to cover their basic needs and they may do so in the context of patron-client relationships. Moreover, poorer individuals are less likely to adhere to the rules and institutions in place if they perceive ethnic inequalities to be the result of the corrupt practices of wealthy ethnic groups, and especially since upward mobility into wealthy ethnic groups is extremely limited due to the relatively immutable nature of ethnicity. In Kyriacou (2013b), I consider the impact of ethnic inequality on governance. I employ data on ethnic group inequalities from Østby (2008), who exploits the Demo-graphic and Health Surveys (DHS) to obtain information on ethnic groups' household assets (economic ethnic inequalities) and years of schooling (social ethnic inequalities). My results, based on a panel of developing countries, support the expectation that economic and social ethnic inequalities undermine the quality of governance.

Bad governance will perpetuate economic inequality

The discussion so far suggests that economic inequality may be inimical to good governance. Sanjeev Gupta *et al.* (2002) turn the direction of causality around when they argue that corruption can worsen inequality and poverty. The basic idea – in line with the material motivation of economic elites discussed earlier – is that the relatively wealthy "buy out" politicians and public administrators to obtain favourable tax and spending decisions. Obviously, corrupt public officials are more likely to be responsive to elite offers than non-corrupt ones. Thus, cor-ruption may reduce both tax pressure and tax progressiveness to the benefit of economic elites and at the cost of less well-off groups. Or it can lead to spend-ing on policies favouring the relatively wealthy to the detriment of spending tar-geting the poor (see also, Shantayanan Devarajan and Ritva Reinikka [2004]). Relatedly, reduced tax pressure means fewer resources for policies that can help equalise market incomes, most notably, public education and health policies.[2]

Another way that corruption can increase income inequality is through the unequal incidence of bribery. Fisman and Golden (2017) suggest that the poor may be more vulnerable to "shake downs" for bribes by public officials because they are less likely to complain than the relatively wealthy. To support this, they report evidence from a study by Brian Fried *et al.* (2010) that showed that Mexican traffic police stopped wealthy and poor drivers (simulated by hired confederates) with equal frequency but were more likely to extort bribes from the latter. In posterior interviews, the police confessed that the reason for this was the expectation that more affluent drivers would complain. Similarly, in another field experiment, this time among traffic police in Malawi, Amanda Robinson and Brigitte Seim (2018) found that fewer bribes were extracted from (confederate) drivers who signalled that they were wealthy and politically connected. Fisman and Golden (2017) add that even if the incidence of bribery were the same across income groups, if public officials seek a fixed bribe for their services, this will hurt poor people more.

From another perspective, corruption can increase inequalities because it reduces popular support for the welfare state (Jan Hanousek and Filip Palda [2004]; Rothstein [2011]; Stefan Svallfors [2013]). If people perceive government as generally efficient, they are more likely to tolerate the higher tax pressure associated with more robust welfare states. Conversely, bad governance is likely to reduce support for social spending and reduce tax morale (including higher tax evasion) to the detriment of economic equality. Good governance – under the guise of a politically independent and meritocratically staffed public administration – may also affect redistributive efficiency. In collaboration with Leonel Muinelo-Gallo and Oriol Roca-Sagalés, I have considered the impact of an effective public administration, on the redistributive efficiency of social transfers and direct taxes (Kyriacou *et al.* [2018]). We measure redistribution as the difference between the market and net income Ginis. Redistributive efficiency is measured in terms of the degree of redistribution attained for a given level of transfers (social benefits in cash) and taxes (payroll and income taxes). We find that more effective public administrations achieve more redistribution for any given level of spending and taxation, even after controlling for a range of potentially confounding variables, including, economic and demographic factors that may impact on the redistributive profile of fiscal policy.

Alberto Chong and Mark Gradstein (2007) examined the two-way relationship between interpersonal economic inequality and governance, and conclude that while the quality of governance does have a negative impact on inequality, "the causal direction from income inequality to institutional quality dominates the linear relationship between these variables regardless of the institutional [see governance] indicators, the sample of countries, and the income distribution variable used" (page 463). This said, the existence of reverse causality alerts us to the real possibility that OLS point estimates of the impact of economic inequality on the quality of governance may be downward biased, since better governance is likely to reduce economic inequality. To account for this, in the empirical analysis I will also report TSLS estimates. TSLS rely on the use of exogenous instruments of economic inequality or, in other words, variables that are correlated with economic inequality but that conceptually cannot be influenced by the quality of governance. A suitable instrumental variable should, moreover, impact on governance through its effect on economic inequality rather than some other unaccounted-for channel.

For such exogenous variables, recall the three biogeographic measures presented in Chapter 3. There, we saw that cool water from Welzel (2013), irrigation potential from Bentzen *et al.* (2016) and the (log) ratio of wheat versus sugar from Easterly (2007) were variously associated with indicators of historical land inequality and the latter were so with contemporary measures of economic inequality. The fact that contemporary governance cannot influence these biogeographic measures satisfies one important requirement of a suitable instrumental variable. Another requirement is that these measures should be correlated with contemporary inequality. In Table 5.1, I regress the different measures of economic inequality on the biogeographic indicators as well as GDP per capita and its square to capture the Kuznets curve. For instruments of ethnic inequalities, I turn to biogeographic measures proposed by Alesina *et al.* (2016) based on five biogeographic dimensions, namely, elevation, land suitability for agriculture, distance to coast, precipitation and temperature. The authors calculate the mean values for each ethnic area and derive Gini coefficients for each dimension at the country level. They then aggregate the resultant Ginis through principal components analysis and propose the first principal component as an instrumental variable for ethnic inequality.

The results reported in Table 5.1 suggest both cool water and the log wheat to sugar ratio as potential instruments for interpersonal inequalities. The exception is perceived economic inequality since cool water is not a significantly associated with it while the wheat to sugar ratio is so but with the wrong sign, a result that is most likely to due to the limited sample that mostly includes European and neo-European (the United States, Australia and New Zealand)

Table 5.1 Biogeography and contemporary inequality

	Cool water	Irrigation potential	Log wheat/ sugar ratio	1st PC Gini geographic endowments (ethnic homeland)
Gini index	−0.187*** (0.040)	0.012 (0.026)	−0.173*** (0.030)	NA
Q5/Q1 ratio	−0.069** (0.032)	−0.022 (0.017)	−0.094*** (0.021)	NA
Middle class share	0.108*** (0.030)	0.019 (0.018)	0.119*** (0.018)	NA
Gini perceived	−0.006 (0.022)	−0.006 (0.017)	0.059*** (0.020)	NA
Inequality of opportunity	−0.188*** (0.057)	−0.048** (0.024)	−0.176*** (0.036)	NA
Ethnic inequality (GREG)	NA	NA	NA	0.064**** (0.008)
Ethnic inequality (ETHG)	NA	NA	NA	0.112*** (0.011)

Notes
Each estimate is the result of the regression of the economic inequality measure on the corresponding biogeographic indicator. All regressions include a constant and control for GDP per capita and GDP per capita squared (not shown). The estimation method is OLS, with White heteroscedasticity consistent standard errors in parentheses. *, **, **** significance at the 10, 5 and 1 per cent levels respectively. NA means not applicable.

countries. Irrigation potential does not seem to be a suitable instrument for interpersonal inequalities except for inequality of opportunity with which it is negatively and statistically significantly associated. On the other hand, the estimates suggest that the first principle component of inequality in biogeographic endowments across ethnic homelands may be a useful instrument for ethnic inequalities. These results must be taken as provisional until we control for a range of confounding variables the inclusion of which may reduce omitted variable bias when estimating the impact of inequality and governance, as well as shore up the exclusion restriction or the requirement that the instrumental variable impact on governance through economic inequality and not through some unaccounted-for channel. The next section is dedicated to a discussion of a range of potentially confounding variables.

Important covariates

Probably the most important confounding variable is the level of economic development. In his review of one decade of cross-country empirical work on the causes of corruption, Treisman (2007) states that "[by] far the strongest and most consistent finding of the new empirical work is that lower perceived corruption correlates closely with higher economic development" (page 223). Economic development may improve governance because richer countries can afford more competent public officials who, being better paid, have less to gain (or more to lose) from abusing their power for private gain. Development may also improve governance insofar as it lengthens individual time horizons and, as a result, leads to demands for governance improvements. Good governance can also contribute towards development by providing an incentive structure that promotes investments in physical and human capital, technology and the more efficient organisation of production. There is also likely to be a two-way relationship between economic development and inequality. The process of economic development may lead, eventually, to a fall in inequality as most workers move away from agriculture and into industry. It can also reduce inequality because richer countries can employ their superior resources and state capacity to fund welfare states. Economic inequality may promote development by sharpening incentives for innovation and entrepreneurship and facilitating saving and investment. But it can also undermine development insofar as it leads to political instability, it means that poorer individuals invest less in human capital and it leads to redistributive schemes that reduce the incentive to work.

Not accounting for the level of economic development is likely to confound the identification of the causal relationship between inequality and governance. If we found that higher inequality is negatively associated with good governance, this could be because of the mechanisms framing the behaviour of relatively wealth and poor individuals as suggested in the previous section, but it could also be partly the result of inequality undermining development and, from there, governance. To control for the level of economic development, I turn to the logarithm of real GDP per capita at constant national prices from the World Penn Tables (Version 9), averaging the values over the period 1996 to 2014 (2014 is the latest year for which this data is available).

A second important control variable is the level of democracy. Democracy has been identified as a robust determinant of good governance, arguably because it can tighten the principal-agent relationship with citizens as principals and public officials as agents. Electoral competition increases the probability that political parties, or leaders within dominant political parties, alternate in office (Montinola and Jackman 2002). The possibility of losing elections or party leadership is expected to make politicians more responsive to citizen demands. Electoral competition also makes it more likely that political elites will reveal information on corruption by opponents (Treisman [2000]; William Heller *et al.* [2016]). Hanna Bäck and Axel Hadenius (2008) propose a quadratic J-shaped relationship linking democracy and good governance. Specifically, the control of public administrators is moderate in autocratic systems because of the existence of top-down hierarchical control, high in developed democracies because press freedom and electoral participation facilitate bottom-up accountability, and lowest in countries transitioning towards democracy because of the relative weakness of either top-down or bottom-up control.

Democracy can also impact on economic inequality. One early and seminal argument is that democratisation or the extension of the voter franchise can lead to redistributive demands by poorer segments of society leading to reduced inequality (Allan Meltzer and Scott Richard [1981]). On the other hand, Acemoglu *et al.* (2015) provide a range of arguments and related empirical evidence for why democracy may not lead to redistribution and an ensuing reduction in inequalities. These include high rates of social mobility, beliefs in a "just world", ethnic or religious cleavages or redistributive policies that favour the middle class (and harm the two ends of the income distribution). Another argument, made in the Introduction of this book, was that the relatively poor may disengage from politics, including abstaining in elections.

Boix (2003) turns the direction of causality around by arguing that a more equal distribution of income makes it more likely that economic elites will not resist democracy in the first place because of the expectation of less intensive redistributive demands. Acemoglu and Robinson (2006) propose an inverted U-shaped relationship between inequality and the likelihood of transition to democracy. At low levels of inequality, citizens have less reason to demand democracy since they are already receiving a share of societal resources. In highly unequal societies, the risk of revolution is high but the fear of strong redistribution in the context of democracy is anathema to economic elites. The weakness of both these mechanisms suggests that democracy is more likely to emerge in societies with intermediate levels of inequality.

Previous work has employed a range of indicators to account for the level of democracy. One popular measure by Freedom House, conceives democracy in terms of political and civil rights:

Political rights enable people to participate freely in the political process, including the right to vote freely for distinct alternatives in legitimate elections, compete for public office, join political parties and organizations, and elect representatives who have a decisive impact on public policies and are accountable to the electorate. Civil liberties allow for the freedoms of expression and belief, associational and organizational rights, rule of law, and personal autonomy without interference from the state.

(Freedom House, 2012)

Another measure comes from the Polity IV Project, and conceives democracy as three interdependent elements: the presence of institutions and procedures through which citizens can express effective preferences about alternative policies and leaders; the existence of institutionalised constraints on the exercise of power by the executive; and the guarantee of civil liberties to all citizens in their daily lives and in acts of political participation (see Monty Marshall *et al.* 2017). While some scholars propose to measure democracy by averaging the two measures (see, for example, Charron and Lapuente, 2010), I will instead turn to the Polity IV indicator since, unlike the Freedom House measure, it does not explicitly incorporate the concept of rule of law that in my analysis is an integral part of good governance. Specifically, I employ the Polity2 variable from Polity IV. This ranges from –10 for autocracies to 10 to full democracies and, again, I employ average values over the period 1996–2016. This said, the results reported here, are robust to the use of the Freedom House measure or when averaging the Freedom House and Polity IV measures. This is not surprising since the simple correlation between them is 0.904 (p-value = 0).

Education is another potential confounding variable. In the previous section, I stated that bad governance in the form of disproportionate influence of economic elites in public decisions, can reduce education levels insofar as it leads to reduced tax pressure and thus fewer public resources available for education policies. Reversing the direction of causality, education is likely to be an important check on bad governance. Both Treisman (2000) and Pellegrini and Gerlagh (2008) suggest that education and literacy can improve governance because they increase the likelihood that malfeasance will be both detected and contested. Consistent with this, Juan Botero *et al.* (2013) provide empirical evidence to support the idea that more educated people complain more about government misconduct. They suggest that this may be because educated people are "more articulate and more knowledgeable about where to go and how to complain" and are less afraid of reprisals by public officials. This is partly "because they know the law and the rules and hence can stand up to officials, but it might also be because they are themselves legal – work formally, occupy their residence formally – and hence do not feel at risk" (pages 966–967).

Education can also improve governance by improving people's employment prospects and thus reducing their dependence on patron-client relationships (recall also Chapter 3 on this subject). In relation to this, Uslaner (2008) points to the creation of the City University of New York (CUNY) in 1847 and its provision of free education for all city residents, as a first important factor contributing to the downfall of patron-client ties in the city in later decades. Interestingly, the creation of CYNY and free tuition is described as a service provided by the political machine to its clients (more on patron-client politics to follow). Perhaps local politicians did not anticipate the possible effect of education on the way local politics would be conducted or, perhaps they calculated that any change would occur long after they retired from politics.

Education and economic inequality are, of course, intimately linked. More economic inequality is likely to translate into education inequality especially if public education is deficient (Corak [2013]). Alternatively, expanding public education will reduce income inequality through its positive effect on equality of opportunity (David Coady and Allan Dizioli [2017]). To account for the link between education and economic inequalities, we require a measure of dispersion in human capital. Amparo Castelló-Climent and Rafael Domenech (2014) report a Gini index based on the years of schooling in the population 15 or 25 years and above over the period 1980–2010. On the other hand, the impact of education on governance is best calibrated by a measure of the average level of education in each country. Such a measure is provided by Robert Barro and Jong-Wha Lee (2013) based on average years of schooling for those above 15 or 25 years of age. In practice, these two indicators are strongly correlated which is not surprising since the Gini measures are constructed from the Barro and Lee data: the correlation between the education Gini and average years of schooling ranges between -0.893 and -0.905 (p-value of 0). Thus, controlling for both indicators is not advisable because it raises the problem of multicollinearity. Because the key outcome variable is the quality of governance, I chose to control for education based on the average level of education attainment for those above 25 years of age. Doing so avoids multicollinearity concerns at the same time as it helps account for education inequalities. This indicator is available for five-year periods between 1950 and 2010 and so I employ average values over the period 1995–2010 (I use version 2.2 published in June 2018).

The relative importance of natural resources (as a share of GDP) is an additional control variable. Previous work has identified the harmful effect of natural resources on governance. Fisman and Golden (2017) suggest that governments flush with resource rents, can buy off voters through government jobs and public resources (see, originally, Michael Ross [2001]). From another perspective, Alberto Ades and Rafael Di Tella (1999), point out that the natural resource sector is characterised by state regulation and large rents and profits that result in part from the absence of competitive market conditions. This combination of rents and regulation creates opportunities for malfeasance by public officials. Empirical work has tended to confirm the link between natural resource endowments and corruption (see, for example, Silje Aslaksen [2009] and Matthias Busse and Steffen Gröning [2013]). Indeed, scholars have described the existence of a "resource curse" whereby natural resources lead to corruption and this hampers a country's growth prospects (Carlos Leite and Jen Weidmann

[2002]; Jonathan Isham *et al.* [2005]; Xavier Sala-i-Martin and Arvind Subramanian [2013]).

Natural resource endowments have also been associated with inequalities. Thorvaldur Gylfason and Gylfi Zoega (2002) argue that natural resource ownership tends to be less equally distributed than other assets leading countries that are more dependent on their natural resources to have greater economic and education inequalities. Philippe Le Billon (2001) suggests that natural resources may affect ethnic group inequalities to the extent that the associated windfall gains accrue disproportionately to the politically dominant ethnic group. Indeed, because of the expected rents, Ruikang Fum and Roland Hodler (2010) argue that ethnic groups have an interest to appropriate natural resources (even violently). In homogenous societies on the other hand, natural resources may be shared more equally or used to support the needy thus reducing economic inequalities.

Consider next, the need to control for a country's legal origin when considering the impact of economic inequality on governance. In their seminal article on the determinants of good governance, La Porta *et al.* (1999) view legal systems as indicators of the relative power of the state vis-à-vis property owners with common law systems being the most protective of property, Soviet systems the least so and civil law systems (divided into French, German and Scandinavian) in between. From another vantage point, they array legal systems from least (common law), moderate (civil law) to most (soviet) interventionist and expect more interventionism to increase the possibility of corruption in the public administration. Treisman (2000) adds that legal origins also pick up "legal culture" that includes expectations about how laws should be enforced. In this context, English common law is characterised by an emphasis on procedural fairness while in other systems the emphasis is on hierarchy and authority. La Porta *et al.* (2008) take a broader view of legal origins as a form of social control. From this perspective, "common law stands for the strategy of social control that seeks to support private market outcomes, whereas civil law seeks to replace such outcomes with state-desired allocations" (page 286).

The differential emphasis placed by different legal systems on the protection of private property and market versus state-desired allocations is likely to have an impact on the degree of economic inequality. All other things being equal, one would expect economic inequality to be highest in common law systems, intermediate in civil law ones and lowest in countries with a Soviet legal origin. Indeed, Scheidel (2017, Chapter 7) discusses at length how the communist revolutions of the twentieth century led to a reduction in economic inequalities in the affected countries. This levelling took the form of mostly violent expropriation of landlords, land redistribution, collectivisation, expropriation of industrialists and urban "bourgeoisie" and nationalisation of businesses. He points to Gini values of 0.27 to 0.28 for the Soviet Union between 1968 and 1991, while in the post-communist Russian federation these oscillate between 0.44 to 0.52 (in my sample, the value is 0.424). He puts the Gini in China at not above 0.40 in 1930 – prior to the communist revolution. By 1984 it was

0.23. With economic liberalisation starting in the 1980s it started to increase (in my data it's 0.400). I account for legal origins by way of dummy variables selecting for common law and socialist legal origin from La Porta *et al.* (1999), leaving civil law as the base category.[3]

Another potential control variable is ethnic heterogeneity typically measured through an ethnic fractionalisation indicator that reflects the probability that two randomly selected individuals from a population, belong to different ethnic or linguistic groups (see Alesina *et al.* [2003]). The impact of ethnicity on governance has been emphasised by several authors who, writing on Africa, describe how the most common form of corruption entails the distribution of rewards, jobs, contracts and promotions on the basis of ethnicity (see, for example, Patrick Chabal and Jean-Pascal Daloz [1999], Morris Szeftel [2000]; Daniel Smith [2003]; Mwangi Kimenyi [2006]). However, Treisman (2000) shows that ethnic fractionalisation does not have a statistically significant impact on governance in the presence of GDP per capita and, indeed, the same thing happens in my cross-country sample. For this reason, in the following empirical analysis I do not control for ethnic fractionalisation although the results reported are very similar to the ones obtained when doing so, regardless of the economic inequality indicator employed.

What does the data say?

In Table 5.2, I report the summary statistics of the continuous variables employed in the empirical analysis in this and the following chapter. The governance and inequality measures have already been shown in Chapter 2 so here I will briefly mention the control variables discussed in the previous section. Real GDP per capita ranges from a low $553 in Burundi to a maximum of $145,551 in Qatar. Many of the very low income countries are in Sub-Saharan Africa, while the high income ones are a mix of Western European and oil producing countries plus the US, Canada, Australia, New Zealand and Japan. Countries around the mean include Argentina, Venezuela, Chile, Malaysia, Gabon and Poland. In my sample, countries like Qatar, Swaziland and Bahrain are autocracies, Armenia, Bangladesh and Malaysia have democracy values around the mean, and a heterogeneous group of countries that include Costa Rica, Lithuania, Mongolia, Greece, Sweden and the United States are fully-fledged democracies. Turning next to mean years of schooling for those above 25 years of age, this ranges from below 2 years for Mozambique, Mali, Niger, Yemen and Senegal to above 12 years in Israel, Slovakia, the Czech Republic and, with the maximum score, the US. Countries around the average value include China, Mexico, Bolivia and Costa Rica. Countries that earn no or very little income from extracting natural resources include Malta, Singapore, Mauritius and Japan while in Liberia, Libya and Congo Republic, natural resources represent more than 40 per cent of GDP. Around the mean value of 7 per cent of GDP, are countries such as Tanzania, Vietnam and Rwanda. While not shown in the table, English and French legal origin radiated out from the UK

Table 5.2 Summary statistics

	Mean	Maximum	Minimum	Std. Dev.	Observations
Quality of governance	-0.022	2.036	-2.096	0.955	204
Gini index	0.390	0.608	0.230	0.078	186
Q5/Q1 ratio	0.084	0.263	0.030	0.046	160
Middle class share	0.471	0.555	0.291	0.053	161
Perceived Gini	0.327	0.390	0.245	0.038	40
Inequality of opportunity	0.060	0.223	0.003	0.057	41
Ethnic inequality (GREG)	0.434	0.963	0.000	0.257	173
Ethnic inequality (ETHG)	0.457	0.979	0.000	0.331	173
Real GDP per capita	16,965.320	145,512.300	553.309	19,900.320	180
Democracy	3.539	10.000	-10.000	6.112	165
Education	7.326	13.040	1.020	3.036	145
Natural resources	0.072	0.486	0.000	0.109	210
Individualism	0.388	0.91	0.06	0.220	102
Power distance	0.643	1	0.11	0.208	102
1st PC col. and power dist.	0	1.639	-2.132	1.005	102
Generalised trust	0.239	0.692	0.035	0.135	98
Respect	0.677	0.903	0.343	0.117	98
1st PC of trust and respect	0	3.301	-2.419	1.081	98

and France through colonisation while Soviet legal origin is a product of communist revolutions. This said, not all colonies have inherited the legal tradition of the coloniser and sometimes non-colonies have adopted these traditions. Treisman (2000) shows this with common law examples. Thus,

> [s]ome former British colonies or mandates do not have a common law legal system: for instance, Jordan, Egypt, Iraq, Kuwait, Malta and Mauritius. And some countries that were never British colonies have nevertheless adopted common law systems, in whole or in part: Thailand, Western Samoa, Liberia, and Namibia.
>
> (Page 403)

In Table 5.3, I report the results obtained when regressing the quality of governance against the different economic inequality measures reviewed in Chapter 2, as well as the full set of covariates discussed in the previous section. The adjusted R^2 from the regressions range between 0.764 and 0.865 indicating that the explanatory variables explain most of the cross-country variation in the quality of governance, something that reduces the risk that the estimates suffer from omitted variable bias.

Insofar as the control variables are concerned, the results confirm the positive association between GDP per capita and democracy on the one hand and governance on the other. Having a common law legal origin is also positive related to governance although the result is not always statistically significant. Alternatively, abundant natural resources and a Soviet legal origin are almost always negatively associated with governance at statistically significant levels. On the other hand, the results presented do not indicate that years of education is related to governance. This does not mean that education is not important. Rather, the statistical insignificance of education probably has more to do with the close correlation between years of education and GDP per capita (0.733, p-value of 0). By way of illustration, when GDP per capita is omitted in the first regression shown in Table 5.3, the estimated impact of education is 0.196 and it is significant at the highest level. This suggests that education does impact on good governance, but its effect is difficult to disentangle from that due to the level of economic development.

Note here that we must be careful to talk about association rather than causation. As previously explained, good governance can also impact on economic development and the provision of public services, including education. It may also be the case that bad governance may undermine democracy perhaps by reducing trust in politics and public institutions more generally (Mark Warren [2004]). Natural resource abundance and legal origins on the other hand, are arguably more exogenous determinants of governance and, as such, we are on surer footing if we interpret the corresponding point estimates and statistical significance in Table 5.3, as indicative of the magnitude of the causal impact of these variables on governance.

Turning now to the relationship between economic inequality and the quality of governance, the results overwhelmingly support the expectation of a

Table 5.3 Inequality and governance (OLS)

	Dependent variable: Quality of governance						
	Gini index	Q5/Q1 ratio	Middle class share	Perceived Gini	Inequality of opportunity	Ethnic inequality (GREG)	Ethnic inequality (ETHG)
Inequality	-3.004***	-3.318***	2.628***	-11.319***	-5.202***	-0.343	-0.342**
	(0.602)	(0.948)	(0.984)	(2.540)	(1.240)	(0.230)	(0.165)
GDP per capita (log)	0.443***	0.410***	0.403***	0.449**	0.401***	0.457***	0.449***
	(0.050)	(0.067)	(0.068)	(0.210)	(0.131)	(0.058)	(0.057)
Democracy	0.026***	0.042***	0.038***	0.068**	0.047**	0.033***	0.033***
	(0.008)	(0.009)	(0.009)	(0.030)	(0.021)	(0.008)	(0.008)
Education	0.027	0.042	0.037	-0.013	0.082*	0.031	0.032
	(0.024)	(0.027)	(0.027)	(0.059)	(0.044)	(0.026)	(0.025)
Natural resources	-1.985***	-1.897***	-1.968***	-5.656	-0.983	-1.718***	-1.702***
	(0.438)	(0.515)	(0.524)	(3.335)	(1.990)	(0.472)	(0.478)
Common law	0.265***	0.147	0.176	0.275	0.182	0.157*	0.172*
	(0.099)	(0.099)	(0.103)	(0.189)	(0.143)	(0.093)	(0.094)
Soviet law	-0.471***	-0.478***	-0.464***	0.252	-0.517**	-0.298***	-0.345***
	(0.111)	(0.133)	(0.130)	(0.286)	(0.193)	(0.122)	(0.128)
N° of observations	126	120	120	38	37	126	126
R² adjusted	0.810	0.789	0.779	0.793	0.865	0.764	0.769

Notes
Regressions displayed vertically. All regressions include a constant (not shown). White heteroscedasticity consistent standard errors in parentheses. *, **, **** significance at the 10, 5 and 1 per cent levels respectively.

negative association between the two in the case of interpersonal inequalities. Regardless of whether we measure interpersonal economic inequalities based on the Gini index, the Q5 to Q1 ratio, the middle class share, the perceived Gini or inequality of opportunity, I always find more inequality to be related to worse governance at statistically significant levels. Alternatively, the negative association between ethnic group inequalities and governance is less robust and, in fact, only emerges when employing the inequality indicator from the Ethnologue source that, recall, does not generally map major immigrant groups and thus is more likely to misrepresent the extent of ethnic inequalities in New World countries. But again, the results in Table 5.3 are silent on the impact of economic inequality on governance. For that, we must turn to Tables 5.4 and 5.5.

Table 5.4 Interpersonal inequality and governance (TSLS)

	Dependent variable: Quality of governance			
	Gini index	*Q5/Q1 ratio*	*Middle class share*	*Inequality of opportunity*
	Panel A1: second stage			
Inequality	−5.916***	−9.687***	8.042***	−12.486***
	(1.535)	(3.632)	(2.479)	(4.873)
N° of observations	119	113	113	37
R² adjusted	0.771	0.684	0.707	0.698
	Panel B1: first stage			
Cool water	−0.197***	−0.115***	0.139***	−0.182**
	(0.048)	(0.039)	(0.034)	(0.087)
F-statistic	11.340	5.366	13.965	4.175
	Panel C1: OLS			
Inequality	−3.184***	−3.429***	2.860***	5.202***
	(0.605)	(0.953)	(1.001)	(1.240)
	Panel A2: second stage			
Inequality	−4.682***	−8.868***	8.331***	−4.432
	(1.359)	(3.115)	(2.746)	(2.250)
N° of observations	93	92	92	33
R² adjusted	0.777	0.691	0.691	0.855
	Panel B2: first stage			
Log wheat/sugar ratio	−0.188***	−0.099***	0.105***	−0.152**
	(0.040)	(0.029)	(0.025)	(0.059)
F-statistic	10.460	4.604	9.074	5.195
	Panel C2: OLS			
Inequality	2.593***	−2.894***	2.331**	−5.034***
	(0.742)	(1.052)	(1.131)	(1.372)

Notes
Regressions displayed vertically. All regressions include a constant and the full set of controls presented in Table 5.3 (not shown). White heteroscedasticity consistent standard errors in parentheses. *, **, **** significance at the 10, 5 and 1 per cent levels respectively. Cool water is employed as an instrument for inequality in panel A1, while the log wheat/sugar ratio is the instrument used in Panel A2.

Table 5.5 Ethnic inequality and governance (TSLS)

	Dependent variable: Quality of governance	
	Ethnic inequality (GREG)	Ethnic inequality (ETHG)
	Panel A: second stage	
Inequality	−0.800**	−0.479*
	(0.395)	(0.251)
N° of observations	126	126
R² adjusted	0.756	0.767
	Panel B: first stage	
1st PC geography	0.057***	0.099***
	(0.007)	(0.012)
F-statistic	24.738	24.513
	Panel C: OLS	
Inequality	−0.343	−0.342**
	(0.230)	(0.165)

Notes
Regressions displayed vertically. All regressions include a constant and the full set of controls presented in Table 5.3 (not shown). White heteroscedasticity consistent standard errors in parentheses. *, **, **** significance at the 10, 5 and 1 per cent levels respectively. The 1st PC of inequality in biogeographic endowments across ethnic homelands is used as an instrument for ethnic inequalities in Panel A.

In Tables 5.4 and 5.5, I report the results from regressing the quality of governance on the interpersonal inequality (Table 5.4) and interethnic inequality (Table 5.5) measures, and applying TSLS. Consistent with my previous discussion, I employ either cool water or the log of wheat/sugar ratio as instruments for interpersonal inequalities, and the first principle components of inequality in biogeographic endowments across ethnic homelands as instruments for ethnic inequalities. In the tables, I report the results across three panels – A, B and C. In panels A, I display the results from the second stage of the TSLS regressions while in panels B, I report the first stage that gives us information on the strength of the instruments. In panels C, I report the OLS estimates but now using the same sample as the TSLS ones.

Reconsider first the strength of the chosen instruments (panels B in the tables). Similar to the results reported in Table 5.1, the corresponding p-values suggest that the instrumental variables are correlated with the economic inequality measures. However, things change slightly when one looks instead at the F-statistics from the first-stage regressions. According to Staiger and Stock (1997), an F-statistic above 10 from the regression of the endogenous variable on the instrument and all the control variables is suggestive of a suitably strong instrument. From this vantage point, and in the context of the regressions reported in Table 5.4 and 5.5, cool water and the log of the wheat/sugar ratio are weak instruments of the Q5 to Q1 ratio and the inequality of opportunity measure. Consequently, the estimated impact of the Q5 to Q1 ratio and inequality of opportunity may be biased towards the OLS estimates (Michael Murray [2006]).[4]

With these qualifications in mind, let's consider now the estimated impact of economic inequality on governance. The second stage regressions provide support for the expectation that economic inequality will undermine good governance. This seems to be the case for both interpersonal inequalities as well as ethnic inequalities. Comparing the statistically significant TSLS estimates with the OLS ones shows that the former are always larger. There are two possible explanations for this. First, reverse causality, since, recall, the expectation that better governance will reduce economic inequalities should bias OLS estimates downwards. A second explanation is measurement error in the economic inequality indicators employed, something that could introduce attenuation bias in the OLS estimates. The presence of measurement error is suggested by what happens when regressing governance on middle class share. If reverse causality were an issue, the OLS estimate should be higher than the TSLS one since better governance should increase the size of the middle class. But, instead, the OLS estimate is lower suggesting that the problem could be attenuation bias due to measurement error. Whatever the reason, the important thing to note is that OLS estimates may represent a lower bound of the impact of economic inequality on governance.

Economic inequality, democracy and governance

The previous analysis suggests that interpersonal and ethnic economic inequality is likely to undermine good governance. This is consistent with the expectation that in more economically unequal settings, economic elites may use their superior resources to bias public decisions in their favour. It also fits with the argument that relatively poor individuals or groups may turn to petty corruption to cover their basic needs. In this section, I will explore the possibility that the impact of economic inequality on governance is likely to be mediated by the level of democracy. Specifically, I will show that the negative impact of interpersonal economic inequality on governance is greater in more democratic countries. Alternatively, I find that ethnic inequality undermines governance in non-democratic countries and has no effect in democratic ones. I will offer a range of reasons that might help explain these results.

In line with Acemoglu *et al.*'s (2005) more general discussion, but now in the context of democratic politics, Jong-sung and Khagram (2005) argue that economic elites can use their superior resources to influence political, administrative and judicial institutions for their economic benefit. In their words:

> [t]he rich, as a class or as interest groups, can use legal lobbying and political contributions or bribery (grand political corruption) to influence lawmaking processes. The rich, as interest groups, as firms, or as individuals, may use bribery or connections to influence law-implementing processes (bureaucratic corruption) and to buy favourable interpretations of the law (judicial corruption).

(Page 138)

Empirical evidence indicating that economic elites may dominate legislative decisions has emerged from the United States. Martin Gilens and Benjamin Page (2014) show that the predicted probability that a policy is adopted, is strongly and positively associated with the preferences of elite citizens defined as those belonging to the ninetieth income percentile. Conversely, the preferences of the average citizen – those belonging to the 50th percentile – had no bearing on policy (for more evidence on the influence of economic elites on legislative outcomes, see Larry Bartels [2008]; Gilens [2012] and Stiglitz [2012, Chapter 8]).

Democracy is, more often than not, likely to increase the incentives of economic elites to undermine good governance. Democracy in unequal settings is likely to bring with it redistributive pressures from the poor and middle classes in the form of progressive taxation and social spending (based, originally, on Meltzer and Richard [1981]). Rather than directly oppose redistribution towards poorer groups, something that may harden calls for greater redistribution, economic elites can employ their resources to subvert legal, regulatory and political institutions to maintain the status quo distribution of resources (see, for example, Acemoglu and Robinson [2008] and Acemoglu *et al.* [2015]). In unequal autocracies on the other hand, either redistributive demands do not emerge or, if they do, elites can resort to repression thus obviating the need to undermine governance structures to protect their interests (Jong-sung and Khagram [2005]).[5]

Democracy in unequal settings can also harm governance if we consider the incentives facing relatively poor individuals. Early on, Scott (1969) points to how "machine politics" feeds on poverty. It is worth citing him at some length on this:

> Perhaps the most fundamental quality shared by the mass clientele of machines is poverty. Machines characteristically rely on suffrage of the poor and, naturally, prosper best when the poor are many and the middle-class few ... Poverty shortens a man's time horizon and maximizes the effectiveness of short-run material inducements. Quite rationally he is willing to accept a job, cash or simply the promise of assistance when he needs it, in return for his vote and that of his family. Attachments to policy goals or to an ideology imply something of a future orientation as well as wide loyalties, while poverty discounts future gains and focuses unavoidably on the here and now.
>
> (Page 1150)

Scott (1969) draws our attention to how patron-client relationships can play out in unequal democracies and does so with reference to the concept of "time preference" previously described. From this vantage point, Charron and Lapuente (2010) show how democracy interacts with a country's level of economic development to affect governance. Specifically, they expect democracy in poorer countries to undermine governance since most people in such countries are likely to have limited time horizons and thus, behave just as Scott (1969) suggests. They are therefore more likely to value immediate (and particularised) benefits from public officials rather than efforts by the latter to improve governance – efforts that are seen to offer uncertain benefits in the distant past. These scholars propose a positive interaction term between democracy and GDP per capita such that at lower levels of development, democracy should be inimical to governance, while the salutary effect of political competition on governance should emerge at higher levels of development.

But another interaction also suggests itself – a negative one between economic inequality and democracy. Now the expectation is that, all other things being equal, inequality is more likely to undermine governance at higher levels of democracy, both because of the high discount rates of poor voters and because of the incentives of economic elites to circumvent redistributive politics (see also, Jong-sung and Khagram [2005]). For this same dynamic to emerge in the case of ethnic inequalities, we require wealthy and underprivileged ethnic groups to be arrayed in a minority-majority pattern. Now relatively wealthy ethnic minorities would have an interest to undermine redistributive pressures coming from relatively underprivileged ethnic majorities. Moreover, voters in the latter group may be motivated to employ their greater leverage during election periods to obtain particularised benefits from coethnics seeking public office.

To be fair, the two mechanisms – patron-client versus programmatic redistributive politics – may conflict with one another (see also, Fukuyama [2014]). In programmatic redistributive politics, voters may be motivated by the desire to change the distribution of income in society for their own benefit, but also for the benefit of others similarly arrayed along the income distribution. In patron-client politics on the other hand, clients vote for patrons in exchange for specific private benefits and not because patrons represent a particular redistributive programme or ideology. In other words, the strength of the patron-client mechanism can mean the potential weakness of the redistributive (spending and taxation) channel. All other things being equal, because economic development will tend to lengthen time horizons on average, it would be reasonable to expect patron-client relationships to be more prominent in poorer countries while the redistributive mechanism should become more relevant as countries develop and if inequality increases in line with the Kuznets curve.[6]

In Table 5.6, I explore the mediating effect of democracy on the impact of inequality on governance by adding an interaction term between inequality and democracy. I do not consider regressions of governance on the perceived Gini or inequality of opportunity indicators because in both cases the samples are severely restricted and are mostly limited to consolidated democracies. The results clearly suggest that democracy may worsen the negative impact of interpersonal inequalities on governance. These results are confirmed in Figure 5.1 where I plot the marginal impact of interpersonal inequality on governance against the level of democracy. I focus on inequality as measured by the Gini index, but a similar story emerges when employing the Q5 to Q1 ratio and the middle class share with the obvious difference that in the case of the latter the

Table 5.6 Inequality, democracy and governance

	Dependent variable: Quality of governance				
	Gini index	Q5/Q1 ratio	Middle class share	Ethnic inequality (GREG)	Ethnic inequality (ETHG)
Inequality	−1.471*	0.377	−1.351	−0.317	−0.276
	(0.884)	(2.159)	(1.613)	(0.243)	(0.180)
Democracy	0.124***	0.083***	−0.240**	0.036**	0.042***
	(0.039)	(0.020)	(0.093)	(0.014)	(0.012)
Interaction	−0.241***	−0.531**	0.599***	0.006	0.019
	(0.098)	(0.255)	(0.194)	(0.026)	(0.021)
Nº of observations	126	120	120	126	126
R² adjusted	0.818	0.797	0.801	0.762	0.768

Notes
Regressions displayed vertically. All regressions include a constant and the full set of controls presented in Table 5.3 (not shown). The estimation method is OLS, with White heteroscedasticity consistent standard errors in parentheses. *, **, **** significance at the 10, 5 and 1 per cent levels respectively. Interaction is inequality multiplied by democracy.

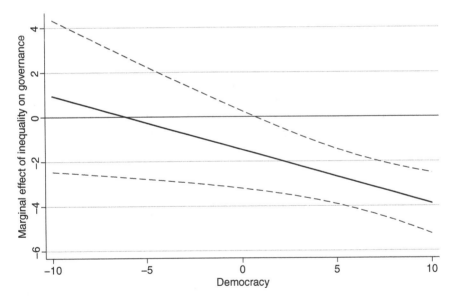

Figure 5.1 Democracy and the impact of inequality on governance.

curve is upward sloping. As Figure 5.1 shows, the marginal effect of inequality on governance is unclear in autocracies since, at Polity2 scores below 0, the estimated marginal effect is not statistically significant. However, as the Polity 2 score moves above 0, the negative effect of economic inequality on governance increases with the level of democracy at statistically significant levels (the dotted lines indicate 95 per cent confidence intervals).

Setting up a horse race between the mediating effect of the level of income and its distribution by adding an interaction term between GDP per capita and democracy is problematic. The reason for this is that the latter is highly correlated with the interaction between inequality and democracy (simple correlation ranges from 0.732 with the Q5 to Q1 ratio/democracy interaction to 0.990 with the middle class share/democracy one). Notwithstanding this, when this interaction is added I find that the inequality/democracy interaction is negative and significant when using the Gini index, the GDP per capita/democracy interaction is positive and significant when using the Q5 to Q1 ratio and both interactions are significant when employing the middle class share (results not shown).[7]

These results, interpreted in the context of Kuznets-curve dynamics of development first increasing and then reducing inequalities, together with the expectation that as countries develop, they shift away from patron-client politics towards more programmatic political contests, suggests the following scenarios. In poor and unequal democracies, high discount rates are likely to make patron-client political relationships a rational survival strategy with the consequent negative impact on good governance. As countries develop and inequalities rise, politics will gradually shift towards programmatic electoral contests, meaning that the negative impact of democracy on governance is increasingly likely to emerge as wealthy elites try to circumvent redistributive pressures. With further development and, assuming, a fall of income inequality, neither patron-client politics nor redistributive demands and elite reactions should emerge with any force, and their absence is likely to contribute towards better governance.

Table 5.6 also shows that the expected deleterious effect of democracy on the relationship between ethnic inequalities and governance does not materialise. To further explore this result, I reconsider the impact of ethnic inequality on governance when splitting the sample between democracies and autocracies based on the dichotomic variable proposed by Cheibub *et al.* (2010). The regressions reported in Table 5.7 show that ethnic inequalities are negatively associated with governance in autocracies, but not in democracies. This result emerges both under OLS and TSLS estimates. Like before, the estimated impact of ethnic inequalities in autocracies is larger when employing TSLS but caution must be applied since the F-statistics from the first stage regression are below the critical threshold.

There are at least three possible and complementary reasons for these results. First, the ethnic inequality measure I employ does not take into account whether the ethnic group is a numerical minority or majority and thus is too coarse to pick up the deleterious effect of ethnic inequalities in democracies. Second, ethnic inequality could be undermining governance through some unaccounted-for channel that works differently in autocracies and democracies. Third, splitting the sample between autocracies and democracies also generally divides countries into those with higher ethnic inequalities and those with lower ones. In fact, the mean values of the ethnic inequality Ginis in autocracies are 0.522 (GREG) and 0.557 (ETHG) while in democracies the values are 0.415

Table 5.7 Ethnic inequality and governance: autocracies versus democracies

	Dependent variable: Quality of governance			
	Autocracies		Democracies	
	Ethnic inequality (GREG)	Ethnic inequality (ETHG)	Ethnic inequality (GREG)	Ethnic inequality (ETHG)
OLS				
Inequality	−0.863***	−0.449*	−0.040	−0.284
	(0.311)	(0.224)	(0.356)	(0.265)
N° of observations	51	51	75	75
R² adjusted	0.661	0.639	0.756	0.761
TSLS: 2nd stage				
Inequality	−1.421**	−0.889*	−0.419	−0.239
	(0.633)	(0.482)	(0.638)	(0.385)
N° of observations	51	51	75	75
R² adjusted	0.636	0.604	0.751	0.761
TSLS: 1st stage				
1st PC geography	0.051***	0.081***	0.056***	0.098***
	(0.013)	(0.022)	(0.009)	(0.012)
F-statistic	8.676	5.249	15.500	26.198

Notes

Regressions displayed vertically. All regressions include a constant and the full set of controls presented in Table 5.3 (not shown). White heteroscedasticity consistent standard errors in parentheses. *, **, **** significance at the 10, 5 and 1 per cent levels respectively. The split between autocracies and democracies follows Cheibub et al. (2010). The 1st PC of inequality in biogeographic endowments across ethnic homelands is used as an instrument for ethnic inequalities in the TSLS regressions.

and 0.340 respectively. This is in line with Houle's (2015) argument that ethnic inequalities create an incentive for wealthy ethnic groups to overthrow democracy to avoid the redistributive pressures that emerge in democratic politics. Thus, the expected deterioration of governance due to ethnic inequalities as we move from autocracies to democracies may not emerge, because ethnic inequalities tend to be smaller in democracies. Similarly, the negative impact of ethnic inequalities on governance in autocracies may be due to the fact that ethnic inequalities are higher in the autocratic sample.[8]

Conclusion

Inequality may undermine good governance because of the actions of relatively wealthy individuals or groups who can use their superior resources to bias public sector decisions in their favour. It may also do so because less privileged individuals or groups may – in the context of patron-client relationships – offer bribes and support to public officials in exchange for material and nonmaterial state benefits. Based on a cross-section of up to 126 countries, the empirical results reported in this chapter show that interpersonal or interethnic economic inequality has a negative impact on the quality of governance even after controlling for a set of potentially confounding variables and the possibility that the quality of governance may affect economic inequalities.

Another significant result obtained is that democracy tends to exacerbate the negative impact of interpersonal inequality on good governance. It may do so because in more democratic but economically unequal settings, economic elites may try to circumvent redistributive pressures that emerge in the normal course of democratic politics by capturing the legislative, judicial, executive and administrative branches of government. It can also do so because relatively poor individuals have an incentive to sell their votes to political patrons in exchange for personalised state benefits. All other thing being equal, this patron-client mechanism is likely to be important in poorer countries while the redistributive mechanism should become more salient as countries develop and – consistent with the Kuznets curve – inequalities grow.

This qualifies the expectation that democracy will improve governance because it introduces political competition and thus potentially tightens the principal-agent relationship with politicians as agents to voters. In relatively poor and unequal democracies, political competition in the context of patron-client politics means that a tighter principal-agent relationship may undermine rather than improve governance. In middle income and highly unequal countries, political competition may lead to strong redistributive pressures that may be indirectly resisted by economic elites by capturing public institutions to ensure public decisions favourable to them.

These results are consistent with Fukuyama's (2014) insight that good governance depends on sequencing (see also, Martin Shefter [1977, 1994]). Specifically, he argues that, historically, the development of a meritocratic civil service prior to democratisation acted as a break on patron-client politics. He contrasts two groups of countries. On the one hand, Prussia, Sweden, Denmark and Japan, where administrative reforms took place after military defeat (recall my discussion in Chapter 3) and, importantly, before democratisation. This limited political patronage when democracy was eventually adopted. On the other, the United States, Italy and Greece, where democratisation happened without a professional civil service and where, consequently, it was difficult to resist political pressures coming from patron-client political relationships. By way of illustration, Greece democratised as early as 1864 in the absence of a professional civil service. Not surprisingly, patron-client political relationships were a basic feature of democratic politics then, and continue to structure politics, to some extent, today (see also, Papakostas [2001]).

The findings reported here must be taken as provisional since they ignore an important determinant of good governance. This determinant is culture or, more precisely, a set of cultural traits that have been identified as important drivers of good governance and that may also be associated with economic inequality. The omission of cultural indicators from the empirical models estimated in this chapter raises the risk of omitted variable bias. It is thus necessary to understand how, if at all, cultural characteristics can impact on the inequality-governance dimension and to this end I will dedicate the next chapter of this book.

Notes

1 It is worth adding here that the under-provision of a specific public service – public legal assistance – may directly undermine the rule of law insofar as it leads to unequal access to legal representation in the judicial system (see, for example, Russell Pearce [2004] and Rebecca Sandefur [2008]).
2 This is compounded by the fact that corruption tends to bias the allocation of public resources towards capital-intensive sectors where corruption opportunities are abundant, to the detriment of other sectors, where the potential rewards are smaller. Empirical evidence has emerged indicating that corrupt countries overinvest in public infrastructure which, moreover, tends to be of lower quality (Vito Tanzi and Hamid Davoodi [1997]), spend less on infrastructure maintenance than on new capital projects, spend more on defence (Gupta *et al.* [2001b]), and less on health and education (Mauro [1997, 1998]; Gupta *et al.* [2001a]; Cheol Liu and John Mikesell [2014]) and social welfare programmes (Zohal Hessami [2014]).
3 Adding German and Scandinavian legal origin does not change the substantive results reported here.
4 This rule of thumb is approximately a 5 per cent test that the worst-case relative bias of TSLS is around 10 per cent or less (Stock and Motohiro Yogo, 2005).
5 This is not to say that redistribution does not occur in autocracies. Acemoglu *et al.* (2015) give several examples of redistribution – such as land reform in Shahist Iran or agrarian reform in Bolivia under a military dictatorship – aimed at increasing regime stability.
6 In my sample, I find strong evidence of the existence of a Kuznets curve among democracies when these are selected based on Polity2 scores above 0, or according to a dummy variable proposed by José Antonio Cheibub *et al.* (2010) that classifies a country as democratic if there is political competition from a viable opposition capable of replacing the government.
7 For additional evidence of the robustness of the inequality-democracy interaction to the use of a range of estimation techniques see Uwe Sunde *et al.* (2008) and, especially, Rainer Kotschy and Uwe Sunde (2017) who employ panel data, strive to deal with the possibility of reverse causality, and control for period and country fixed effects.
8 Recall from Chapter 1 that Houle's (2015) full argument is that ethnic inequalities undermine democracy but the effect is stronger in the presence of low within-group inequalities since these make ethnic groups more cohesive. The differential effect of ethnic inequalities in autocracies also emerges when I split the sample between countries with a Polity2 score at or below zero (31 countries) and above zero (95 countries).

6 Culture, economic inequality and governance

Introduction

In an innovative article, Fisman and Edward Miguel (2007) document the existence of a "culture of corruption" driving individual behaviour. Typically, attempts to identify the impact of such a culture are confounded by the influence of legal enforcement. Thus, corruption may be observed in countries both because of specific cultural traits but also because of ineffective legal enforcement. To overcome this identification problem, they turn to an environment that controls for enforcement and varies the cultural dimension. Specifically, they consider the behaviour of diplomats accredited to the United Nations in New York. Prior to November 2002, diplomats and their families enjoyed diplomatic immunity, which meant among other things that they could avoid paying parking fines. Accumulated parking violations is a proxy for corrupt behaviour since corruption is typically defined as the abuse of public power for private gain. They find that diplomats from countries that, according to World Bank's Control of Corruption indicator, are more corrupt, tend to accumulate significantly more traffic violations. Conversely, those from countries where corruption is relatively low did not incur traffic citations despite the benefits of diplomatic immunity. This suggests that cultural norms related to corruption do impact on individual behaviour. In this chapter I will focus on how culture relates to economic inequality and the quality of governance.[1]

When discussing the emergence of good governance from a long-run perspective in Chapter 3, I argued that as social groups increase in size, individuals faced with uncertainty in social interaction will turn to a set of strategies that make social life more predictable. One response was to maintain personal relationships by structuring them hierarchically. Another was symbolic marking or the classification of individuals as members of demarcated ingroups. I argued that, historically, the rule of law was less likely to emerge where social hierarchies were steep and ingroup ties were strong. The steepness of social hierarchies and the strength of ingroup ties were, moreover, seen to depend on a range of factors ultimately related to biogeography, namely, the disease environment, societal size, intra and intergroup conflict and the nature of production.

In this chapter, I will argue that social hierarchy and ingroup bias can impact on the quality of governance in contemporary settings because they express themselves as specific cultural traits that are inimical to good governance – specifically, traits that reflect the extent to which individuals accept the existence of unequal power relationships as legitimate, and ones that capture the importance afforded to individual versus group objectives.

Culture has been defined as "those customary beliefs and values that ethnic, religious, and social groups transmit fairly unchanged from generation to generation", (Guiso *et al.* [2006], page 23). Alternatively, and in line with my approach here, Boyd and Richerson (1985, 2005) "define culture as decision-making heuristics or rules of thumb that have evolved to serve our need to make decisions in complex and uncertain environments" (in the words of Alesina and Paola Giuliano [2016], page 901). Similarly, Greif (1994, page 915) sees culture as "the ideas and thoughts common to several people that govern interaction ... [P]ast cultural beliefs provide focal points and coordinate expectations, thereby influencing equilibrium selection" (see also, Tabellini [2008]). From this vantage point, cultural norms that incorporate expectations of (un)ethical behaviour by others are basic drivers of the alternative governance equilibria we saw in Chapter 4.

North (1990, 2005) identifies informal institutions – norms of behaviour, conventions and self-imposed codes of conduct – as an integral part of culture: "culture consists of the intergenerational transfer of norms, values, and ideas" (2005, page 50). Together with formal institutions that include written laws and constitutions, informal rules emerge to reduce uncertainty by channelling choice into a smaller set of actions (see, for example, North, [1991]). While formal constraints or institutions may change suddenly due, for example, to a revolution or imposition by a conquering power, informal institutions or culture change more gradually (Oliver Williamson [2000]; Gérard Roland [2004]). In fact, empirical evidence suggests that cultural values can persist over decades and even centuries (see Alesina and Guiliano [2015] and Guiso *et al.* [2016]). This means that formal institutions can be undermined by informal rules that provide an alternative source of predictability although, over time, both formal and informal rules can converge (North [1990]). In this vein, Rothstein and Teorell (2008) make the important point that the effectiveness of formal rules enshrining impartiality depends on the existence of cultural norms that similarly reflect the notion of impartiality or equality before the law.

In this chapter, I will explore the impact on governance of cultural traits reflecting hierarchical social relationships on the one hand, and the strength of ingroups on the other. In the next section I will describe the main cultural indicators that will be employed and explore some preliminary associations between them and the quality of governance. Having done so, I will review work that has explored the relationship between these cultural traits and governance as well as that between these traits and economic inequality. I will then empirically explore the impact of culture and economic inequality on governance. In this empirical investigation, I will strive to reduce biases that may emerge from the omission of potentially confounding covariates and from the possibility that the quality of governance may also impact on culture. I will conclude with the main findings and implications.

Measures of culture

Social psychologists have identified cross-societal differences along a range of cultural dimensions (for reviews, see Amir Licht *et al.* [2007] and Yuriy Gorodnichenko and Roland [2011]). As already reported in Chapter 3, two of these are directly related to the notion of hierarchical social relationships and ingroup bias: power distance and individualism versus collectivism (Hofstede [1980]; Shalom Schwartz [1990]; Triandis [1995]). According to Hofstede (1980), power distance refers to the extent to which the less powerful members of institutions and organisations within a country expect and accept that power is distributed unequally. Regarding the individualism-collectivism dimension, in collectivist societies, people are born into tightly knit ingroups that protect them in exchange for unquestioning loyalty, while in individualist ones, ties between individuals are loose and everyone is expected to look after themselves and their immediate family. Collectivist societies impose mutual obligations and expectations in the context of ingroups that are perceived to have common fates and goals, while individualist societies put rights above duties and emphasise personal control, autonomy and accomplishments.

To get a better appreciation of the nature of these cultural traits consider Hofstede's online description of two representative countries.[2] First power distance:

> Australia scores low on [power distance]. Within Australian organizations, hierarchy is established for convenience, superiors are always accessible and managers rely on individual employees and teams for their expertise. Both managers and employees expect to be consulted and information is shared frequently. At the same time, communication is informal, direct and participative.

> Angola is a hierarchical society. This means that people accept a hierarchical order in which everybody has a place and which needs no further justification. Hierarchy in an organisation is seen as reflecting inherent inequalities, centralisation is popular, subordinates expect to be told what to do and the ideal boss is a benevolent autocrat.

Next, individualism-collectivism:

> Australia … is a highly [i]ndividualist culture. This translates into a loosely-knit society in which the expectation is that people look after themselves and their immediate families. In the business world, employees are expected

to be self-reliant and display initiative. Also, within the exchange-based world of work, hiring and promotion decisions are based on merit or evidence of what one has done or can do.

Angola ... is considered a collectivistic society. This is evident in a close, long-term commitment to the member "group", be that a family, extended family, or extended relationships. Loyalty in a collectivist culture is paramount and overrides most other societal rules and regulations. The society fosters strong relationships where everyone takes responsibility for fellow members of their group. In collectivist societies: offence leads to shame and the loss of face, employer/employee relationships are perceived in moral terms (like a family link), hiring and promotion decisions take account of the employee's in-group and management is the management of groups.

The two dimensions are strongly correlated. The simple correlation between power distance and collectivism across 102 countries, is 0.652 with a p-value of 0 (0.553, p-value of 0 when controlling for GDP per capita since this is a potentially important determinant of both – more on this to follow). This association is illustrated in Figure 6.1 that plots one dimension against the other. Most countries are located at either end of the fitted line. This suggests that the two stylised societal types represented in Figure 3.1 of Chapter 3 – one collectivist and with a steep social hierarchy and the other individualist and with more symmetric vertical relationships – tend to be descriptive of many contemporary societies. In the words of Hofstede *et al.* (2010),

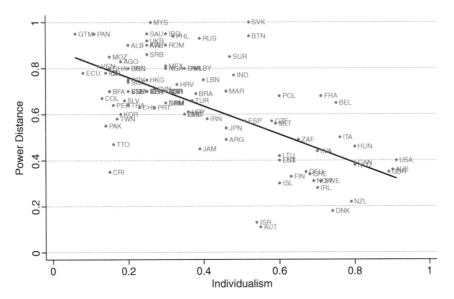

Figure 6.1 Power distance versus individualism.

[i]n cultures in which people are dependent on in-groups, these people are *usually* also dependent on power figures … In cultures in which people are relatively independent from in-groups, they are *usually* also less dependent on powerful others.

(Pages 103–104, italics in the original)

While in the following empirical analysis I employ each dimension separately, because of the strong correlation between these two dimensions, I also employ the first principle component that emerges when combining them (see also, Mariko Klasing [2013]). This component explains 82.61 per cent of the variance of the two sub-components. Power distance and collectivism are very strong in countries like Guatemala, Panama and Ecuador while, on the other end, individualism and egalitarianism are strong in the UK, Australia and the US.[3]

To capture the strength of ingroup ties I, moreover, turn to two variables provided by the World Values Survey. First, generalised trust, which is based on responses to the question: "Generally speaking, would you say that most people can be trusted or that you can't be too careful when dealing with others?" People can choose between two possible answers, namely, "Most people can be trusted" or "Need to be very careful". The other variable, labelled respect, emerges from asking people whether they consider "tolerance and respect for other people" to be important qualities that children can be encouraged to learn at home. The wording "most people can be trusted" has been interpreted to reflect "generalised trust" or trust in strangers, the opposite of which is particularised trust or trusting only members of identified ingroups (Uslaner [2002]). As such, generalised trust could be used as an alternative measure of the weakness of ingroup ties. The link between "tolerance and respect for others" and ingroup ties is more tenuous since the "others" are not specified in any way. In practice however, tolerance and respect for others is more closely correlated with collectivism than generalised trust is (simple correlation of –0.516 compared to –0.439 – p-value of 0 – respectively). As such, it is probably safe to expect that tolerance and respect for others should proxy to some extent for weaker ingroup ties.[4]

Tabellini (2008) combines the trust and respect variables to capture the notion of generalised morality that reflects the idea "that individual values support a generalised application of norms of good conduct in a society of abstract individuals entitled to specific rights" (page 257). Generalised morality is connected with two ideas that are intimately related to notion of individualism and egalitarianism:

First, the conviction that the individual is entitled to a set of basic rights that others should not violate. Second, the idea that we are all equal, in the limited sense that the same principles of justice should be applied equally towards everybody.

(Page 272)

Tabellini takes the notion of generalised morality from Platteau (1994, 2000), who distinguishes between generalised and limited morality. In the case of the latter, individuals restrict the application of ethical standards to ingroups and opportunistic behaviour is morally acceptable outside these groups. With generalised morality, the same ethical or moral standards are extended to ingroups and strangers. Before that, Banfield (1958) had coined the concept of "amoral familism" to describe the application of moral behaviour within the nuclear family and the abandonment of considerations of right and wrong outside this context (recall also my discussion in Chapter 3).

To measure generalised trust and respect, I compute the share of people who consider that most people can be trusted and those who think tolerance and respect is an important value, respectively. I also employ the first principle component that emerges when combining these two variables. This component explains 57.81 per cent of the variance of the two sub-components. The correlation between this variable and the 1st PC that results from combining power distance with collectivism is –0.654 (p-value of 0). This suggests that the notion of "generalised morality" as measured by generalised trust and respect may be a useful alternative indicator of the strength (or weakness) of ingroup ties: it is correlated with the Hofstede measure but not excessively so, thus, offering a possibility to check the robustness of the results that emerge when employing the individualism-collectivism cleavage.[5]

In Figures 6.2 and 6.3, I plot my measure of the quality of governance against these two aggregate cultural indicators and after controlling for GDP per capita. In Chapter 3, I already indicated the need to control for the level of economic development when considering the impact of cultural traits capturing

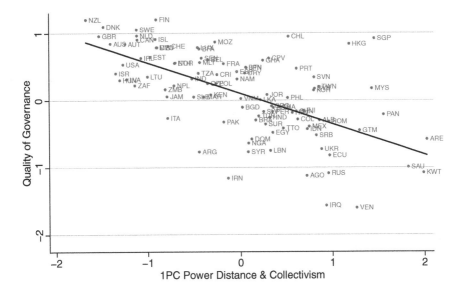

Figure 6.2 Quality of governance and culture I (controlling for GDP pc).

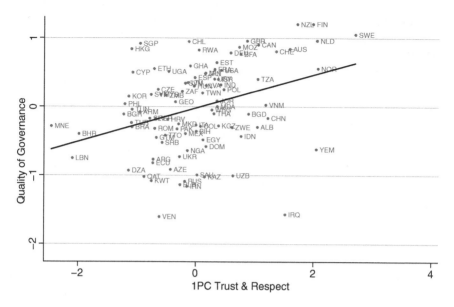

Figure 6.3 Quality of governance and culture II (controlling for GDP pc).

the strength of ingroups. To reiterate, modernisation theory indicates that development reduces existential security and consequently the need to rely on ingroups to enhance one's survival prospects. Greater existential security, reduces individuals' reliance on powerful others and, as such, is likely to undermine social acceptance of significant power asymmetries. Thus, economic development will tend to be negatively associated with collectivism and power distance and positively associated with generalised trust and respect for others. Given the positive association between GDP per capita and the quality of governance discussed elsewhere in this book, failing to account for economic development is likely to lead us to overestimate the association between governance and these cultural traits. This said, the two figures clearly indicate that, even after controlling for GDP per capita, power distance-collectivism is negatively associated with good governance while generalised trust-respect is positively so. In fact, the simple correlations between the governance measure on the one hand, and power distance-collectivism and trust-respect on the other are respectively –0.749 and 0.572 and after accounting for GDP per capita they are –0.599 and 0.417 (p-value always 0).

The causal links

To understand how economic inequality and culture can impact on governance consider Figure 6.4. Chapter 5 was devoted to fleshing out the relationship indicated by the top-left arrow in this figure – that between economic inequality and

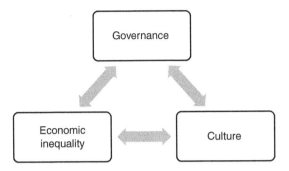

Figure 6.4 The causal relationships.

governance. We saw that economic inequality may undermine good governance because individuals or groups at the top end of the income distribution will employ their superior resources to skew governance outcomes in their favour. Relatively underprivileged individuals or groups on the other hand may contribute to bad governance because they are pushed towards petty corruption and supporting public officials in exchange for highly valued material and nonmaterial state benefits. Democracy can potentially aggravate these problems. This is because economic elites have an incentive to bias public decisions in their favour to neutralise redistributive pressures that may emerge in the course of electoral politics. And public officials facing re-election, may provide specific benefits to constituents in exchange for their electoral support. Bad governance was also deleterious to a more egalitarian income distribution since corrupt public officials are more likely to "shake down" poorer people as well as accommodate economic elites seeking to reduce both tax pressure and tax progressiveness. In addition, corruption may reduce popular support for social spending and taxation. Together, these effects will hollow-out the capacity of the state to provide public goods that could offer a degree of equality of opportunity and, ultimately, economic equality.

Consider next the upper-right arrow, that linking culture to the quality of governance. In Chapter 3, I argued that from a long-term historical perspective, the rule of law was more likely to emerge in societies with flatter social hierarchies and weaker ingroup ties. In the context of this chapter, the important thing to consider is that the influence of these fundamental drivers of good governance will persist in contemporary settings in the form of individualistic and egalitarian cultures. Egalitarianism flows directly into the expectation of equality before the law (see also, Licht *et al.* [2007]), while individualism or weak ingroup ties is associated with the tendency to resort to formal rules that structure impersonal exchange with strangers (Greif [1994]). Together, individualism and egalitarianism set the stage for a Weberian state described by impersonal rules applied equally and impartially to all citizens.

Consistent with this, several authors have provided empirical evidence on the direct impact of the cultural traits I focus on here on governance. Thus, Licht *et al.* (2007) show that individualism and egalitarianism are positively related to good governance and democratic accountability and, moreover, provide evidence of the causal impact of individualism. Klasing (2013) finds that these cultural traits – combined by taking their first principal component – make a significant positive contribution towards the quality of governance. Tabellini (2008) considers the impact of generalised morality – as measured by generalised trust and respect for others – on governance. He argues that good governance is likely to rise with generalised morality, since the extension of norms of good behaviour to strangers means that,

> law enforcement is easier because citizens are more likely to be law-abiding; bureaucrats are more likely to refrain from corruption; and voters expect and demand higher standards of behaviour from political representatives and are more inclined to vote based on general social welfare rather than personal benefit criteria.
>
> (Page 261)

He finds that generalised morality has a positive impact on a range of governance indicators. Finally, in Kyriacou (2016), I relate individualism to good governance and show that the impact of individualism on economic development passes through the quality of governance.

The previous discussion illuminates the extent to which culture can influence impartial governance. But good governance can also potentially impact on the cultural traits reviewed here. Impartial governance that, by definition, implies equality before the law, is likely to promote a more egalitarian cultural outlook. People treated equally by public authority are less likely to perceive power asymmetries as acceptable. Moreover, in societies characterised by the rule of law, the absence of corruption and meritocratic public administrations, there is less need for identified ingroups and personal hierarchical relationships as sources of predictability in social interaction. Good governance allows individuals to interact with strangers beyond ingroup boundaries since it reduces the risk that such interaction may end up harming them. Rothstein (2000) says as much in the context of generalised trust:

> In a civilized society, institutions of law and order have one particularly important task: to detect and punish people who are "traitors", that is, those who break contracts, steal, murder and do other such non-cooperative things and therefore should not be trusted. Thus, if you think (i.e., if your cognitive map is) that these particular institutions do what they are supposed to do in a fair and effective manner, then you also have reason to believe that the chance people have of getting away with such treacherous behaviour is small. If so, you will believe that people will have very good reason to refrain from acting in a treacherous manner, and you will therefore believe that "most people can be trusted".
>
> (Pages 491–492)

Empirical evidence indicating that good governance can undermine ingroup ties has been provided by, among others, by Jan Delhey and Kenneth Newton (2005) and Rothstein and Dietlind Stolle (2008) who associate more impartial institutions with more generalised trust. In addition, Hruschka and Henrich (2013) report that good governance has a negative impact on the strength of ingroup ties as measured through several indicators, including those from Hofstede. Thus, in the following empirical analysis where I examine the possible incidence of culture on governance, some effort will be made to account for the possibility of a two-way relationship between the quality of governance and the strength of ingroup ties. Specifically, in TSLS regressions of the former on the latter, I will employ instrumental variables for the power distance-collectivism cultural dimension as well as the generalised trust-respect one.

Consider finally the bottom arrow, that linking economic inequality with culture. Economic inequality can affect the cultural traits reviewed here in several ways. At the most basic level, income inequality may strengthen ingroup ties because it increases uncertainty in social interaction (see Kyriacou and Pedro Trivin [2018]). Income inequality is one dimension of social heterogeneity and, like ethnic or religious diversity, makes it more difficult to predict the behaviour of others thus increasing the rationality of ingroup bias. This is especially so since, in unequal settings, wealthy individuals may expect relatively poorer ones to defect from cooperative agreements that perpetuate the status quo (Boix and Daniel Posner [1998]).

Consistent with this reasoning, previous work has reported a negative association between income inequality and generalised trust (for example, Knack and Philip Keefer [1997]; Alesina and Eliana La Ferrara [2002]; Delhey and Newton [2005]; Rothstein and Uslaner [2005]; Andrew Leigh [2006]; Christian Bjørnskov [2007]; Pickett and Wilkinson [2009]; Gugl0mo Barone and Sauro Mocetti [2016]). Moreover, in Kyriacou and Francisco José López-Velásquez (2015), we show that inequality has a negative impact on a cultural variable that includes both generalised trust and respect for others. Finally, in Kyriacou and Trivin (2018), we provide empirical evidence to support the idea that while economic development may increase generalised trust because it reduces existential uncertainty, this positive effect is mitigated in the presence of income inequality, since the latter increases social uncertainty and thus the rationality of ingroup bias. In addition, one would expect economic inequality to reinforce the power-distance cultural trait. One reason is, again, that inequality increases uncertainty in social interaction and personal hierarchical relationships can be a source of predictability. Another is, simply, that economic equality will grate against the social acceptance of steep inequalities in the distribution of power across society.

Like the other two bivariate relationships shown in Figure 6.4 the possibility exists for the cultural traits described here to affect the degree of economic inequality. The reason is that when people consider others, including strangers, as part of their moral community, they may be inclined to contribute towards public policies that provide a degree of social security. Conversely, if ingroup ties are strong or, in other words, people adhere to the notion of particularised morality, they are less likely to support social welfare programmes that underpin a more egalitarian distribution of income. Moreover, in cultures where power asymmetries are generally accepted, people may be more likely to perceive economic inequalities as legitimate. Empirical evidence has been provided that shows how historical levels of generalised trust determine contemporary government spending and revenues (Andreas Bergh and Bjørnskov [2011]; Bjørnskov and Gert Svendsen [2013]). In addition, indirect evidence of the impact of culture on welfare policies has emerged from empirical work identifying a (causal) relationship from individualism or generalised trust to lower economic inequalities (see respectively, Boris Nikolaev *et al.* [2017] and Bergh and Bjørnskov [2014]).

The impact of inequality and culture on governance

Time now to empirical consider the impact of economic inequality and culture on the quality of governance. In Table 6.1, I report OLS regressions of governance on both inequality and culture as well as the full set of control variables employed in Chapter 5. Recall that one potential confounding variable when calibrating the effect of inequality on governance is ethnic heterogeneity given the expectation that impartiality may be abandoned for the benefit of one's ethnic group. It is important to consider that ethnic heterogeneity has also been found to be negatively associated with generalised trust (see Alesina and La Ferrara [2000] and Delhey and Newton [2005]) and as such is a potentially confounding covariate in regressions that include generalised trust as an explanatory variable. This said, when adding ethnic heterogeneity as an explanatory variable in the regressions shown in this section, I do not find it to be statistically significant nor does it alter the estimated impact and statistical significance of inequality or culture. Because of this, I omit it from the empirical analysis.

The first four numerical columns of Table 6.1 report results when using individualism and power distance from Hofstede, while the last four columns employ generalised trust and respect for others from the World Values Survey. In the "Common sample" columns, I reproduce the OLS regressions shown in Table 5.3, but now adjusting the sample so that it corresponds to that available when calibrating the effect of culture. I do so to minimise the risk that the results reported in Table 6.1 are different to those in Table 5.3 because of the different samples employed. As can be seen, both the point estimates and the statistical significance of interpersonal economic inequality are broadly the same – if anything, the estimated effect is larger in this more reduced sample. In the case of ethnic inequalities, reducing the sample also reduces the strength of the relationship with governance but these results are not statistically significant.

Consider next what happens when the different cultural variables are added to the regressions. Overwhelmingly, the economic and statistical association between inequality and governance is reduced, while the cultural variables are almost always associated with governance at statistically significant levels. This said, interpersonal inequality is still significantly associated with lower quality of

Table 6.1 Inequality, culture and governance (OLS)

	Dependent variable: Quality of governance							
	Common sample	Individualism	Power distance	1st PC collectivism and power distance	Common sample	Generalised Trust	Respect	1st PC trust and respect
Gini index	-3.240*** (0.768)	-2.422*** (0.737)	-2.617*** (-0.752)	-2.248*** (0.739)	-2.887*** (0.982)	-2.130** (0.988)	-2.679*** (0.944)	-1.916** (0.941)
Culture		0.908*** (0.288)	-0.921*** (0.258)	-0.244*** (0.063)		0.980*** (0.346)	1.787*** (0.457)	0.203*** (0.044)
N° of observations	87	87	87	87	78	78	78	78
R² adjusted	0.783	0.806	0.806	0.816	0.744	0.756	0.768	0.777
Q5/Q1 ratio	-3.869*** (1.119)	-2.595*** (0.894)	-3.111*** (0.995)	-2.460*** (0.892)	-3.975*** (1.411)	-2.533** (1.223)	-3.435** (1.362)	-2.078* (1.185)
Culture		1.246*** (0.292)	-1.270*** (0.303)	-0.339*** (0.069)		1.233*** (0.409)	1.998*** (0.476)	0.243*** (0.046)
N° of observations	83	83	83	83	74	74	74	74
R² adjusted	0.774	0.814	0.819	0.834	0.747	0.765	0.780	0.793
Middle class share	3.003** (1.195)	1.842* (1.065)	2.276** (1.075)	1.703 (1.040)	2.727*** (1.400)	1.312 (1.287)	2.215 (1.353)	0.961 (1.259)
Culture		1.338*** (0.299)	-1.322*** (0.310)	-0.357*** (0.071)		1.429*** (0.420)	2.078*** (0.493)	0.264*** (0.049)
N° of observations	83	83	83	83	74	74	74	74
R² adjusted	0.759	0.806	0.807	0.826	0.731	0.757	0.766	0.787
Perceived Gini	-12.211*** (2.518)	-12.007*** (2.727)	-11.310*** (2.777)	-11.207*** (2.877)	-12.326*** (2.907)	-8.433** (3.252)	-10.655*** (2.673)	-6.747** (2.831)
Culture		0.177 (0.420)	-0.813** (0.368)	-0.172** (0.081)		1.280** (0.580)	2.087** (0.752)	0.267*** (0.061)
N° of observations	37	37	37	37	34	34	34	34

continued

Table 6.1 Continued

	Dependent variable: Quality of governance							
	Common sample	Individualism	Power distance	1st PC collectivism and power distance	Common sample	Generalised Trust	Respect	1st PC trust and respect
R² adjusted	0.804	0.798	0.823	0.813	0.778	0.790	0.810	0.824
Inequality of opportunity	-4.852***	-4.649***	-4.394***	-4.362***	-5.509***	-3.949**	-4.158**	-3.069*
	(1.399)	(1.281)	(1.328)	(1.243)	(1.896)	(1.701)	(2.011)	(1.636)
Culture		0.550	-1.022***	-0.231***		1.878***	1.600*	0.300***
		(0.445)	(0.224)	(0.075)		(0.554)	(0.822)	(0.071)
N° of observations	34	34	34	34	28	28	28	28
R² adjusted	0.849	0.853	0.884	0.878	0.855	0.908	0.867	0.921
Ethnic inequality (GREG)	-0.084	-0.133	-0.092	-0.121	-0.139	-0.371	-0.154	-0.372
	(0.313)	(0.274)	(0.277)	(0.259)	(0.312)	(0.269)	(0.278)	(0.245)
Culture		1.211***	-1.183***	-0.310***		1.435***	1.804***	0.257***
		(0.290)	(0.263)	(0.061)		(0.389)	(0.439)	(0.048)
N° of observations	88	88	88	88	79	79	79	79
R² adjusted	0.740	0.787	0.782	0.800	0.713	0.746	0.740	0.771
Ethnic inequality (ETHG)	-0.252	-0.195	-0.171	-0.159	-0.355	-0.458	-0.411	-0.503***
	(0.216)	(0.177)	(0.187)	(0.170)	(0.236)	(0.211)	(0.206)	(0.189)
Culture		1.186***	-1.156***	-0.304***		1.438***	1.902***	0.266***
		(0.286)	(0.265)	(0.061)		(0.393)	(0.434)	(0.049)
N° of observations	88	88	88	88	79	79	79	79
R² adjusted	0.744	0.789	0.783	0.802	0.723	0.757	0.753	0.785

Notes

Regressions displayed vertically. All regressions include a constant and the full set of controls presented in Table 5.3 (not shown). White heteroscedasticity consistent standard errors in parentheses. *, **, *** significance at the 10, 5 and 1 per cent levels respectively.

governance. But the results suggest that the cultural traits I explore here may be even more important determinants of governance. Focusing on the regression of governance on the Gini index and the 1st PC of power distance and collectivism, the estimates show that a one standard deviation increase in economic inequality leads to a 0.175 point reduction in the quality of governance or 18.36 per cent of a standard deviation of the governance measure. On the other hand, a one standard deviation increase in the cultural indicator leads to a 0.245 point reduction in the quality of governance or 25.67 per cent of a standard deviation in the governance indicator. With just a couple of exceptions, the relatively larger impact of culture emerges regardless of the inequality or cultural measure employed. It seems then, that culture, as I define it here, is a more important determinant of good governance than economic inequality.

Of course, to be able to state this with greater certainty one needs to deal with the real possibility, previously raised, that the quality of governance may also affect the strength of ingroup ties and power asymmetries. In what remains in this section I will strive to address this issue. To deal with the possibility of reverse causality I will, as before, turn to instrumental variables and TSLS. The discussion in Chapters 3 and 5 brought to light two possible instruments for interpersonal economic inequality, namely, cool water from Welzel (2013) and the (log) ratio of wheat versus sugar from Easterly (2007). I choose cool water because it increases the available sample but the following results reported also generally stand when employing the instrument proposed by William Easterly. For interethnic inequalities, I again turn to the biogeographic measures proposed by Alesina *et al.* (2016).

One potential instrument for the individualist-collectivist cultural dimension is pathogen prevalence. Recall from Chapter 3 that historical pathogen burden is both theoretically and empirical linked to the strength of ingroups and, in particular, the greater the burden the more collectivist societies tend to be. Unfortunately, historical pathogen prevalence is not a suitable instrument for culture in regressions that include inequality because it is correlated with both inequality and the cool water instrument. In fact, the correlation between pathogen prevalence and interpersonal inequality ranges from 0.285 (with the Q5 to Q1 ratio) to –0.501 (with middle class share) and that between pathogens and cool water is 0.794, always at statistically significant levels. Cool water is also correlated with the cultural variables employed, with statistically significant correlations ranging from 0.385 (with generalised trust) to 0.662 (with individualism). This makes it unlikely that one would be able to identify the two endogenous variables – economic inequality and culture – with each instrument (John Shea [1997]). And indeed, this is suggested by the Shea partial R^2 values that are 0.023 and 0.022 respectively when regressing the quality of governance on interpersonal inequality and culture and the full set of controls in the context of TSLS.[6]

Thus, I must turn elsewhere for alternative instruments for the cultural variables. Fortunately, religion and more specifically, membership of one of the main monotheistic religions can be helpful here. In Chapter 3, I explained that, from a historical perspective, important differences emerged between Christianity and Islam regarding marriage practices – the Christian church was against marriage with close kin while Islam encouraged such unions – and these differences tended to reinforce individualism in the former and collectivism in the latter. I also described differences within Christianity in that Protestantism prioritised the individual while Catholicism and Eastern Orthodoxy favour kin and close friends. In the words of Weber (1951), Protestantism helped to "shatter the fetters of the sib [kinship group]" (page 237).

Beside the possible incidence of these monotheistic religions on the strength of ingroup ties, it is interesting to consider that Islam, Catholicism and Eastern Orthodoxy have also been identified as "hierarchical religions" (Putnam *et al.* [1993]; La Porta *et al.* [1997, 1999]). In the words of Putnam *et al.* (1993, page 107) "[ve]rtical bonds of authority are more characteristic of the Italian Church than horizontal bonds of fellowship". It is not unreasonable to expect that this religious heritage is likely to inculcate a culture of obedience to authority whereas Protestantism with its emphasis on individual responsibility will tend to produce more contestation of public authority (Treisman [2000]). From this vantage point, religion may impact on governance through its influence on both the strength of ingroup ties and general acceptance of power asymmetries. As such, it is potentially a useful instrumental variable for the cultural variables employed here. As a result, I use the share of people in each country that can be identified as Protestants, Catholics, Eastern Orthodox and Muslims in the year 1900 as instruments.[7]

In Table 6.2, I report the results from TSLS regressions of the quality of governance on economic inequality and culture. Panels A1 and A2 report the TSLS results when measuring culture based on the 1st principal component of, respectively, power distance-collectivism and generalised trust-respect. In panels B1 and B2, I report the corresponding OLS estimates (holding the sample constant). The TSLS results are revealing. Economic inequality almost never has a statistically significant impact on governance. The exception is ethnic inequality when culture is measured by way of the trust-respect measure. On the other hand, culture's impact on governance is confirmed: collectivism and power distance undermine good governance while generalised trust and respect for others influences governance positively. If reverse causality were a problem, the point estimates of the power distance-collectivism variable should be smaller with OLS while the estimates of the trust-respect variable should be larger (good governance promotes egalitarianism and reduces reliance on ingroups or, conversely, promotes outgroup interactions). The fact that the estimated effect of culture is always larger when applying TSLS, indicates instead the presence of attenuation bias due to measurement error in the cultural indicators. Recall from Chapter 5 that this was also a potential problem affecting the economic inequality indicators.

Thus, the OLS estimates are likely to underestimate the impact of economic inequality and culture on governance. To get a better idea of the relative impact of these two variables consider the TSLS regressions of governance on ethnic

Table 6.2 Inequality, culture and governance (TSLS)

	Dependent variable: Quality of governance					
	Gini index	Q5/Q1 ratio	Middle class share	Inequality of opportunity	Ethnic inequality (GREG)	Ethnic inequality (ETHG)
Panel A1: TSLS						
Inequality	-2.832*	-1.673	1.141	-1.298	-0.793*	-0.277
	(1.432)	(2.055)	(2.156)	(3.468)	(0.563)	(0.367)
1st PC power distance and collectivism	-0.373***	-0.556***	-0.578***	-0.631***	-0.535***	-0.525***
	(0.099)	(0.123)	(0.128)	(0.202)	(0.140)	(0.128)
N° of observations	85	81	81	34	88	88
R² adjusted	0.796	0.806	0.797	0.758	0.751	0.767
Shea partial R²						
Inequality	0.181	0.233	0.215	0.204	0.385	0.442
1st PC	0.204	0.241	0.234	0.246	0.252	0.256
F-statistic from 1st stage						
Inequality	8.614	4.863	8.223	4.893	11.227	12.142
1st PC	13.737	15.276	15.276	9.265	12.772	12.291
Panel B1: OLS						
Inequality	-2.287***	-2.560***	1.786*	-4.362***	-0.121	-0.159
	(0.746)	(0.895)	(1.044)	(1.243)	(0.259)	(0.170)
1st PC power distance and collectivism	-0.231***	-0.325***	-0.345***	-0.231***	-0.310***	-0.304***
	(0.065)	(0.072)	(0.074)	(0.075)	(0.061)	(0.061)

continued

Table 6.2 Continued

	Dependent variable: Quality of governance					
	Gini index	Q5/Q1 ratio	Middle class share	Inequality of opportunity	Ethnic inequality (GREG)	Ethnic inequality (ETHG)
Panel A2: TSLS						
Inequality	-1.116	0.383	-0.500	-3.253*	-1.267**	-0.757**
	(2.720)	(2.933)	(2.986)	(2.850)	(0.592)	(0.348)
1st PC trust and respect	0.364***	0.474***	0.476***	0.379***	0.509***	0.472***
	(0.093)	(0.097)	(0.095)	(0.098)	(0.107)	(0.082)
N° of observations	76	72	72	28	79	79
R² adjusted	0.755	0.749	0.750	0.913	0.693	0.744
Shea partial R²						
Inequality	0.107	0.279	0.241	0.252	0.358	0.458
1st PC	0.244	0.399	0.392	0.565	0.390	0.434
F-statistic from 1st stage						
Inequality	6.247	4.603	7.085	3.579	10.553	12.349
1st PC	11.435	10.798	10.798	17.091	11.648	10.853
Panel B2: OLS						
Inequality	-1.673*	-1.918	0.705	-3.069*	-0.372	-0.503***
	(0.973)	(1.173)	(1.250)	(1.636)	(0.245)	(0.189)
1st PC trust and respect	0.202***	0.237***	0.259***	0.300***	0.257***	0.266***
	(0.042)	(0.045)	(0.49)	(0.071)	(0.048)	(0.049)

Notes

Regressions displayed vertically. All regressions include a constant and the full set of controls presented in Table 5.3 (not shown). White heteroscedasticity consistent standard errors in parentheses. *, **, **** significance at the 10, 5 and 1 per cent levels respectively. In the TSLS regressions, interpersonal economic inequality is instrumented with cool water while ethnic inequality is instrumented with the 1st PC of inequality in biogeographic endowments across ethnic homelands. The cultural variable is instrumented with the share of the population that can be classified as Catholic, Muslim, Orthodox and Protestant in the year 1900.

inequality and the trust-respect cultural traits. Both inequality and culture are estimated at statistically significant levels. The results when using the GREG and Ethnologue inequality indicators reveal that a one standard deviation increase in ethnic inequality reduces governance by between 26 and 34 per cent of a standard deviation of the governance measure respectively. Alternatively, a one standard deviation increase in the cultural indicator increases the governance measure in a much larger range – from 53 to 57 per cent. Like the OLS results reported in Table 6.1, this suggests that the impact of inequality on governance is weaker than that of culture.[8]

Culture, democracy and governance

Having provided evidence indicating the importance of cultural traits reflecting the strength of ingroup ties and the general acceptance of power asymmetries, I will now reconsider the mediating role of democracy on the impact of economic inequality on governance. In Chapter 5, I showed that democracy may amplify the negative impact of inequality on good governance. I suggested that this may be the case because economic elites faced with redistributive demands from the electorate may use their superior resources to neutralise redistributive policies. The deleterious effect of democracy may also emerge because, in the context of patron-client relationships, relatively poorer individuals exchange their support for those seeking public office for private material and nonmaterial benefits.

However, that analysis ignored the potentially confounding effect of culture. It is not unreasonable to expect the negative effect of the cultural traits reviewed in this chapter to be stronger in more democratic settings. In collectivist, high power distance cultures, patron-client relationships are more likely, with those seeking or holding public office acting as patrons to specific ingroup needs. Collectivism means that public decisions in these settings may respond to the specific needs of ingroups rather than some notion of the general interest. Power distance means that politicians will enjoy a large measure of discretion in the exercise of public power. Conversely, in more individualist and egalitarian cultures, politics will tend to be more programmatic or, in other words, more about competing interpretations of the general or public good. And politicians in this context are more likely to be held accountable by voters.

In Panels A and B of Table 6.3, I reconsider the mediating effect of democracy on the relationship between economic inequality and governance. I focus on interpersonal inequalities since the factors identified in Chapter 5 potentially clouding the effect of ethnic inequalities – most notably the fact that the relevant indicators don't reflect on majority-minority patterns – continue to be relevant here. In numerical columns 1, 3 and 5, I reproduce the estimates shown in Table 5.6, but now for samples corresponding to the cultural variables I employ: panel A shows the results when the sample is limited by the power distance-collectivist indicator while panel B does the same for the trust-respect one. The mediating effect of democracy – as captured by the interaction term between inequality and democracy – emerges weakly in panel A and strongly in

Table 6.3 Culture, democracy and governance

	Dependent variable: Quality of governance		
	Gini index	Q5/Q1 ratio	Middle class share
Panel A: culture is 1st PC of power distance and collectivism			
Inequality*Democracy	-0.328*	-0.302	0.951*
	(0.193)	(0.627)	(0.515)
	-0.150	-0.226	0.677
	(0.170)	(0.484)	(0.415)
Culture*Democracy	-0.046***	-0.039**	-0.043**
	(0.016)	(0.017)	(0.017)
N° of observations	87	83	83
R² adjusted	0.785	0.772	0.768
	0.827	0.839	0.837
Panel B: culture is 1st PC of generalised trust and respect for others			
Inequality*Democracy	-0.514***	-0.677	0.871***
	(0.190)	(0.625)	(0.265)
	-0.338*	-0.308	0.531**
	(0.178)	(0.524)	(0.256)
Culture*Democracy	0.022**	0.024**	0.019**
	(0.011)	(0.010)	(0.009)
N° of observations	78	74	74
R² adjusted	0.762	0.753	0.759
	0.789	0.803	0.808

Panel C: culture is 1st PC of power distance and collectivism			
GDP per capita*Democracy	-0.008	0.052***	0.056***
	(0.011)	(0.016)	(0.018)
Culture*Democracy	-0.049***	-0.013	-0.014
	(0.016)	(0.022)	(0.021)
N° of observations	87	83	83
R² adjusted	0.827	0.854	0.849
Panel D: culture is 1st PC of generalised trust and respect for others			
GDP per capita*Democracy	-0.005	0.036***	0.036***
	(0.011)	(0.013)	(0.013)
Culture*Democracy	0.027**	0.015	0.017*
	(0.012)	(0.009)	(0.017)
N° of observations	78	74	74
R² adjusted	0.782	0.822	0.818

Notes

Regressions displayed vertically. All regressions include a constant and the full set of controls presented in Table 5.3 and the corresponding inequality measure added separately (not shown). The estimation method is OLS with White heteroscedasticity consistent standard errors in parentheses. *, **, *** significance at the 10, 5 and 1 percent levels respectively.

panel B when measuring economic inequality by way of the Gini index and the middle class share.

Consider now what happens when I add an interaction term between the cultural variables and democracy. Adding this term raises the possibility of multicollinearity but this is not in fact a problem since its correlation with the inequality-democracy interaction is, generally, not statistically significant and when it is, as is the case when inequality is measured by way of middle class share, it is a relatively low 0.327. Now the inequality-democracy interaction is never significant in panel A, while in panel B the size of the estimated coefficients and their statistical significance are reduced. On the other hand, the interaction between culture and democracy is always negative and statistically significant. The negative interaction term between culture and democracy is consistent with the idea that the harmful effect of a power distance-collectivist culture on governance is stronger in more democratic settings.

In Figure 6.5, I show the marginal effect of culture on impartial governance as one varies the level of democracy (Table 6.3, panel A, regression in numerical column 2). It indicates that at higher levels of democracy (above around 6 on the Polity2 scale that remember ranges from –10 to 10), a stronger power distance-collectivist culture has a negative impact on governance (again, within 95 per cent confidence intervals).[9]

These results suggest that, all other things being equal, in societies with large economic inequalities and, especially, in ones with a culture reflecting strong ingroup ties and the acceptance of asymmetric power relationships, democracy is likely to undermine good governance. In other words, stronger political

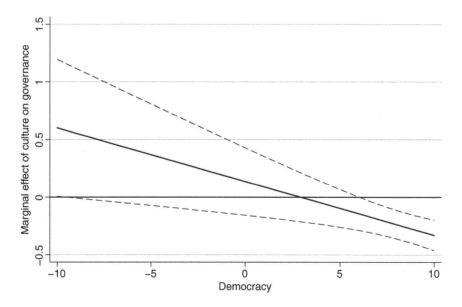

Figure 6.5 Democracy and the impact of culture on governance.

competition in the context of democratising reforms has the potential to improve governance, but this potential is more likely to be realised in societies with a more egalitarian distribution of income and ones whose members are less accepting of power asymmetries and more open to interactions with strangers.

Before closing here, in panels C and D of Table 6.3, I also check what happens to the culture-democracy interaction when adding a GDP per capita-democracy one (instead of the inequality-democracy interaction). I do so because of the possibility that rather than patron-client relationships being driven by the cultural dimensions I propose, they may depend on the discount rates of voters that, recall, also vary with the level of economic development. This examination is possible because, again, the two interaction terms are not strongly correlated: the simple correlations are –0.220 and 0.294 (both statistically significant), when measuring culture by way of power distance-collectivism or trust-respect, respectively. The results are mixed. When controlling for economic inequality by way of the Gini index, only the culture-democracy interactions are statistically significant (and with the expected signs). Alternatively, when inequality is measured based on income shares, either the GDP per capita-democracy interaction is statistically significant or both are. This suggests that, all other things being equal, democracies may underperform because of patron-client relationships that are buttressed by both hierarchical and collectivist cultures and the high discount rates of voters.

Conclusion

In Chapter 5, we saw that economic inequality can undermine governance because of the behaviour of societal members at both ends of the income distribution. Economic elites use their superior resources to maintain or improve their relative position while underprivileged individuals can turn to malfeasance to obtain much needed but scarce public resources. The associated empirical evidence, although weaker, is generally maintained when, moreover, we account for the confounding influence of culture as I do in this chapter. Thus, both economic inequalities and a power distance-collectivist culture can undermine good governance although, I find, that the estimated impact of the latter is stronger.

A culture where asymmetric power relationships are not deemed to be acceptable or "normal" and where individuals do not bias their interactions towards identified ingroups, is an important basis for impartial governance. Egalitarianism translates into the expectation of equal treatment before the law. Weak ingroup ties lead to outgroup interactions in the context of impersonal formal rules. Together, egalitarianism and outgroup interactions underpin impartial treatment in the context of formal rules. Conversely, in cultures where power asymmetries are generally accepted and ingroups are strong, public authority is more likely to be exercised for the benefit of ingroup members and in the context of personal and informal patron-client relationships. Democracy, more often than not, is likely to amplify the negative effect of these cultural traits on governance.

Reconsider now the two-way relationships displayed in Figure 6.4. Impartial governance is less likely in societies with a power distance-collectivist culture and economic inequalities. The absence of impartiality will in turn, perpetuate both this cultural mix and economic inequalities. Moreover, economic inequality may contribute towards the general acceptance of asymmetric social relationships and increase the rationality of ingroup bias, while these cultural traits may reduce support for public policies aimed at reducing income inequalities. This analysis points to the possibility that societies may be trapped in "wrong" culture-high inequality-low governance equilibria. In this vein, Rothstein and Uslaner have put economic inequality and/or bad governance at the beginning of a causal chain generating this type of social trap (Rothstein and Uslaner [2005]; Uslaner [2008]; Rothstein [2011]). Rothstein and Uslaner (2005) put it as follows:

> Equality and honesty in government stand at the beginning of our causal chain. Both are necessary to create trust and the universalistic social policies that lead to a greater level of equality and social cohesion. The reinforcing effects of inequality and honesty on trust and social policy – and the "feedback" to greater trust and less inequality – lead to a positive equilibrium for societies that initially take steps to adopt universalistic social welfare policies. But they lead to a negative equilibrium – an inequality trap – for countries with high or increasing inequality and corrupt governments. *While equality and honest government come first, the reciprocal effects we posit make it difficult (at best) for countries to escape the inequality trap.*
>
> (Pages 44–45, italics in the original)

This leads these authors to the pessimistic conclusion that countries may be trapped in a high inequality, bad governance and low trust equilibrium or, alternatively, may be blessed with a low inequality, good governance and high trust one. This idea fits with the notion, explained in Chapter 4, of high and low corruption societies as two stable equilibria. Recall that in corrupt settings there are more potential partners in corruption, the probability of getting caught is lower, foregoing corruption raises the risk of being priced out from obtaining valued public resources and the prevalence of corruption reduces the psychological cost of breaking the law. Moving from a corrupt setting to an honest one is a coordination problem since to abstain from corruption, an individual would require that most other people do similarly. The discussion in this chapter provides two additional reasons for why societies may find themselves in either equilibrium, namely, economic inequality (equality) and a culture generally accepting (intolerant) of power asymmetries and with strong (weak) ingroup ties.

Consistent with the existence of a social trap, Rothstein and Uslaner (2005) provide evidence on the "stickiness" of economic inequality, corruption and generalised trust. This evidence is based on relatively strong correlations between initial and final values of each variable in a panel of countries. Applying the same approach using all the data available at the time of writing yields the following correlations: 0.917 for the quality of governance over the period 1996 to 2016, 0.839 for the SWIID-based Gini index from 1960 to 2016 and 0.772 for generalised trust from 1980 to 2014. The stickiness of culture has also been reported by work reporting high correlations in trust levels between parents and children, and between second-generation immigrants and current inhabitants of the country of origin (both are consistent with the inter-generational transmission of cultural values), as well as contributions that trace contemporary trust levels to long-term historical factors (for discussions and related citations, see Alesina and Giuliano [2015], Guiso *et al.* [2016] and Johannes Buggle and Ruben Durante [2017]). Of course, I have also related the cultural traits discussed in this chapter to the impact of geographic conditions on early societies as well as religious traditions.

But evidence has also emerged that the cultural traits I focus on here do evolve over time. Sjoerd Beugelsdijk *et al.* (2015) exploit data from the World Values Survey to consider if Hofstede's cultural dimensions – including individualism-collectivism and power distance – have evolved over time. To do this they compare responses to a set of questions that are related to these cultural traits from two age cohorts; one born between 1902 and 1958 – corresponding to the population potentially sampled by Hofstede's original surveys conducted between 1969 and 1973 – and another cohort born after 1958. Among their findings, they report that societies have become, on average, more individualist and less tolerant of power asymmetries. Importantly, these changes are absolute rather than relative or, in other words, the changes emerge when tracking their evolution within rather than between countries. Consistent with the modernisation hypothesis, Danko Tarabar (2019) employs the same data to show that this cultural change is driven, in part, by economic development.

Obviously more work is needed if we are to fully understand if and how cultural traits reflecting social power hierarchies and group ties change over time and, to the extent that they do, in what time frame. This said, modernisation theory raises the more optimistic prospect that a cultural environment more conducive towards better governance may eventually emerge in countries that experience sustained economic growth rates.

Notes

1 They also report a sizeable generalised reduction in parking violations after November 2002, when the city of New York started legally enforcing the traffic tickets by potentially revoking the official diplomatic plates of vehicles with three or more outstanding violations, and deducting the owed amount (with penalisation included) from the US foreign aid to the diplomat's country. This suggests that both culture and legal enforcement impact on corruption.

2 These descriptions, as well as the latest Hofstede data, can be found at www.hofstede-insights.com/product/compare-countries/. This data was originally collected in the late 1960s and early 1970s for around 40 countries, but has since then been expanded and currently covers 102.

3 Triandis (1995) recognises that most countries can be classified as either collectivist with high power distance or individualist with low power distance. At the same time,

he explains that two additional types are conceptually possible, namely, collectivist with low power distance or individualist and high power distance (see also, Theodore Singelis *et al.* [1995] and Triandis and Michele Gelfand [1998]). Figure 6.1 shows that Costa Rica is an example of the former, while France and Belgium are examples of the latter.

4 I employ waves 3 to 6, starting in 1995–1998 and ending in 2010–2014. At the time of writing, the 7th wave covering the period 2017–2019 was underway.

5 The notion of limited morality resembles what is typically understood by collectivism, but generalised morality does not necessarily map neatly with individualism that also refers to self-reliance, personal control, autonomy and initiative (Kyriacou [2016]).

6 Pathogen prevalence is not correlated with the ethnic inequality indicators or the associated biogeographic instruments thus making prevalence a potentially useful instrument. The results for ethnic inequality reported here are maintained when instrumenting with historical pathogen burden.

7 I also check what happens when additionally controlling for affiliation in these religions in 2000 – data from North *et al.* (2013) – in an effort to reinforce the exclusion restriction or, in other words, ensure that religion does not impact on governance directly or through other unaccounted for channels. The substantive results – although not reported here – are similar. I am not the first to employ religion as an instrument for culture. La Porta *et al.* (1997) and Guiso *et al.* (2006) use contemporary affiliation of main religions as an instrument for generalized trust. Arguably, the use of historical religious affiliation is a more rigorous empirical strategy.

8 The Shea partial R^2s are always above 0.100 indicating that both ethnic inequality and trust-respect are separately identified with the corresponding instruments. The F-statistics from the first stage indicate that the instruments are sufficiently strong reducing the risk that TSLS point estimates are biased towards the OLS ones: Stock and Yogo (2005) report that when there are two endogenous regressors and five instruments (the case here), the 5 per cent test that the worse-case relative bias of TSLS is equal or below 5 per cent, 10 per cent, 20 per cent or 30 per cent is, respectively, 13.97, 8.78, 5.91 and 4.79.

9 Countries that have democracy scores above 6 and that have a collectivist-power distance score above the mean value of 0 are Albania, Brazil, Bulgaria, Cabo Verde, Chile, Colombia, Dominican Republic, El Salvador, Guatemala, Honduras, India, Mexico, Panama, Peru, the Philippines, Portugal, Romania, Serbia, Slovakia, Slovenia, South Korea, Taiwan and Trinidad and Tobago. Except for Portugal, Taiwan, Slovenia and South Korea, with governance scores around 1, the rest have relatively modest scores (remember that the maximum possible value is 2.5, and in my sample, it is 2.036 corresponding to Denmark).

7 Conclusion

Governance refers to the exercise of public authority and, specifically, good governance means that public sector agents act impartially or, in other words, without regards to personal relationships and preferences. It expresses itself in the form of an independent and professional public administration, equality before the law, and checks on the misuse of public power for private or political gain. Good governance can contribute towards the achievement of a range of desirable social outcomes including economic development, better health and education, environmental quality and happiness.

In the previous pages, I have focused on one potentially important determinant of the quality of governance, namely, economic inequality. Specifically, I have examined the relationship between economic inequality and governance from three perspectives. First, a long-run historical one that exploits anthropological data on pre-industrial societies. Second, based on experimental work conducted by social psychologists and behavioural economists. Third, through cross-country empirical analysis drawn from a large sample of contemporary societies. The research has brought to light the causal mechanisms linking inequality and governance. An understanding of these mechanisms may be helpful when considering which policies to adopt to improve the quality of governance. In these final pages, I will first summarise the key insights generated by the analysis and, based on this, then consider what we can do.

What have we learnt?

From a (very) long-run historical perspective, we have seen that cross-society differences in governance are the result of different societal responses to the uncertainty emerging from social interaction. In large group settings, people respond to such uncertainty by entering personal hierarchical relationships and by reinforcing ingroup ties. The move towards the rule of law has occurred in societies with flatter social hierarchies and weaker ingroup ties. The steepness of hierarchies and the strength of ingroups evolved over time in the context of four fundamental and interrelated factors, namely, disease, population growth, conflict and production. A heavier disease burden, increased societal size, greater intensity of conflict, the availability of storable food surpluses and the need for

social coordination to obtain these, all contributed towards steeper social hierarchies and stronger ingroup ties. We have also seen that these variables are, in
turn, affected by biogeographic conditions thus making biogeography an ultimate determinant of governance.

The experimental evidence reviewed confirms the tendency of people to
identify with ingroups even in the absence of competition for resources. Ingroup
favouritism leads people to support leaders who discriminate outgroups, makes it
more likely that they act unethically, and less likely that they criticise or report
unethical behaviour from members of their ingroup. Limited social mobility and
the perception that inequality is illegitimate because of unequal opportunities,
corruption or chance, is likely to reinforce ingroup bias in low status groups. High
status groups have an interest to expound ideologies that help legitimise social
inequalities. In societies where upward mobility is expected but not possible due
to unequal opportunities, low status individuals may reduce their adherence to the
law. Powerful people tend to view subordinates instrumentally and through the
application of negative stereotypes. They are also more likely to act unethically,
especially if primed to think in terms of self-interest rather than social welfare.

The experimental evidence also suggests that individual behaviour is driven
by the expected behaviour of others. This can lead to good or bad governance
equilibria. If one expects others to act unethically, he or she does likewise for a
range of reasons, including, the relative abundance of partners in crime, a
smaller probability of getting caught, a reduced psychological cost of unethical
behaviour and, finally, to avoid being priced out from accessing public services
or public resources more generally. Alternatively, if I expect everyone else to
behave ethically, it is much more difficult for me not to do so. While it may be
in everyone's interest to shift to the good governance equilibrium, no one has
an incentive to act ethically unless most other people behave similarly. Thus, a
poorly governed country may be stuck in the bad equilibrium.

The analysis of contemporary societies suggests that inequality may undermine good governance because of the behaviour of societal members at either
end of the income distribution. First, the actions of relatively wealthy individuals
or groups who can use their superior resources to bias public sector decisions in
their favour. Second, the behaviour of relatively poor people who, in the context
of patron-client relationships, may bribe or support public officials to obtain
much needed material and nonmaterial state benefits. Both these mechanisms
are amplified in democratic settings. On the one hand, economic elites may try
to circumvent redistributive pressures that emerge in the normal course of
democratic politics by capturing government. On the other hand, the relatively
poor can sell their votes to political patrons in exchange for state benefits. Everything else equal, the patron-client mechanism is likely to be more important in
poorer countries where existential uncertainty is greater, while the redistributive
channel will become more salient as countries develop and if economic inequalities increase along the lines of the Kuznets curve.

The negative impact of economic inequality on governance persists when
additionally accounting for the effect of culture, although the results suggest

that the impact of the latter tends to be stronger. Impartiality in governance is more likely in egalitarian cultures where asymmetric power relationships are not deemed acceptable or "normal" and in individualist cultures where individuals do not bias their interactions towards identified ingroups. Egalitarianism translates into the expectation of equal treatment before the law. Individualism facilitates outgroup interactions in the context of impersonal formal rules. The analysis also points to the danger of ignoring culture when democratising. In cultures with large power asymmetries and strong ingroup ties, democratic politics is likely to be structured according to patron-client relationships and, as such, will be inimical to good governance.

The analysis of how economic inequality and culture relate to governance reinforces the notion of good and bad governance equilibria. It suggests the existence of feedback effects between the level of economic inequality, the nature of cultural traits and the quality of governance – effects that keep countries in either equilibrium. Thus, good governance goes hand-in-hand with lower inequalities and more egalitarian and individualist cultures. Alternatively, countries with bad governance also tend to have higher economic inequalities and cultures described by power asymmetries and ingroup bias. Higher economic inequalities will undermine good governance because of the behaviour of individuals or groups on either end of the income distribution. Poor governance will feed back into greater inequalities because corrupt governments are more likely to accommodate economic elites (for a price) and because corruption will reduce popular support for social spending and taxation. It will also reinforce power distance and collectivism since the absence of impartiality, increases the attractiveness of ingroups and personal hierarchical relationships as alternative sources of predictability. Moreover, by increasing uncertainty in social interaction, economic inequality is likely to reinforce both collectivism and hierarchical social relationships. These cultural traits will contribute towards greater inequality since ingroup bias will hamper redistributive programmes that include outgroups, and the social acceptance of power asymmetries may feed into the legitimation of economic inequality.

What can be done?

In light of this discussion, what, if anything, can we do to improve governance?[1] The experimental evidence pointing towards good and bad governance as alternative equilibria suggests that the road towards good governance requires changing individual expectations about the behaviour of others and, in particular, people should expect that others shall respect the rule of law. This leads Fisman and Golden (2017) to favour "big bang" rather than gradualist approaches to reform. The strength of the big bang approach lies in its capacity to change individual expectations more fully. Both gradual and radical approaches are likely to be resisted by those with an interest in the status quo, but because the stakes are higher in the case of the latter, so is the risk of political instability due to opposition from those negatively affected by the changes.

Both the potential effectiveness and risks of the big-bang approach will increase further if, as suggested by Rothstein (2011), reforms target most if not all public institutions including the public administration and the courts.

Relatedly, we have seen that countries can be trapped in a bad equilibrium described by high inequalities, collectivist and power distance cultural traits and bad governance. This certainly reinforces the view that governance improvements – whether gradualist or across the board – are difficult to implement. But the relationships described and estimated in this book are probabilistic rather than deterministic. This allows some scope for human agency. Public officials with a genuine interest in introducing governance reforms are not completely helpless, especially if they are supported by civil society organisations with the same agenda. The scope for reform can be broadened by the international community, provided that international institutions can leverage their influence in badly governed countries to support domestic reform efforts.

With this in mind, the key policy implication of the analysis is that reducing economic inequalities can help improve governance. It can do so because it reduces the capacity of elites to capture public sector agents as well as their incentive to do so since, in more equal countries, redistributive demands will be weaker. It can also do so, especially when coupled with economic development, because it reduces the existential uncertainty faced by the relatively poor and thus their need to rely on personal patron-client relationships that are antithetical to impartial governance. In other words, good governance is more likely to emerge in countries that can achieve more inclusive or equitable growth spells in the long term.

Is this a pipe dream? In Chapter 1, we saw that extensive redistribution may be inimical to growth. However, we also saw that economic inequality may undermine growth because – in the presence of imperfect credit markets – it reduces human capital accumulation. Thus, a redistributive policy that can promote the accumulation of human capital can also promote growth. This highlights the importance of health and education policies that can level the playing field. By facilitating the accumulation of human capital, equal opportunity policies can contribute towards economic growth. But they can also improve governance insofar as they contribute towards the reduction of economic inequalities. Better governance will in turn facilitate the attainment of a range of desirable social outcomes, including sustainable growth.

The importance of equality in education opportunities cannot be overstated. We have seen that education can reduce peoples' reliance on asymmetric patron-client power relationships and increase the possibility that misgovernance will be detected and effectively contested. It can weaken patron-client ties by improving individuals' market prospects, while more detection and effective contestation emerge from the likelihood that educated people are more knowledgeable, more articulate and less fearful of official reprisals. Education can also impact favourably on governance because it can undermine ingroup ties or, conversely, strengthen ties across groups, as suggested by empirical evidence that has established a positive relationship between education and generalised trust (see, for example, Knack and Keefer [1997], Uslaner [2002], Helliwell and Putnam [2007], Jian Huang *et al.* [2011]). Equal opportunity in education is not simply a matter of equal spending per student. Rather, it means assigning resources so as to minimise the impact of factors beyond a child's control on his or her educational achievement (Roemer [1998]).

According to Nelson Mandela, "education is the most powerful weapon which you can use to change the world" (Susan Ratcliffe [2017]). The exploration of the link between inequality and governance undertaken in this book suggests that equal access to education opportunities harbours the potential to deliver both economic growth and better governance. Education could be the key that allows countries to escape the high-inequality-"wrong" culture-bad governance trap.

Note

1 I will only refer here to policy implications emerging from the main findings I have discussed in this book. See Fisman and Golden (2017), for a critical discussion of a range of policies that can potentially improve governance including, higher government salaries, independent anticorruption authorities and greater government transparency.

Appendix

Country codes and samples

Country code	Country name	Gini index	Q5/Q1 ratio	Middle class share	Perceived Gini	Inequality of opportunity	Ethnic inequality (GREG and ETHG)
AFG	Afghanistan	•					•
AGO	Angola	•	•	•			•
ALB	Albania	•	•	•			•
ARE	United Arab Emirates	•					•
ARG	Argentina	•	•	•	•		•
ARM	Armenia	•	•	•			•
ATG	Antigua and Barbuda	•					•
AUS	Australia	•	•	•	•		•
AUT	Austria	•	•	•	•	•	•
AZE	Azerbaijan	•	•	•			•
BDI	Burundi	•	•	•			•
BEL	Belgium	•	•	•	•	•	•
BEN	Benin	•	•	•			•
BFA	Burkina Faso	•	•	•			•
BGD	Bangladesh	•	•	•			•
BGR	Bulgaria	•	•	•	•		•
BHR	Bahrain						•
BHS	Bahamas, The	•					•
BIH	Bosnia and Herzegovina	•	•	•			•
BLR	Belarus	•	•	•			•
BLZ	Belize	•	•	•			•
BOL	Bolivia	•	•	•			•
BRA	Brazil	•	•	•		•	•
BRB	Barbados	•					
BRN	Brunei Darussalam						•
BTN	Bhutan	•	•	•			•
BWA	Botswana	•	•	•			•
CAF	Central African Republic	•	•	•			•

Country code	Country name	Gini index	Q5/Q1 ratio	Middle class share	Perceived Gini	Inequality of opportunity	Ethnic inequality (GREG and ETHG)
CAN	Canada	•	•	•			•
CHE	Switzerland	•	•	•	•		•
CHL	Chile	•	•	•	•		•
CHN	China	•	•	•	•		•
CIV	Côte d'Ivoire	•	•	•		•	•
CMR	Cameroon	•	•	•			•
COG	Congo, Rep.	•	•	•			•
COL	Colombia	•	•	•		•	•
COM	Comoros	•	•	•			•
CPV	Cabo Verde	•	•	•			•
CRI	Costa Rica	•	•	•			•
CUB	Cuba						•
CYP	Cyprus	•	•	•	•	•	•
CZE	Czech Republic	•	•	•	•	•	•
DEU	Germany	•	•	•	•	•	•
DJI	Djibouti	•	•	•			•
DMA	Dominica	•					•
DNK	Denmark	•	•	•	•	•	•
DOM	Dominican Republic	•	•	•			•
DZA	Algeria	•	•	•			•
ECU	Ecuador	•	•	•		•	•
EGY	Egypt, Arab Rep.	•	•	•		•	•
ERI	Eritrea						•
ESP	Spain	•	•	•	•	•	•
EST	Estonia	•	•	•	•	•	•
ETH	Ethiopia	•	•	•			•
FIN	Finland	•	•	•	•	•	•
FJI	Fiji	•	•	•			•
FRA	France	•	•	•	•	•	•
FSM	Micronesia, Fed. Sts.	•	•				
GAB	Gabon	•	•	•			•
GBR	United Kingdom	•	•	•	•	•	•
GEO	Georgia	•	•	•			•
GHA	Ghana	•	•	•		•	•
GIN	Guinea	•	•	•		•	•
GMB	Gambia, The	•	•	•			•
GNB	Guinea-Bissau	•	•	•			•
GNQ	Equatorial Guinea	•					•
GRC	Greece	•	•	•		•	•
GRD	Grenada	•					•
GTM	Guatemala	•	•	•		•	•

continued

Country code	Country name	Gini index	Q5/Q1 ratio	Middle class share	Perceived Gini	Inequality of opportunity	Ethnic inequality (GREG and ETHG)
GUY	Guyana	•	•	•			•
HKG	Hong Kong SAR, China	•					
HND	Honduras	•	•	•			•
HRV	Croatia	•	•	•	•		•
HTI	Haiti	•	•	•			•
HUN	Hungary	•	•	•	•	•	•
IDN	Indonesia	•	•	•			•
IND	India	•	•	•			•
IRL	Ireland	•	•	•		•	•
IRN	Iran, Islamic Rep.	•	•	•			•
IRQ	Iraq		•	•			•
ISL	Iceland	•	•	•	•	•	•
ISR	Israel	•	•	•	•		•
ITA	Italy	•	•	•	•	•	•
JAM	Jamaica	•	•	•			•
JOR	Jordan	•	•	•			•
JPN	Japan	•	•	•	•		•
KAZ	Kazakhstan	•	•	•			•
KEN	Kenya	•	•	•			•
KGZ	Kyrgyz Republic	•	•	•			•
KHM	Cambodia	•					•
KIR	Kiribati	•	•	•			
KNA	St. Kitts and Nevis	•					•
KOR	Korea, Rep.	•	•	•	•		
KSV	Kosovo	•	•	•			
KWT	Kuwait	•					•
LAO	Lao PDR	•	•	•			•
LBN	Lebanon	•	•	•		•	•
LBR	Liberia	•	•	•			•
LBY	Libya	•					
LCA	St. Lucia	•					
LKA	Sri Lanka	•	•	•			•
LSO	Lesotho	•	•	•			•
LTU	Lithuania	•	•	•			•
LUX	Luxembourg	•	•	•		•	•
LVA	Latvia	•	•	•	•	•	•
MAR	Morocco	•	•	•			•
MDA	Moldova	•	•	•			•
MDG	Madagascar	•	•	•		•	•
MDV	Maldives	•	•	•			•
MEX	Mexico	•	•	•			•
MKD	Macedonia, FYR	•	•	•			•

Country code	Country name	Gini index	Q5/Q1 ratio	Middle class share	Perceived Gini	Inequality of opportunity	Ethnic inequality (GREG and ETHG)
MLI	Mali	•	•	•			•
MLT	Malta	•					•
MMR	Myanmar	•	•	•			•
MNE	Montenegro	•	•	•			
MNG	Mongolia	•	•	•			•
MOZ	Mozambique	•	•	•			•
MRT	Mauritania	•	•	•			•
MUS	Mauritius	•	•	•			•
MWI	Malawi	•	•	•			•
MYS	Malaysia	•	•	•			•
NAM	Namibia	•	•	•			•
NER	Niger	•	•	•			•
NGA	Nigeria	•	•	•			•
NIC	Nicaragua	•	•	•			•
NLD	Netherlands	•	•	•		•	•
NOR	Norway	•	•	•	•	•	•
NPL	Nepal	•	•	•			•
NRU	Nauru	•					
NZL	New Zealand	•			•		•
OMN	Oman						•
PAK	Pakistan	•	•	•			•
PAN	Panama	•	•	•		•	•
PER	Peru	•	•	•		•	•
PHL	Philippines	•	•	•	•		•
PLW	Palau	•					
PNG	Papua New Guinea	•	•	•			•
POL	Poland	•	•	•	•	•	•
PRI	Puerto Rico	•					
PRT	Portugal	•	•	•	•	•	•
PRY	Paraguay	•	•	•			•
QAT	Qatar	•					•
ROM	Romania	•	•	•			•
RUS	Russian Federation	•	•	•	•		•
RWA	Rwanda	•	•	•			•
SAU	Saudi Arabia		•	•			
SDN	Sudan	•	•	•			•
SEN	Senegal	•	•	•			•
SGP	Singapore	•					•
SLB	Solomon Islands	•	•	•			
SLE	Sierra Leone	•	•	•			•
SLV	El Salvador	•	•	•			•
SMR	San Marino	•	•	•			•
SOM	Somalia	•					•

continued

Country code	Country name	Gini index	Q5/Q1 ratio	Middle class share	Perceived Gini	Inequality of opportunity	Ethnic inequality (GREG and ETHG)
SRB	Serbia	•	•	•			
SSD	South Sudan	•	•	•			
STP	São Tomé and Principe	•	•	•			
SUR	Suriname	•		•			•
SVK	Slovak Republic	•	•	•	•	•	•
SVN	Slovenia	•	•	•	•	•	•
SWE	Sweden	•	•	•	•	•	•
SWZ	Swaziland	•	•	•			•
SYC	Seychelles	•	•	•			•
SYR	Syrian Arab Republic	•	•	•			•
TCA	Turks and Caicos Islands	•					
TCD	Chad	•	•	•			•
TGO	Togo	•	•	•			•
THA	Thailand	•	•	•			•
TJK	Tajikistan	•	•	•			•
TKM	Turkmenistan	•	•	•			•
TMP	Timor-Leste	•	•	•			
TON	Tonga	•	•	•			•
TTO	Trinidad and Tobago	•					•
TUN	Tunisia	•	•	•			•
TUR	Turkey	•	•	•	•	•	•
TUV	Tuvalu	•	•	•			
TWN	Taiwan, China	•			•		
TZA	Tanzania	•	•	•			•
UGA	Uganda	•	•	•		•	•
UKR	Ukraine	•	•	•	•		•
URY	Uruguay	•	•	•			•
USA	United States	•	•	•	•	•	•
UZB	Uzbekistan	•	•	•			•
VCT	St. Vincent and the Grenadines	•					•
VEN	Venezuela, RB	•	•	•	•		•
VNM	Vietnam	•	•	•			•
VUT	Vanuatu	•	•	•			•
WBG	West Bank and Gaza	•	•	•			
WSM	Samoa	•	•	•			•
YEM	Yemen, Rep.	•	•	•			
ZAF	South Africa	•	•	•	•	•	•
ZAR	Congo, Dem. Rep.	•	•	•			•
ZMB	Zambia	•	•	•			•
ZWE	Zimbabwe	•	•	•			•

References

Acemoglu, Daron and James Robinson. (2006). *Economic Origins of Dictatorship and Democracy*. New York: Cambridge University Press.

Acemoglu, Daron and James Robinson. (2008). Persistence of power, elites and institutions. *American Economic Review* 98: 267–291.

Acemoglu, Daron and James Robinson. (2012). *Why Nations Fail: The Origins of Power, Prosperity and Poverty*. New York: Crown Business.

Acemoglu Daron, Simon Johnson and James Robinson. (2001). The colonial origins of comparative development: An empirical investigation. *American Economic Review* 91(5): 1369–1401.

Acemoglu Daron, Simon Johnson and James Robinson. (2005). Institutions as a Fundamental Cause of Long-run Growth. In: Philippe Aghion and Steven Durlauf (eds), *Handbook of Economic Growth*. Amsterdam: Elsevier, pp. 385–472.

Acemoglu, Daron, Suresh Naidu, Pascual Restrepo and James Robinson. (2015). Democracy, Redistribution and Inequality. In: Anthony Atkinson and François Bourguignon (eds), *Handbook of Income Distribution*, vol. 2B. Boston: Elsevier, pp. 1885–1966.

Ades, Alberto and Rafael Di Tella. (1999). Rents, competition and corruption. *American Economic Review* 89(4): 982–993.

Aldenderfer, Mark. (2010). Gimme that old time religion: Rethinking the Role of Religion in the Emergence of Social Inequality. In Douglas Price and Gary Feinman (eds), *Pathways to Power New Perspectives on the Emergence of Social Inequality*. London: Springer, pp. 77–94.

Alesina, Alberto and Paola Giuliano. (2015). Culture and institutions. *Journal of Economic Literature* 53(4): 898–944.

Alesina, Alberto and Eliana La Ferrara. (2002). Who trusts others? *Journal of Public Economics* 85(2): 207–234.

Alesina, Alberto, Arnaud Devleeschauwer, William Easterly, Sergio Kurlat and Romain Wacziarg. (2003). Fractionalization. *Journal of Economic Growth* 8: 155–194.

Alesina, Alberto, Stelios Michalopoulos and Elias Papaioannou. (2016). Ethnic inequality. *Journal of Political Economy* 124(2): 428–488.

Alvaredo, Facundo, Lucas Chancel, Thomas Piketty, Emmanuel Saez and Gabriel Zucman. (2018). *World Inequality Report*. World Inequality Lab.

Ames, Kenneth. (1994). The northwest coast: Complex hunter-gatherers, ecology, and social evolution. *Annual Review of Anthropology* 23: 209–229.

Andreski, Stansislav. (1968). *The Military Organization of Society*. Berkeley and Los Angeles: University of California Press.

Andvig, Jens Christopher. (1991). The economics of corruption: A survey. *Studi Economici* 1(43): 57–94.

Aristotle (n.d./1992). *The Politics.* New York: Penguin Books.

Arruñada, Benito. (2010). Protestants and Catholics: Similar work ethic, different social ethic. *The Economic Journal* 120: 890–918.

Ashraf, Quamrul and Oded Galor. (2018). The macrogenoeconomics of comparative development. *Journal of Economic Literature* 56(3): 1119–1155.

Aslaksen, Silje. (2009). Corruption and oil: evidence from panel data. Mimeo: Department of Economics, University of Oslo.

Atkinson, Anthony. (2015). *Inequality: What Can Be Done?* Cambridge, MA: Harvard University Press.

Atkinson, Anthony and Andrea Brandolini. (2011). On the identification of the "middle class". Working Paper 217, ECINEQ, Society for the Study of Economic Inequality.

Atkinson, Anthony, Thomas Piketty and Emmanuel Saez. (2011). Top incomes in the long run of history. *Journal of Economic Literature* 49(1): 3–71.

Axelrod, Robert. (1984). *The Evolution of Cooperation.* New York: Basic Books.

Bäck, Hanna and Axel Hadenius. (2008). Democracy and state capacity: Exploring a j-shaped relationship. *Governance* 21(1): 1–24.

Baldwin, Kate and John Huber. (2010). Economic versus cultural differences: Forms of ethnic diversity and public good provision. *American Political Science Review* 104(4): 644–662.

Banfield, Edward. (1958). *The Moral Basis of a Backward Society.* New York: Free Press.

Bardhan, Pranab. (1997). Corruption and development: A review of issues. *Journal of Economic Literature* 35(3): 1320–1346.

Barone, Guglielmo and Sauro Mocetti. (2015). Inequality and trust: New evidence from panel data. *Economic Inquiry* 54(2): 794–809.

Barro, Robert and Jong-Wha Lee. (2013). A new data set of educational attainment in the world, 1950–2010. *Journal of Development Economics* 104: 184–198.

Bartels, Larry. (2008). *Unequal Democracy: The Political Economy of the New Gilded Age.* Princeton: Russell Sage Foundation and Princeton University Press.

Becker, Gary. (1968). Crime and punishment: An economic approach. *Journal of Political Economy* 76: 169–217.

Bellah, Robert. (2011). *Religion in Human Evolution: From the Paleolithic to the Axial Age.* Cambridge, MA: Harvard University Press.

Bentzen, Jeanet, Nicolai Kaarsen and Asger Wingender. (2016). Irrigation and autocracy. *Journal of the European Economic Association* 15(1): 1–53.

Berg, Andrew, Jonathan Ostry, Charalambos Tsangarides and Yorbol Yakhshilikov. (2018). Redistribution, inequality, and growth: New evidence. *Journal of Economic Growth* 23(3): 259–305.

Bergh, Andreas and Christian Bjørnskov. (2011). Historical trust levels predict the current size of the welfare state. *Kyklos* 64(1): 1–19.

Bergh, Andreas and Christian Bjørnskov. (2014). Trust, welfare states and income equality: Sorting out the causality. *European Journal of Political Economy* 35: 183–199.

Beugelsdijk, Sjoerd, Robbert Maseland and André van Hoorn. (2015). Are scores on Hofstede's dimensions of national culture stable over time? A cohort analysis. *Global Strategy Journal* 5(3): 223–240.

Bittles, Alan. (1994). The role and significance of consanguinity as a demographic variable. *Population and Development Review* 20(3): 561–584.

Bjørnskov, Christian. (2007). Determinants of generalized trust: A cross-country comparison. *Public Choice* 130(1): 1–21.

Bjørnskov, Christian and Gert Tinggaard Svendsen. (2013). Does social trust determine the size of the welfare state? Evidence using historical identification. *Public Choice* 157(1/2): 269–286.

Bloch, Marc. (1961). *Feudal Society*. Chicago: University of Chicago Press.

Bockstette, Valerie, Areendam Chanda and Louis Putterman. (2002). States and markets: The advantage of an early start. *Journal of Economic Growth* 7: 347–369.

Boehm, Christopher. (1999). *Hierarchy in the Forest: The Evolution of Egalitarian Behaviour*. Cambridge, MA: Harvard University Press.

Boehm, Christopher. (2012). Ancestral hierarchy and conflict. *Science* 336: 844–847.

Boix, Carles. (2003). *Democracy and Redistribution*. New York: Cambridge University Press.

Boix, Carles. (2015). *Political Order and Inequality: Their Foundations and their Consequences for Human Welfare*. New York: Cambridge University Press.

Boix, Carles and Daniel Posner. (1998). Social capital: Explaining its origins and effects on government performance. *British Journal of Political Science* 28(4): 686–693.

Borsch, Stuart. (2005). *The Black Death in Egypt and England: A Comparative Study*. Austin: University of Texas Press.

Botero, Juan, Alejandro Ponce and Andrei Shleifer. (2013). Education, complaints, and accountability. *Journal of Law and Economics* 56(4): 959–996.

Bourguignon, François. (2017). World changes in inequality: An overview of facts, causes, consequences and policies. BIS Working Paper No. 654.

Bowles, Samuel and Herbert Gintis. (2002). The inheritance of inequality. *Journal of Economic Perspectives* 16(3): 3–30.

Bowles, Samuel and Jung-Kyoo Choi. (2013). Coevolution of farming and private property during the early Holocene. *Proceedings of the National Academy of Sciences* 110(22): 8830–8835.

Boyd, Robert and Peter Richerson. (1985). *Culture and the Evolutionary Process*. Chicago and London: University of Chicago Press.

Boyd, Robert and Peter Richerson. (2005). *Not by Genes Alone: How Culture Transformed Human Evolution*. Chicago: University of Chicago Press.

Bruce, Steve. (2004). Did Protestantism create democracy? *Democratization* 11(4): 3–20.

Brunori, Paolo, Francisco Ferreira and Vito Peragine. (2013). Inequality of Opportunity, Income Inequality, and Economic Mobility: Some International Comparisons. In: Eva Paus (ed.), *Getting Development Right*. New York: Palgrave Macmillan, pp. 85–115.

Buggle, Johannes and Ruben Durante. (2017). Climate risk, cooperation, and the co-evolution of culture and institutions. CEPR Discussion Paper No. DP12380.

Busse, Matthias and Steffen Gröning. (2013). The resource curse revisited: Governance and natural resources. *Public Choice* 154(1–2): 1–20.

Cadsby, Bram, Ninghua Du and Fei Song. (2016). In-group favoritism and moral decision-making. *Journal of Economic Behaviour & Organization* 128: 59–71.

Callan, Mitchell, James Olson and Will Shead. (2011). Personal relative deprivation, delay discounting, and gambling. *Journal of Personality and Social Psychology* 101(5): 955–973.

Carneiro, Robert. (1970). A theory of the origin of the state. *Science* 169: 733–738.

Castelló-Climent, Amparo and Rafael Doménech. (2014). Human capital and income inequality: Some facts and some puzzles. Banco Bilbao Vizcaya Argentaria, Working Paper no. 12/28. Madrid: BBVA.

Cederman, Lars-Erik, Kristian Gleditsch and Nils Weidmann. (2011). Horizontal inequalities and ethno-nationalist civil war: A global comparison. *American Political Science Review* 105(3): 478–495.

Cederman, Lars-Erik, Nils Weidmann and Nils-Christian Bormann. (2015). Triangulating horizontal inequality: Toward improved conflict analysis. *Journal of Peace Research* 52(6): 806–821.

Chabal, Patrick and Jean-Pascal Daloz. (1999). *Africa Works: Disorder as Political Instrument*. Oxford: James Currey for the International African Institute.

Charron, Nicholas and Victor Lapuente. (2010). Does democracy produce quality of government? *European Journal of Political Research* 49: 443–470.

Charron, Nicholas and Victor Lapuente. (2013). Why do some regions in Europe have a higher quality of government? *Journal of Politics* 75(3): 567–582.

Cherry, Todd, Peter Frykblom and Jason Shogren. (2002). Hardnose the dictator. *American Economic Review* 92: 1218–1221.

Childe, Gordon. (1936). *Man Makes Himself*. London: Watts & Co.

Chong, Alberto and Mark Gradstein. (2007). Inequality and institutions. *Review of Economics and Statistics* 89(3): 454–465.

Clark, Andrew and Conchita D'Ambrosio. (2015). Attitudes to Income Inequality: Experimental and Survey Evidence. In: Anthony Atkinson and François Bourguignon (eds), *Handbook of Income Distribution*, vol. 2A. Boston: Elsevier, pp. 1147–1208.

Coady, David and Allan Dizioli. (2017). Income inequality and education revisited: Persistence, endogeneity, and heterogeneity. IMF Working Paper WP/17/126.

Corak, Miles. (2013). Income inequality, equality of opportunity, and intergenerational mobility. *Journal of Economic Perspectives* 27(3): 79–102.

Costa-Lopes, Rui, John Dovidio, Cicero Roberto Pereira and John Jot. (2013). Social psychological perspectives on the legitimation of social inequality: Past, present and future. *European Journal of Social Psychology* 43: 229–237.

Cowell, Frank. (2008). *Measuring Inequality*. Oxford: Oxford University Press.

Cupit, Geoffrey. (2000). When does justice require impartiality? Presented at the Political Studies Association–UK 50th Annual Conference, London.

Dabla-Norris, Era, Kalpana Kochhar, Nujin Suphaphiphat, Frantisek Ricka and Evridiki Tsounta. (2015). Causes and consequence of income inequality: A global perspective. IMF Staff Discussion Note SDN/15/13.

Davidai, Shai and Thomas Gilovich. (2015). Building a more mobile America – one income quintile at a time. *Perspectives on Psychological Science* 10(1): 60–71.

Deininger, Klaus and Lyn Squire. (1996). A new data set measuring income inequality. *World Bank Economic Review* 10(3), 565–591.

Delhey, Jan and Kenneth Newton. (2005). Predicting cross-national levels of social trust: Global pattern or Nordic exceptionalism? *European Sociological Review* 21(4): 311–327.

Devarajan, Shantayanan and Ritva Reinikka. (2004). Making services work for the poor. *Journal of African Economies* 13(1): 142–166.

Diamond, Jared. (1997), *Guns, Germs, and Steel: The Fates of Human Societies*. New York: W.W. Norton & Co.

Dong, Bin, Uwe Dulleck and Benno Torgler. (2012). Conditional corruption. *Journal of Economic Psychology* 33(3): 609–627.

Dunbar, Robin. (1992). Neocortex size as a constraint on group size in primates. *Journal of Human Evolution* 22(6): 469–493.

Easterly, William. (2001). The middle class consensus and economic development. *Journal of Economic Growth* 6(4): 317–336.

Easterly, William. (2007). Inequality does cause underdevelopment: Insights from a new instrument. *Journal of Development Economics* 84(2007): 755–776.

Efferson, Charles, Rafael Lalive and Ernst Fehr. (2008). The coevolution of cultural groups and ingroup favoritism. *Science* 321(5897): 1844–1849.

Eisenkopf, Gerald, Urs Fischbacher and Franziska Föllmi-Heusi. (2011). Unequal opportunities and distributive justice. *Journal of Economic Behaviour & Organization* 93: 51–61.

Engel, Christoph. (2011). Dictator games: A meta study. *Experimental Economics* 14: 583–610.

Engerman, Stanley and Kenneth Sokoloff. (1997). Factor Endowments, Institutions, and Differential Paths of Growth among New World Economies: A View from Economic Historians of the United States. In: Stephen Haber (ed.), *How Latin America Fell Behind: Essays on the Economic Histories of Brazil and Mexico, 1800–1914.* Stanford: Stanford University Press, pp. 260–304.

Engerman, Stanley and Kenneth Sokoloff. (2002). Factor endowments, inequality, and paths of development among New World economies. *Economia*: 41–88.

Etty, John. (2007). Russia's climate and geography. *History Review* 58: 48–51.

Evans, Peter and James Rauch. (1999). Bureaucracy and growth: A cross-national analysis of the effects of "Weberian" state structures on economic growth. *American Sociological Review* 64(5): 748–765.

Fehr, Ernst and Urs Fischbacher. (2005). The Economics of Strong Reciprocity. In: Herbert, Gintis, Samuel Bowles, Richard Boyd and Ernst Fehr (eds), *Moral Sentiments and Material Interests: The Foundations for Cooperation in Economic Life.* Cambridge, MA: MIT Press, pp. 151–192.

Fehr, Ernst and Klaus Schmidt. (1999). A theory of fairness, competition and co-operation. *Quarterly Journal of Economics* 114: 817–868.

Ferrer-i-Carbonell, Ada and Xavier Ramos. (2014). Inequality and happiness. *Journal of Economic Surveys* 28: 1016–1027.

Fincher, Corey, Randy Thornhill, Damian Murray and Mark Schaller. (2008). Pathogen prevalence predicts human cross-cultural variability in individualism/collectivism. *Proceedings of the Royal Society B* 275: 1279–1285.

Finer, Samuel. (1997). *The History of Government*, 3 volumes. Oxford: Oxford University Press.

Fiske, Susan. (1993). Controlling other people: The impact of power on stereotyping. *American Psychologist* 48(6): 621–628.

Fisman, Ray and Miriam Golden. (2017). *Corruption. What Everyone Needs to Know.* New York: Oxford University Press.

Fisman, Ray and Edward Miguel. (2007). Corruption, norms, and legal enforcement: Evidence from diplomatic parking tickets. *Journal of Political Economy* 115(6): 1020–1048.

Flannery, Kent and Joyce Marcus. (2012). *The Creation of Inequality: How Our Prehistoric Ancestors Set the Stage for Monarchy, Slavery, and Empire.* Cambridge, MA: Harvard University Press.

Frank, Robert. (1985). *Choosing the Right Pond: Human Behaviour and the Quest for Status.* New York: Oxford University Press.

Frankema, Ewout. (2010). The colonial roots of land inequality. Geography, factor endowments, or institutions? *Economic History Review* 63(2): 418–451.

Freedom House. (2018). Freedom in the World 2018. Methodology. Source: https://freedomhouse.org/report/methodology-freedom-world-2018, accessed on 25 August 2018.

Fried, Brian, Paul Lagunes and Atheendar Venkataramani. (2010). Corruption and inequality at the crossroad: A multimethod study of bribery and discrimination in Latin America. *Latin American Research Review* 45(1): 76–97.

Fukuyama, Francis. (2011). *The Origins of Political Order: From Prehuman Times to the French Revolution*. London: Profile Books.

Fukuyama, Francis. (2013). What is governance? *Governance* 26: 347–368.

Fukuyama, Francis. (2014). *Political Order and Political Decay: From the Industrial Revolution to the Globalisation of Democracy*. New York: Farrar, Straus and Giroux.

Fum, Ruikang and Roland Hodler. (2010). Natural resources and income inequality: The role of ethnic divisions. *Economics Letters* 107: 360–363.

Gallego, Aina. (2015). *Unequal Political Participation Worldwide*. New York: Cambridge University Press.

Gallup, John, Jeffrey Sachs and Andrew Mellinger. (1999). Geography and economic development. *International Regional Science Review* 22(2): 179–232.

Galor, Oded, Omer Moav and Dietrich Vollrath. (2009). Inequality in landownership, the emergence of human-capital promoting institutions, and the Great Divergence. *Review of Economic Studies* 76: 143–179.

Gilens, Martin. (2012). *Affluence and Influence: Economic Inequality and Political Power in America*. Princeton: Princeton University Press and Russell Sage Foundation.

Gilens, Martin and Benjamin Page. (2014). Testing theories of American politics: Elites, interest Groups, and average citizens. *Perspectives on Politics* 12(3): 564–581.

Gimpelson, Vladimir and Treisman Daniel. (2018). Misperceiving inequality. *Economics and Politics* 30: 27–54.

Gino, Francesca, Shahar Ayal and Dan Ariely. (2009). Contagion and differentiation in unethical behaviour the effect of one bad apple on the barrel. *Psychological Science* 20(3): 393–398.

Gintis, Herbert, Carel van Schaik and Christopher Boehm. (2015). Zoon Politikon: The evolutionary origins of human political systems. *Current Anthropology* 56(3): 327–353.

Glaeser, Edward, Jose Scheinkman and Andrei Shleifer. (2003). The injustice of inequality. *Journal of Monetary Economics* 50: 199–222.

Goldsmith, Arthur. (2007). Is governance reform a catalyst for development? *Governance* 20(2): 165–186.

Goody, Jack. (1971). *Technology, Tradition and State in Africa*. New York: Cambridge University Press.

Goody, Jack. (1983). *The Development of the Family and Marriage in Europe*. New York: Cambridge University Press.

Gorodnichenko, Yuriy and Gerard Roland. (2011). Which dimensions of culture matter for long-run growth? *American Economic Review* 101(3): 492–498.

Greif, Avner. (1994). Cultural beliefs and the organization of society: A historical and theoretical reflection on collectivist and individualist societies. *Journal of Political Economy* 102(5): 912–950.

Greif, Avner and Guido Tabellini. (2017). The clan and the corporation: Sustaining cooperation in China and Europe. *Journal of Comparative Economics* 45(1): 1–35.

Gruenfeld, Deborah, M. Ena Inesi, Joe Magee and Adam Galinsky. (2008). Power and the objectification of social targets. *Journal of Personality and Social Psychology* 95(1): 111–127.

Guiso, Luigi, Paola Sapienza and Luigi Zingales. (2006). Does culture affect economic outcomes? *Journal of Economic Perspectives* 20(2): 23–48.

Guiso, Luigi, Paola Sapienza and Luigi Zingales. (2016). Long-term persistence. *Journal of the European Economic Association* 14: 1401–1436.

Gupta, Sanjeev, Hamid Davoodi and Erwin Tiongson. (2001a). Corruption and the Provision of Healthcare and Education Services. In: Arvind Jain (ed.), *The Political Economy of Corruption*. London: Routledge, pp. 111–141.

Gupta, Sanjeev, Luiz de Mello and Raju Sharan. (2001b). Corruption and military spending. *European Journal of Political Economy* 17(4): 749–777.

Gupta, Sanjeev, Hamid Davoodi and Rosa Alonso-Terme. (2002). Does corruption affect income inequality and poverty? *Economics of Governance* 3: 23–45.

Gylfason, Thorvaldur and Gylfi Zoega. (2002). Inequality and economic growth: Do natural resources matter? CESifo Working Paper No. 712(5).

Haber, Stephen. (2012). Rainfall and democracy: Climate, technology, and the evolution of economic and political institutions. Unpublished paper.

Hamilton, William. (1964a). The genetical evolution of social behaviour. I. *Journal of Theoretical Biology* 7(1): 1–16.

Hamilton, William. (1964b). The genetical evolution of social behaviour. II. *Journal of Theoretical Biology* 7(1): 17–52.

Hanousek, Jan and Filip Palda. (2004). Quality of government services and the civic duty to pay taxes in the Czech and Slovak republics, and other transition countries. *Kyklos* 57: 237–252.

Hanson, Victor. (1998). *Warfare and Agriculture in Classical Greece*. Berkeley: University of California Press.

Harvey, Simon-Pierre and Richard Bourhis. (2013). Discrimination between the rich and the poor under contrasting conditions of wealth stratification. *Journal of Applied Social Psychology* 43: E351–E366.

Hayden, Brian. (1995). Pathways to Power. In: Douglas Price and Gary Feinman (eds), *Foundations of Social Inequality*. New York: Springer, pp. 15–86.

Heller, William, Andreas Kyriacou and Oriol Roca-Sagalés. (2016). Institutional checks and corruption: The effect of formal agenda access on governance. *European Journal of Political Research* 55: 681–701.

Helliwell, John and Robert Putnam. (2007). Education and social capital. *Eastern Economic Journal* 33(1): 1–19.

Henrich, Joseph, Robert Boyd, Samuel Bowles, Colin Camerer, Ernst Fehr and Herbert Gintis (eds). (2004). *Foundations of Human Sociality: Economic Experiments and Ethnographic Evidence from Fifteen Small-Scale Societies*. Oxford: Oxford University Press.

Henrich, Joseph, Jean Ensminger, Richard McElreath, Abigail Barr, Clark Barrett, Alexander Bolyanatz, Juan Camilo Cardenas, Michael Gurven, Edwins Gwako, Natalie Henrich, Carolyn Lesorogol, Frank Marlowe, David Tracer and John Ziker. (2010). Markets, religion, community size, and the evolution of fairness and punishment. *Science* 327: 1480–1484.

Hessami, Zohal. (2014). Political corruption, public procurement, and budget composition: Theory and evidence from OECD countries. *European Journal of Political Economy* 34: 372–389.

Hicken, Allen. (2011). Clientelism. *Annual Review of Political Science* 14: 289–310.

Hirschman, Albert. (1970). *Exit, Voice and Loyalty: Responses to Decline in Firms, Organizations and States*. Cambridge, MA: Harvard University Press.

Hoben, Ashley, Abraham Buunk, Corey Fincher, Randy Thornhill and Mark Schaller. (2010). On the adaptive origins and maladaptive consequences of human inbreeding: Parasite prevalence, immune functioning, and consanguineous marriage. *Evolutionary Psychology: An International Journal of Evolutionary Approaches to Psychology and Behavior* 8(4): 658–676.

Hoffman, Elisabeth, Kevin McCabe, Keith Shachat and Vernon Smith. (1994). Preferences, property rights, and anonymity in bargaining games. *Games and Economic Behaviour* 7: 346–380.

Hofstede, Geert. (1980). *Culture's Consequences*. Beverly Hills: Sage.

Hofstede, Geert, Gert Jan Hofstede and Michael Minkov. (2010). *Cultures and Organizations: Software of the Mind*, 3rd edition. Maidenhead: McGraw-Hill Education.

Hooper Paul, Hillard Kaplan and James Boone. (2010). A theory of leadership in human cooperative groups. *Journal of Theoretical Biology* 265: 633–646.

Houle, Christian. (2015). Ethnic inequality and the dismantling of democracy: A global analysis. *World Politics* 67(3): 469–505.

Houle, Christian. (2017). Inequality, ethnic diversity, and redistribution. *Journal of Economic Inequality* 15: 1–23.

Hruschka, Daniel and Henrich Joseph. (2013). Institutions, parasites and the persistence of in-group preferences. *PLoS ONE* 8(5): e63642.

Huang, Jian, Henriëtte Maassen van den Brink and Wim Groot. (2011). College education and social trust: An evidence-based study on the causal mechanisms. *Social Indicators Research* 104(2): 287–310.

Inesi, M. Ena, Deborah Gruenfeld and Adam Galinsky. (2012). How power corrupts relationships: Cynical attributions for others' generous acts. *Journal of Experimental Social Psychology* 48(4): 795–803.

Inglehart, Ronald and Christian Welzel. (2005). *Modernization, Cultural Change, and Democracy. The Human Development Sequence*. Cambridge: Cambridge University Press.

Isham, Jonathan, Michael Woolcock, Lant Pritchett and Gwen Busby. (2015). The varieties of resource experience: Natural resource export structures and the political economy of economic growth. *World Bank Economic Review* 19(2): 141–174.

ISSP. (2009). International social survey program questionnaire. Manheim, Germany: ISSP.

Jensen, Nathan and Aminur Rahman. (2015). The Silence of Corruption: Identifying Underreporting of Business Corruption through Randomized Response Techniques. In: Paul Heywood (ed.), *Routledge Handbook of Political Corruption*. London and New York: Routledge, pp. 154–171.

Jetten, Jolanda, Zhechen Wang, Niklas Steffens, Frank Mols, Kim Peters and Maykel Verkuyten. (2017). A social identity analysis of responses to economic inequality. *Current Opinion in Psychology* 18: 1–5.

Johnson, Allen and Timothy Earle. (2000). *The Evolution of Human Societies. From Foraging Group to Agrarian State*, 2nd edition. Stanford: Stanford University Press.

Jones, Eric. (1981). *The European Miracle: Environments, Economies, and Geopolitics in the History of Europe and Asia*. New York: Cambridge University Press.

Jong-sung, You and Sanjeev Khagram. (2005). A comparative study of inequality and corruption. *American Sociological Review* 70: 136–157.

Jost, John. (2001). Outgroup Favoritism and the Theory of System Justification: A Paradigm for Investigating the Effects of Socioeconomic Success on Stereotype Content. In: Gordon Moskowitz (ed.), *Cognitive Social Psychology: The Princeton Symposium on the Legacy and Future of Social Cognition*. Mahwah: Lawrence Erlbaum Associates, pp. 89–102.

Jost, John and Mahzarin Banaji. (1994). The role of stereotyping in system-justification and the production of false consciousness. *British Journal of Social Psychology* 33: 1–27.

Jost, John, Brett Pelham, Oliver Sheldon and Bilian Sullivan. (2003). Social inequality and the reduction of ideological dissonance on behalf of the system: Evidence of enhanced system justification among the disadvantaged. *European Journal of Social Psychology* 33: 13–36.

Karklins, Rasma. (2005). *The System Made Me Do It: Corruption in Post-Communist Societies*. Armonk: M.E. Sharpe.

Kaufmann, Daniel, Aart Kraay and Massimo Mastruzzi. (2010). The worldwide governance indicators. Methodology and analytical issues. Policy Research Working Paper 5430. Washington, DC: The World Bank.

Kay, Aaron and Justin Friesen. (2011). On social stability and social change: Understanding when system justification does and does not occur. *Current Directions in Psychological Science* 20(6): 360–364.

Kedourie Elie. (1989). Crisis and revolution in modern Islam. *Times Literary Supplement* 19–25 May: 549.

Kelly, Robert. (1995). *The Foraging Spectrum. Diversity in Hunter-Gatherer Lifeways.* Washington and London: Smithsonian Institution Press.

Keltner, Dacher. (2016). *The Power Paradox: How We Gain and Lose Influence.* New York: Penguin Press.

Kimenyi, Mwangi. (2006). Ethnicity, governance and the provision of public goods. *Journal of African Economies* 15(1): 62–99.

Kipnis, David. (1972). Does power corrupt? *Journal of Personality and Social Psychology*, 24: 33–41.

Klasing, Mariko. (2013). Cultural dimensions, collective values and their importance for institutions. *Journal of Comparative Economics* 41(2): 447–467.

Klosko, George. (1992). *The Principle of Fairness and Political Obligation.* Lanham: Rowman and Littlefield.

Knack, Stephen, and Philip Keefer. (1997). Does social capital have an economic payoff? A cross-country investigation. *Quarterly Journal of Economics* 112(4): 1251–1288.

Knauft, Bruce. (1991). Violence and sociality in human evolution. *Current Anthropology* 32(4): 391–409.

Knight, Frank. (1921). *Risk, Uncertainty, and Profit.* Boston: Hart, Schaffner & Marx; Houghton Mifflin Company.

Köbis, Nils, Jan-Willem Prooijen, Francesca Righetti and Paul Van Lange. (2015). Who doesn't? The impact of descriptive norms on corruption. *PLoS ONE* 10(6): e0131830.

Kotschy, Rainer and Uwe Sunde. (2017). Democracy, inequality, and institutional quality. *European Economic Review* 91: 209–228.

Kraus, Michael and Dacher Keltner. (2013). Social class rank, essentialism, and punitive judgment. *Journal of Personality and Social Psychology* 105(2): 247–261.

Kteily, Nour, Jennifer Sheehy-Skeffington and Arnold Ho. (2017). Hierarchy in the eye of the beholder: (Anti-)egalitarianism shapes perceived levels of social inequality. *Journal of Personality and Social Psychology* 112(1): 136–159.

Kuznets, Simon. (1955). Economic growth and income inequality. *American Economic Review* 45(1): 1–28.

Kyriacou, Andreas. (2005). Rationality, ethnicity and institutions: A survey of issues and results. *Journal of Economics Surveys* 19(1): 23–42.

Kyriacou, Andreas. (2010). Intrinsic motivation and the logic of collective action: The impact of selective incentives. *American Journal of Economics and Sociology* 69(2): 823–839.

Kyriacou, Andreas. (2013a). Government quality. In Jürgen Backhaus (ed.), *Encyclopedia of Law and Economics*. New York: Springer.

Kyriacou, Andreas. (2013b). Ethnic group inequalities and governance: Evidence from developing countries. *Kyklos* 66(1): 78–101.

Kyriacou, Andreas. (2016). Individualism–collectivism, governance and economic development. *European Journal of Political Economy* 42(C): 91–104.

Kyriacou, Andreas and Francisco José López-Velásquez. (2015). Inequality and culture in a cross section of countries. *Journal of Institutional Economics* 11(1): 141–166.

Kyriacou, Andreas and Pedro Trivin. (2018). Economic development, inequality and generalized trust. MPRA Paper 91651, University Library of Munich, Germany.

Kyriacou, Andreas, Leonel Muinelo-Gallo and Roca-Sagalés Oriol. (2018). Redistributive efficiency in 28 developed economies. *Journal of European Social Policy* 28(4): 370–385.

Langbein Laura and Stephen Knack. (2010). The worldwide world governance indicators: Six, one, or none? *Journal of Development Studies* 46(2): 350–370.

Lammers, Joris, Diederik Stapel and Adam Galinsky. (2010). Power increases hypocrisy: Moralizing in reasoning, immorality in behaviour. *Psychological Science* 21(5): 737–744.

La Porta, Rafael, Florencio Lopez-de-Silanes and Andrei Shleifer. (2008). The economic consequences of legal origins. *Journal of Economic Literature* 46: 285–332.

La Porta, Rafael, Florencio Lopez-de-Silanes, Andrei Shleifer and Robert W. Vishny. (1997). Trust in large organizations. *American Economic Review* 87(2): 333–338.

La Porta, Rafael, Florencio Lopez-de-Silanes, Andrei Shleifer and Robert W. Vishny. (1999). The quality of government. *Journal of Law, Economics and Organization* 15(1): 222–279.

Lawrance, Emily. (1991). Poverty and the rate of time preference: Evidence from panel data. *Journal of Political Economy* 99(1): 54–77.

Le Billon, Philippe. (2001). The political ecology of war: Natural resources and armed conflicts. *Political Geography* 20: 561–584.

Leigh, Andrew. (2006). Does equality lead to fraternity? *Economics Letters* 93(1): 121–125.

Leite, Carlos and Jens Weidmann. (2002). Does Mother Nature Corrupt? Natural Resources, Corruption and Economic Growth. In: George Abed and Sanjeev Gupta (eds), *Governance, Corruption and Economic Performance*. Washington, DC: IMF, pp. 159–196.

Lerner, Melvin. (1980). *The Belief in a Just World: A Fundamental Delusion*. New York: Plenum Press.

Levitt, Steven and John List. (2007). What do laboratory experiments measuring social preferences reveal about the real world? *Journal of Economic Perspectives* 21: 153–174.

Licht, Amir, Chanan Goldschmidt and Shalom H. Schwarz. (2007). Culture rules: The foundations of the rule of law and other norms of governance. *Journal of Comparative Economics* 35(4): 659–688.

Liu Cheol and John Mikesell. (2014). The impact of public officials' corruption on the size and allocation of U.S. state spending. *Public Administration Review* 74(3): 346–359.

Mann, Michael. (1986). *The Sources of Social Power: Volume 1, A History of Power from the Beginning to AD 1760*. New York: Cambridge University Press.

Marmot, Michael. (2004). *Status Syndrome*. London: Bloomsbury.

Marshall, Monty, Ted Gurr and Keith Jaggers. (2017). *Polity IV Project: Political Regime Characteristics and Transitions 1800–2016*. Dataset Users' Manual. Center for Systemic Peace.

Mauro, Paolo. (1995). Corruption and growth. *Quarterly Journal of Economics* 110(3): 681–712.

Mauro, Paolo. (1997). The Effects of Corruption on Growth, Investment, and Government Expenditure: A Cross-Country Analysis. In: Kimberly Elliott (ed.), *Corruption and the Global Economy*. Washington, DC: Institute for International Economics, pp. 83–107.

Mauro, Paolo. (1998). Corruption and the composition of government expenditure. *Journal of Public Economics* 69: 263–279.

Mayshar, Joram, Omer Moavz, Zvika Neeman and Luigi Pascali. (2016). Cereals, appropriability and hierarchy. Unpublished paper.

Mazar, Nina and Pankaj Aggarwal. (2011). Greasing the palm: Can collectivism promote bribery? *Psychological Science* 22(7): 843–884.

McCleary, Rachel. (2007). Salvation, damnation and economic incentives. *Journal of Contemporary Religion* 22(1): 49–74.

McNeill, William. (1982). *The Pursuit of Power*. Chicago: University of Chicago Press.

Meltzer, Allan and Scott Richard. (1981). A rational theory of the size of government. *Journal of Political Economy* 89: 914–927.

Merton, Robert. (1938). Social structure and anomie. *American Sociological Review* 3(5): 672–682.

Michalopoulos, Stelios, Alireza Naghavi and Giovanni Prarolo. (2016). Islam, inequality and pre-industrial comparative development. *Journal of Development Economics* 120: 86–98.

Miller, William. (2006). Corruption and corruptibility. *World Development* 34(2): 371–380.

Montinola, Gabriella and Robert Jackman. (2002). Sources of corruption: A cross-country study. *British Journal of Political Science* 32: 147–170.

Moscatelli, Silvia, Flavia Albarello, Francesca Prati and Monica Rubini. (2014). Badly off or better off than them? The impact of relative deprivation and relative gratification on intergroup discrimination. *Journal of Personality and Social Psychology* 107(2): 248–264.

Mungiu-Pippidi, Alina. (2015). *The Quest for Good Governance: How Societies Develop Control of Corruption*. Cambridge: Cambridge University Press.

Murray, Michael. (2006). Avoiding invalid instruments and coping with weak instruments. *Journal of Economic Perspectives* 20(4): 111–132.

Murdock, George. (1967). *Ethnographic Atlas*. Pittsburgh: University of Pittsburgh Press.

Murdock, George and Douglas White. (1969). Standard cross-cultural sample. *Ethnology* 8(4): 329–369.

Murray, Damian and Mark Schaller. (2010). Historical prevalence of infectious diseases within 230 geopolitical regions: A tool for investigating origins of culture. *Journal of Cross-Cultural Psychology* 41(1): 99–108.

Newman, Benjamin, Christopher Johnston and Patrick Lown. (2015). False consciousness or class awareness? Local income inequality, personal economic position, and belief in American meritocracy. *American Journal of Political Science* 59: 326–340.

Nikolaev, Boris, Christopher Boudreaux and Rauf Salahodjaev. (2017). Are individualistic societies less equal? Evidence from the parasite stress theory of values. *Journal of Economic Behaviour & Organization* 138: 30–49.

Nolan, Patrick and Gerhard Lenski. (2009). *Human Societies: An Introduction to Macrosociology*, 11th edition. Boulder: Paradigm Publishers.

North, Charles, Wafa Orman and Carl Gwin. (2013). Religion, corruption, and the rule of law. *Journal of Money, Credit and Banking* 45(5): 757–779.

North, Douglass. (1981). *Structure and Change in Economic History*. New York, London: W.W. Norton.

North, Douglass. (1990). *Institutions, Institutional Change and Economic Performance*. Cambridge: Cambridge University Press.

North, Douglass. (1991). Institutions. *Journal of Economic Perspectives* 5(1): 97–112.

North, Douglass. (2005). *Understanding the Process of Economic Change*. Princeton: Princeton University Press.

North, Douglass, John Wallis and Barry Weingast. (2009). *Violence and Social Orders: A Conceptual Framework for Interpreting Recorded Human History*. New York: Cambridge University Press.

Norton, Michael and Dan Ariely. (2011). Building a better America – one wealth quintile at a time. *Perspectives on Psychological Science* 6(1): 9–12.

Nunn, Nathan. (2009). The importance of history for economic development. *Annual Review of Economics* 1: 65–92.

Nunn, Nathan. (2014). Historical Development. In: Philippe Aghion and Steven Durlauf (eds), *Handbook of Economic Growth*, 1st edition. London: Elsevier, pp. 347–402.

Okun, Arthur. (1975). *Equality and Efficiency: The Big Tradeoff*. Washington, DC: The Brookings Institution.

Olsson, Ola and Christopher Paik. (2016). Long-run cultural divergence: Evidence from the neolithic revolution. *Journal of Development Economics* 122: 197–213.

Østby, Gudrun. (2008). Polarization, horizontal inequalities and violent civil conflict. *Journal of Peace Research* 45: 143–162.

Ott, Jan. (2010). Good governance and happiness in nations: Technical quality precedes democracy and quality beats size. *Journal of Happiness Studies* 11: 353–368.

Ott, Jan. (2011). Government and happiness in 130 nations: Good governance fosters higher level and more equality of happiness. *Social Indicators Research* 102: 3–22.

Papakostas, Apostolis. (2001). Why Is There No Clientelism in Scandinavia? A Comparison of the Swedish and Greek Sequences of Development. In: Simona Piattoni (ed.), *Clientelism, Interests and Democratic Representation*. Cambridge: Cambridge University Press, pp. 31–53.

Patriquin, Larry. (2015). *Economic Equality and Direct Democracy in Ancient Athens*. New York: Palgrave Macmillan.

Piff, Paul, Daniel Stancato, Stéphane Côté, Rodolfo Mendoza-Denton and Dacher Keltner. (2012). Higher social class predicts increased unethical behaviour. *Proceedings of the National Academy of Sciences* 109(11): 4086–4091.

Pearce, Russell. (2004). Redressing inequality in the market for justice: Why access to lawyers will never solve the problem and why rethinking the role of judges will help. *Fordham Law Review* 73(3): 969–981.

Pellegrini, Lorenzo and Reyer Gerlagh. (2007). Causes of corruption: A survey of cross-country analyses and extended results. *Economics of Governance* 9(3): 245–263.

Persson, Anna, Rothstein Bo and Jan Teorell. (2013). Why anticorruption reforms fail – systemic corruption as a collective action problem. *Governance* 26: 449–471.

Pickett, Kate and Richard Wilkinson. (2009). *The Spirit Level: Why Greater Equality Makes Societies Stronger*. New York: Bloomsbury Press.

Platow, Michael, Stephanie Hoar, Scott Reid, Keryn Harley and Dianne Morrison. (1997). Endorsement of distributively fair and unfair leaders in interpersonal and intergroup situations. *European Journal of Social Psychology* 27: 465–494.

Platteau, Jean-Philippe. (1994). Behind the market stage where real societies exist – part I: The role of public and private order institutions. *Journal of Development Studies* 30(3): 533–577.

Platteau, Jean-Philippe. (2000). *Institutions, Social Norms, and Economic Development.* Amsterdam: Harwood Academic Publishing.

Platteau, Jean-Philippe and Yujiro Hayami. (1998). Resource Endowments and Agricultural Development: Africa versus Asia. In: Yujiro Hayami and Masahiko Aoki (eds), *The Institutional Foundations of East Asian Economic Development.* Basingstoke: International Economic Association and Palgrave Macmillan, pp. 357–412.

Powelson, John. (1997). *Centuries of Economic Endeavor.* Ann Arbor: University of Michigan Press.

Putnam, Robert, Robert Leonardi and Raffaella Nanetti. (1993). *Making Democracy Work: Civic Traditions in Modern Italy.* Princeton: Princeton University Press.

Ratcliffe, Susan. (2017). *Oxford Essential Quotations (5th Edition).* Online: Oxford University Press.

Robinson, Amanda and Brigitte Seim. (2018). Who is targeted in corruption? Disentangling the effects of wealth and power on exposure to bribery. *Quarterly Journal of Political Science* 13: 313–331.

Roemer, John. (2008). *Equality of Opportunity.* Cambridge, MA: Harvard University Press.

Rogowski, Ronald and Duncan MacRae. (2004). Inequality and Institutions: What Theory, History, and (Some) Data Tell Us. In: Pablo Beramendi and Christopher Anderson (eds), *Democracy, Inequality and Representation.* New York: Russell Sage Foundation, pp. 354–386.

Roland, Gérard. (2004). Understanding institutional change: Fast-moving and slow-moving institutions. *Studies in Comparative International Development* 38(4): 109–131.

Ross, Michael. (2001). Does oil hinder democracy? *World Politics* 53(3): 325–361.

Rothstein, Bo. (2000). Trust, social dilemmas, and collective memories. *Journal of Theoretical Politics* 12: 477–501.

Rothstein, Bo. (2011). *The Quality of Government. Corruption, Social Trust, and Inequality in International Perspective.* Chicago and London: Chicago University Press.

Rothstein, Bo and Dietlind Stolle. (2008). The state and social capital: An institutional theory of generalized trust. *Comparative Politics* 40(4): 441–459.

Rothstein, Bo and Jan Teorell. (2008). What is quality of government? A theory of impartial government institutions. *Governance* 21: 165–190.

Rothstein, Bo and Jan Teorell. (2015a). Getting to Sweden, part I: War and malfeasance 1720–1850. *Scandinavian Political Studies* 38: 217–237.

Rothstein, Bo and Jan Teorell. (2015b). Getting to Sweden, part II: Breaking with corruption in the 19th century. *Scandinavian Political Studies* 38: 238–254.

Rothstein, Bo and Eric Uslaner. (2005). All for all: Equality, corruption and social trust. *World Politics* 58(3): 41–73.

Rotondi, Valentina and Luca Stanca. (2015). The effect of particularism on corruption: Theory and empirical evidence. *Journal of Economic Psychology* 51: 219–235.

Runciman, Walter. (1966). *Relative Deprivation and Social Justice.* London: Routledge Kegan Paul.

Rustichini, Aldo and Alexander Vostroknutov. (2014). Merit and justice: An experimental analysis of attitude to inequality. *Plos One* 9: e114512.

Sachdev, Itesh and Richard Bourhis. (1987). Status differentials and intergroups behaviour. *European Journal of Social Psychology* 17: 277–293.

Sala-i-Martin, Xavier and Arvind Subramanian. (2013). Addressing the natural resource curse: An illustration from Nigeria. *Journal of African Economies* 22(4): 570–615.

Sandefur, Rebecca. (2008). Access to civil justice and race, class and gender inequality. *Annual Review of Sociology* 34: 339–358.

Schattschneider, Elmer. (1960). *The Semisovereign People: A Realist's View of Democracy in America*. New York: Holt, Reinhart and Winston.

Scheidel, Walter. (2017). *The Great Leveler: Violence and the History of Inequality from the Stone Age to the Twenty-First Century*. Princeton: Princeton University Press.

Scholz John and Mark Lubell. (1998). Trust and taxpaying: Testing the heuristic approach to collective action. *American Journal of Political Science* 42(2): 398–417.

Schwartz Shalom. (1990). Individualism–collectivism: Critique and proposed refinements. *Journal of Cross-Cultural Psychology* 21: 139–157.

Scott, James. (1969). Corruption, machine politics, and political change. *American Political Science Review* 63(4): 1142–1158.

Scott, James. (1972). Patron-client politics and political change in Southeast Asia. *American Political Science Review* 66(1): 91–113.

Seaford, Richard. (2004). *Money and the Early Greek Mind: Homer, Philosophy, Tragedy*. Cambridge: Cambridge University Press.

Selway, Joel. (2011). The measurement of cross-cutting cleavages and other multi-dimensional cleavage structures. *Political Analysis* 19(1): 48–65.

Service, Elman. (1975). *Origins of the State and Civilization: The Process of Cultural Evolution*. New York: W.W. Norton and Company.

Shea, John. (1997). Instrument relevance in multivariate linear models: A simple measure. *Review of Economics and Statistics* 79: 348–352.

Shefter, Martin. (1977). Party and patronage: Germany, England, and Italy. *Politics and Society* 7(4): 403–451.

Shefter, Martin. (1994). *Political Parties and the State*. Princeton: Princeton University Press.

Sherif, Muzafer, OJ Harvey, Jack White, William Hood and Carolyn Sherif. (1961). *Intergroup Conflict and Cooperation: The Robbers Cave Experiment*. Norman: University Book Exchange.

Shleifer, Andrei and Robert Vishny. (1993). Corruption. *Quarterly Journal of Economics* 108: 599–616.

Sidanius, Jim and Felicia Pratto. (1999). *Social Dominance: An Intergroup Theory of Social Hierarchy and Oppression*. New York: Cambridge University Press.

Singelis, Theodore, Harry Triandis, Dharm Bhawuk and Michele Gelfand. (1995). Horizontal and vertical dimensions of individualism and collectivism: A theoretical and measurement refinement. *Cross-Cultural Research: The Journal of Comparative Social Science* 29(3): 240–275.

Smith, Daniel. (2003). Patronage, per diems and the "workshop mentality": The practice of family planning programs in southeastern Nigeria. *World Development* 31(4): 703–715.

Smith, Eric, Monique Borgerhoff-Mulder, Samuel Bowles, Michael Gurven, Tom Hertz, and Mary Shenk. (2010). Production systems, inheritance, and inequality in premodern societies: conclusions. *Current Anthropology* 51: 85–94.

Smith, Heather, Thomas Pettigrew, Gina Pippin and Silvana Bialosiewicz. (2012). Relative deprivation A theoretical and meta-analytic review. *Personality and Social Psychology Review* 16(3): 203–232.

Sokoloff, Kenneth and Stanley Engerman. (2000). History lessons: Institutions, factors endowments, and paths of development in the new world. *Journal of Economic Perspectives* 14(3): 217–232.

Solt, Frederick. (2008). Economic inequality and democratic political engagement. *American Journal of Political Science* 52(1): 48–60.

Solt, Frederick. (2010). Does economic inequality depress electoral participation? Testing the Schattschneider hypothesis. *Political Behaviour* 32: 285–301.

Solt, Frederick. (2016). The standardized world income inequality database. *Social Science Quarterly* 97: 1267–1281.

Sowell, Thomas. (1978). *Ethnic America: A History.* New York: Basic Books.

Spolaore, Enrico and Romain Wacziarg. (2013). How deep are the roots of economic development? *Journal of Economic Literature* 51(2): 325–369.

Staiger, Douglas and James Stock. (1997). Instrumental variables regression with weak instruments. *Econometrica* 65: 557–586.

Stewart, Frances. (2000). Crisis prevention: Tackling horizontal inequalities. *Oxford Development Studies* 28(3): 245–262.

Stiglitz, Joseph. (2012). *The Price of Inequality: How Today's Divided Society Endangers Our Future.* New York: W.W. Norton & Company, Kindle Edition.

Stock James and Motohiro Yogo M. (2005). Testing for Weak Instruments in Linear IV Regression. In: Donald Andrews and James Stock (eds), *Identification and Inference for Econometric Models: Essays in Honor of Thomas Rothenberg.* Cambridge: Cambridge University Press, pp. 80–108.

Sunde, Uwe, Matteo Cervellati and Piergiuseppe Fortunato. (2008). Are all democracies equally good? The role of interactions between political environment and inequality for rule of law. *Economics Letters* 99(3): 552–556.

Svallfors, Stefan, (2013). Government quality, egalitarianism, and attitudes to taxes and social spending: A European comparison. *European Political Science Review* 5(3): 363–380.

Szeftel, Morris. (2000). Clientelism, corruption and catastrophe. *Review of African Political Economy* 27(85): 427–441.

Tabellini, Guido. (2008). Institutions and culture. *Journal of the European Economic Association* 6(2–3): 255–294.

Tajfel, Henri. (1970). Experiments in intergroup discrimination. *Scientific American* 223(5): 96–102.

Tajfel, Henri and John Turner. (1986). The social identity theory of intergroup behaviour. *Psychology of Intergroup Relations* 5: 7–24.

Tajfel, Henri, Michael Billig, R. Bundy and Claude Flament. (1971). Social categorization and intergroup behaviour. *European Journal of Social Psychology* 1(2): 149–178.

Talhelm, Thomas, Xuemin Zhang, Shigehiro Oishi, Chen Shimin, Dechao Duan, Xuezhao Lan and Shinobo Kitayama. (2015). Large-scale psychological differences within China explained by rice versus wheat agriculture. *Science* 344 (6184): 603–608.

Tanaka, Tomomi, Colin Camerer and Quang Nguyen. (2010). Risk and time preferences: Linking experimental and household survey data from Vietnam. *American Economic Review* 100(1): 557–571.

Tannenberg, Marcus. (2014). On the road to better governance. The "middle class particularism" and quality of government. University of Gothenburg, The Quality of Government Institute Working Paper Series.

Tanzi, Vito and Hamid Davoodi. (1997). Corruption, public investment, and growth. International Monetary Fund Working Paper 97/139.

Tarabar, Danko. (2019). Does national culture change as countries develop? Evidence from generational cleavages. *Journal of Institutional Economics*, 15(3): 397–412.

Thornhill, Randy and Corey, Fincher. (2014). *The Parasite-Stress Theory of Values and Sociality: Infectious Disease, History and Human Values Worldwide*. New York: Springer Science & Business Media.

Tilly, Charles. (1975). *The Formation of National States in Western Europe*. Princeton: Princeton University Press.

Treisman, Daniel. (2000). The causes of corruption: A cross-national study. *Journal of Public Economics* 76: 399–457.

Treisman, Daniel. (2007). What have we learned about the causes of corruption from ten years of cross-national empirical research? *Annual Review of Political Science* 10(1): 211–244.

Treisman, Daniel. (2015). What Does Cross-National Empirical Research Reveal about the Causes of Corruption? In: Paul Heywood (ed.), *Routledge Handbook of Political Corruption*. London and New York: Routledge, pp. 95–109.

Triandis, Harry. (1995). *Individualism and Collectivism*. Boulder: Westview Press, Boulder.

Triandis, Harry and Michele Gelfand. (1998). Converging measurement of horizontal and vertical individualism and collectivism. *Journal of Personality and Social Psychology* 74(1): 118–128.

Trigger, Bruce. (2003). *Understanding Early Civilization: A Comparative Study*. Cambridge: Cambridge University Press.

Trivers, Robert. (1971). The Evolution of Reciprocal Altruism. *Quarterly Review of Biology*, 46: 35–57.

Turchin, Peter. (2006). *War and Peace and War: The Rise and Fall of Empires*. New York: Penguin Group.

Turchin, Peter. (2016). *Ultrasociety: How 10,000 Years of War Made Humans the Greatest Cooperators on Earth*. Kindle Edition. Storrs: Beresta Books.

Turchin, Peter and Sergey Gavrilets. (2009). Evolution of complex hierarchical societies. *Social Evolution & History* 8(2): 167–198.

Turchin, Peter and Sergey Nefedov. (2009). *Secular Cycles*. Princeton: Princeton University Press.

Tyler, Tom. (1990). *Why People Obey the Law*. New Haven and London: Yale University Press.

Tyler, Tom. (2011). Procedural justice shapes evaluations of income inequality: Commentary on Norton and Ariely (2011). *Perspectives on Psychological Science* 6: 15–16.

Tyler, Tom and John Jost. (2007). Psychology and the Law: Reconciling Normative and Descriptive Accounts of Social Justice and System Legitimacy. In: Arie Kruglanski and Tory Higgins (eds), *Social Psychology: Handbook of Basic Principles*, 2nd edition. New York: Guilford Press, pp. 807–825.

Uslaner, Eric. (2002). *The Moral Foundations of Trust*. Cambridge: Cambridge University Press.

Uslaner, Eric. (2008). *Corruption, Inequality and the Rule of Law*. Cambridge: Cambridge University Press.

Uslaner Eric and Bo Rothstein. (2012). The roots of corruption: Mass education, economic inequality and state building. Presented at the Workshop "Building State

Capacity: The Other Side of Political Development" Radcliffe Institute, Harvard University, 4–5 May 2012.

Uslaner, Eric and Bo Rothstein. (2016). The historical roots of corruption: State building, economic inequality, and mass education. *Comparative Politics* 48(2): 227–248.

Vanhanen, Tatu. (1997). *Prospects of Democracy: A Study of 172 Countries*. London: Routledge.

Van Rijckeghem, Caroline and Beatrice Weder. (2001). Bureaucratic corruption and the rate of temptation: Do wages in the civil service affect corruption, and by how much. *Journal of Development Economics* 65(2): 307–331.

Voigt Stefan. (2013). How (not) to measure institutions. *Journal of Institutional Economics* 9(1): 1–26.

Voigt, Stefan, Jerg Gutmann and Lars Feld. (2015). Economic growth and judicial independence, a dozen years on: Cross-country evidence using an updated set of indicators. *European Journal of Political Economy* 38: 197–211.

Wang, Fand and Xunwei Sun. (2015). Absolute power leads to absolute corruption? Impact of power on corruption depending on the concepts of power one holds. *European Journal of Social Psychology* 46: 77–89.

Warren, Mark. (2004). What does corruption mean in a democracy? *American Journal of Political Science* 48(2): 328–343.

Waytz, Adam, James Dungan and Liane Young. (2013). The whistleblower's dilemma and the fairness–loyalty tradeoff. *Journal of Experimental Social Psychology* 49(6): 1027–1033.

Weber, Max. (1922/1978). *Economy and Society: An Outline of Interpretive Sociology*. Berkeley: University of California Press.

Weber, Max. (1951). *The Religion of China: Confucianism and Taoism*. Glencoe: The Free Press.

Welzel, Christian. (2013). *Freedom Rising: Human Empowerment and the Quest for Emancipation*. Cambridge: Cambridge University Press.

White, Lynn. (1962). *Medieval Technology and Social Change*. Oxford: Clarendon Press.

Williamson, Oliver. (2000). The new institutional economics: Taking stock, looking ahead. *Journal of Economic Literature* 38(3): 595–613.

Wilkinson, Richard and Kate Pickett. (2017). The enemy between us: The psychological and social costs of inequality. *European Journal of Social Psychology* 47: 11–24.

Wittfogel, Karl. (1957). *Oriental Despotism: A Comparative Study of Total Power*. New Haven: Yale University Press.

Woodburn, James. (1982). Egalitarian societies. *Man: New Series* 17(3): 431–451.

Zhang, Nan. (2015). Changing a "culture" of corruption: Evidence from an economic experiment in Italy. *Rationality and Society* 27(4): 387–413.

Index

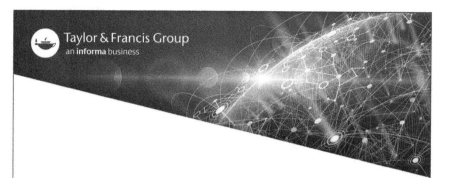